Truth and the Church in a Secular Age

Truth and the Church in a Secular Age

Edited by
David Jasper
and
Jenny Wright

scm press

© The Editors and Contributors 2019

Published in 2019 by SCM Press
Editorial office
3rd Floor, Invicta House,
108–114 Golden Lane,
London EC1Y 0TG, UK

www.scmpress.co.uk

SCM Press is an imprint of Hymns Ancient & Modern Ltd
(a registered charity)

Hymns Ancient & Modern® is a registered trademark of
Hymns Ancient & Modern Ltd
13A Hellesdon Park Road, Norwich,
Norfolk NR6 5DR, UK

All rights reserved. No part of this publication may be reproduced,
stored in a retrieval system, or transmitted,
in any form or by any means, electronic, mechanical,
photocopying or otherwise, without the prior permission of
the publisher, SCM Press.

The Authors have asserted their right under the Copyright, Designs and
Patents Act 1988 to be identified as the Authors of this Work

Unless otherwise stated, the Scripture quotations contained herein are
from The New Revised Standard Version of the Bible, Anglicized Edition,
copyright © 1989, 1995 by the Division of Christian Education of the
National Council of the Churches of Christ in the United States of America,
and are used by permission. All rights reserved.

British Library Cataloguing in Publication data

A catalogue record for this book is available
from the British Library

978-0-334-05816-8

Typeset by Regent Typesetting Ltd

Contents

Contributors	vii
Foreword by the Most Revd Mark Strange	ix
Introduction	xi
David Jasper and Jenny Wright	

1	Truth and the Biblical Tradition Nicholas Taylor	1
2	The Origins of Truth in Philosophy, Theology, and Theory David Jasper	17
3	Seeing As: Wittgenstein's Approach to Truth Scott Robertson	33
4	Truth and Christian Theology Jenny Wright	52
5	Tangling the Fibres of the Threefold Cord: Truth and the Anglican Tradition Trevor Hart	67
6	Liturgy as a Repository of Truth John Reuben Davies	84
7	Truth and Experience: Prayer and Ascetic Practice John McLuckie	102
8	Rudolf Otto: Truth and the Holy Steven Ballard	114
9	Truth, Non-Truth and Reality in the Pastoral Context Robert A. Gillies	130
10	Sciences and Truth: A Scientist's View Eric Priest	146

11 Sciences and Truths: A Theologian's View   162
    Michael Fuller

12 Today's Church and the Politics of Post-Truth   177
    Alison Jasper

Afterword   190
  Jochen Schmidt
Index of Biblical References   195
Index of Names and Subjects   197

Contributors

Steven Ballard is Assistant Priest at St John's Dumfries in the Diocese of Glasgow and Galloway. He completed his doctoral thesis on Rudolf Otto at the Philipps University of Marburg in 1998.

John Reuben Davies is Research Fellow in History in the University of Glasgow, where he also lectures for Theology and Religious Studies. He is Convener of the Liturgy Committee of the Scottish Episcopal Church.

Michael Fuller is a Senior Teaching Fellow at New College, University of Edinburgh. He holds degrees in Theology and in Chemistry.

Robert Gillies was Bishop of Aberdeen and Orkney in the Scottish Episcopal Church. He retired in 2016. He is an Honorary Research Fellow at the University of Glasgow.

Trevor Hart is Rector of St Andrew's Episcopal Church, St Andrews. He was Professor of Divinity, University of St Andrews from 1995.

Alison Jasper is a Senior Lecturer in Religion and Gender in the University of Stirling. She gained her PhD from the University of Glasgow in 1998.

David Jasper is Professor Emeritus, formerly Professor of Literature and Theology at the University of Glasgow. He is Convener of the Doctrine Committee of the Scottish Episcopal Church and Canon Theologian of St Mary's Cathedral, Glasgow.

John McLuckie is Vice Provost of St Mary's Cathedral, Edinburgh. He is Convener of the Inter-Church Relations Committee of the Scottish Episcopal Church.

Eric Priest, is Emeritus Professor, having held previously the Gregory Chair of Mathematics and a Bishop Wardlaw Professorship at the University of St Andrews. He has served on the Board of Trustees of the John Templeton Foundation.

Scott Robertson is Rector of St Margaret of Scotland, Newlands in the Diocese of Glasgow and Galloway. He is a Canon of St Mary's Cathedral, Glasgow.

Jochen Schmidt is Professor for Systematic Theology, Ethics and Philosophy of Religion at the Faculty of Arts and Humanities, University of Paderborn.

Nicholas Taylor is Rector of St Aidan's, Clarkston, in the Diocese of Glasgow and Galloway, and Canon Theologian of Mutare Cathedral, Zimbabwe since 1999.

Jenny Wright is Associate Priest of Christchurch, Morningside in the Diocese of Edinburgh. She gained her PhD from Stellenbosch University, South Africa, in 2011.

Foreword

BY THE MOST REVD MARK STRANGE

'Tell the Truth'

This is a phrase that immediately springs into my mind when I think of my parents' response to any story I was telling them about why I had found myself in trouble: 'Tell the Truth.'

I always realized that telling the truth sometimes required courage and always an acceptance of consequences. What I learned as I developed was the difference between truth and deception and the rightness of the first and the danger of the second.

I now find myself in a world where it seems acceptable to say whatever works for you and to then persuade someone that it is true. With the development of digital media, we now have a world where discovering the truth among the news stories becomes more and more difficult.

As a Christian I am confronted by those who ask me to tell them the truth about faith, while they are being bombarded by theory wrapped up as truth. I find it, at times, frustrating and difficult.

I am therefore very thankful for those from the Scottish Episcopal Church Doctrine Committee who have spent time in theological study and discussion in producing this book. I hope it will enable more of us to be able to discern the truth revealed in our faith.

The Most Revd Mark Strange
Bishop of Moray, Ross and Caithness
Primus of the Scottish Episcopal Church

Introduction

We live in a world in which the claims of truth are being challenged at every level. This condition is complex and the threat to our humanity is very real. Living by the demands of truth, as Pontius Pilate recognizes at the trial of Jesus (John 18:38), is often neither easy nor comfortable. We are under no delusions about this. The authors of this book, however, all of them practising members of the Scottish Episcopal Church, hold in common the non-negotiable belief in the necessary pursuit of truth in both our personal and social lives. Most, though not all, are members of the Doctrine Committee of that Church. In the Fourth Gospel Jesus says to his disciples, 'I am the way, and the truth, and the life' (14:6), and it is in the light of this statement that these essays are written and have been debated. Truth, we believe, is not something that is self-evident but is to be pursued, cared for, and treasured. It is in this spirit that we offer these essays.

Much has been written in recent months concerning truth and 'post-truth'. Within our political and democratic social structures truth is under threat. Henry Tam has recently written in the *Journal* of the Royal Society of Arts of three necessary areas in which truth must be preserved and protected. First, we need to maintain responsible forms of communication. In Tam's words, 'No democratic country allows the freedom of speech to become a licence to lie.'[1] Second, we need to ensure a proper programme of citizenship education in our schools and within society, reversing its current marginalization. Finally, for a democracy to function properly there must be robust electoral regulation. As Tam concludes:

> If systemic deception is allowed to continue, ignorance of politics and public policies persist, and electoral arrangements are left to unscrupulous manipulation, we would simply end up with more people voting for what would be damaging for them, their communities and the country.[2]

Such thoughts form the immediate background for the essays in this book. But their concerns will be rather different, rooted first in a theological and religious perspective and covering a wide range of disciplines. They seek to explore the central place of truth within the Christian tradition and the church and how this plays its role in our current precarious position.

Some of our essays will draw upon the work of philosophers like Simon Blackburn and others, while over all of them looms the shadow of our current political world with its dangerous simplifications, its lack of real debate and its apparent lack of care or integrity. Books appear on an almost daily basis, but many of them are simply reactions to the current mendacity in public life, lacking the necessary sense of the complexity of the idea of truth in our history and culture. Our book is determinedly interdisciplinary, examining the place of truth in theology, philosophy, science, spirituality, pastoral experience, liturgy and so on. We all subscribe to the importance of ideas, and above all the idea of truth, and we hope to contribute to the creating of an atmosphere of informed discussion and thought, debating our differences in love and charity. Each chapter represents the viewpoint of its author and the editors have not attempted to impose an artificial uniformity on the book.

The first essay, by Nicholas Taylor, grounds the whole discussion in biblical origins. There was never any doubt that we should begin here. The next two essays, by David Jasper and Scott Robertson, expand the discussion into the philosophical tradition and in particular the philosophy of Ludwig Wittgenstein in the twentieth century. From here, in the essays of Jenny Wright and Trevor Hart, we bring theology itself into the debate, and above all the theology of the Anglican tradition from which we speak. This is then developed in a consideration by John Davies of liturgy as a place for truth. John McLuckie and Steven Ballard expand this more broadly in considerations of truth in spirituality, and, in Ballard's essay, the place in today's fractured society for the idea of the Holy, as it was discussed early in the twentieth century by the German theologian Rudolf Otto.

But all of these discussions are rooted, finally, in the daily pastoral ministry of the church, and it is to this that Robert Gillies gives his particular attention. It is here that the truth is to be sought and must direct all of our concerns.

We knew from the beginning that none of this would be complete without the contribution of science, and the essays by Eric Priest and Michael Fuller are from two scientists, each with a different perspective, who are also members of the Doctrine Committee of the Scottish Episcopal Church. The final essay, by Alison Jasper, is written from a more cultural perspective, discussing the place of the church today within the politics of post-truth.

INTRODUCTION

The German theologian Jochen Schmidt provides an Afterword as someone who works outside the Scottish Anglican tradition that the rest of the authors have in common, although he has experience of Scotland having studied theology for some time at the University of Glasgow.

These essays are offered with humility and a sense of urgency. They do not claim to represent any position in the Scottish Episcopal Church, and they are neither dogmatic nor conclusive. They are the result of many meetings and often vigorous discussions and they constitute a small element in the search for truth, without which we are in danger of perishing as a people and a civilization.

David Jasper
Jenny Wright

Notes

1 Henry Tam, 'Democracy Endangered?' *RSA Journal*, Issue 3, 2018, p. 17. Henry Tam is former Head of Civil Renewal at the Home Office.
2 Ibid., p. 19.

I

Truth and the Biblical Tradition

NICHOLAS TAYLOR

'I am the way, and the truth, and the life. No one comes to the Father except through me.' (John 14:6)

Christians of most persuasions view Scripture as a repository of truth, but they differ as to the nature and authority of that truth. They differ also as to how truth is to be discerned. A further complication is that Christians do not agree the parameters of Scripture, or the relationship between the component parts of the biblical canon. Some consideration of the nature of Scripture is therefore needed, before issues to do with truth in the Bible can be discussed.

The nature of Scripture

It is widely assumed that the early Church inherited without question the Hebrew Scriptures now generally known as the Old Testament, to which Christian documents now termed the New Testament were added during the first century or so. We need to be aware that this is an over-simplification of a lengthy, complex, and contested process. By the first century CE the documents broadly known as the Old Testament were circulating in Hebrew and in Greek, with significant differences in the content of each: the Greek tradition included the books that Protestants know as the Apocrypha, as integral to the canon, not as an appended and liminal collection of ambiguous value; furthermore, the Greek texts are not simply a translation of the Hebrew, but represent in places quite divergent traditions.[1] In addition there were the Aramaic *Targumim*, which extrapolated as well as translated the Hebrew texts.[2] It was the Greek text, known as the Septuagint, which became definitive for Christianity in the Hellenistic world, until Jerome produced the Latin Vulgate in the late fourth century. In the meanwhile, Hebrew and especially Syriac texts formed the Scripture of Oriental Christians.[3] It was not until the Reformation that the Hebrew text became normative for Western Protestant Christians, and formed the basis for most subsequent translations of the Old Testament into vernacular languages. While the early church condemned attempts by the second-century Marcion and others to repudiate the Old Testament,[4] its parameters and contents, and its relationship to the New Testament, have since the earliest days of the church been matters of disagreement among Christians.[5]

The New Testament is, at least superficially, a much less complicated entity. Notwithstanding the divergent textual traditions,[6] there is a recognized and agreed canon, at least among most Christian denominations. However, it was a far from uniform process over several centuries before such consensus was achieved.[7] Jewish Christians revered gospels written in Hebrew or Aramaic, and repudiated the Pauline corpus, until the rise of Islam.[8] Gnostic and other groups revered yet other gospels, books of apostolic actions, letters, and apocalypses attributed to various of the disciples of Jesus,[9] and some of these continue to be received as Scripture among Oriental Christians. The consensus that was achieved among churches within the Roman Empire was premised upon the ascription of apostolic authorship and authority, much of which has been brought into question by subsequent Christian scholarship.[10] Once the premise has been dismissed, the authority in defining Scripture is seen to have rested essentially with church leaders whose judgement has been questioned, not only on questions of attribution but also of theological and political agenda. Quite apart from whether other surviving ancient Christian writings may witness more or at least as authentically to the voice of the early church, it is profoundly problematic for some Protestant Christians that the canon was defined by the church of the third and fourth centuries rather than being self-evidently those books of divine authorship and inspiration.

Recognizing the complexity of the history of the development of the biblical canon requires that we recognize also that Scripture is the creation of the church, which accepted some documents and rejected others, as well as of the authors, editors, and compilers of those documents. It is therefore not merely naïve and simplistic to regard Scripture as *ipsissima verba Dei*, but an evasion of the Christian responsibility to discern within the received texts those doctrines, values, and truths which are of enduring authority and relevance for the church today. The Bible reflects and gives expression to human attempts to discern the way of God and to proclaim it, within a distinctive but broad and far from monolithic Judaeo-Christian tradition. Scripture functions within specific faith communities which have mutated quite significantly over the centuries, and live today in contexts and cultures far from the ancient societies in which their spiritual forebears grappled to discover the truth of God. For Anglicans/Episcopalians, the canon of Scripture was redefined at the Reformation, creating the anomalous category of Apocrypha, and elevating the Hebrew Masoretic text to the definitive basis for vernacular translations of the Old Testament. This did not settle how Scripture was to be interpreted and its authority appropriated in the life of the church, but it did establish some parameters of theological debate and critical engagement with the text in subsequent centuries. The perceived testimony of Scripture to divine truth is the basis of its authority in the life of the church, but complex issues of interpretation remain. To these we will return after exploring ways in which Scripture speaks of truth.

Truth in Scripture

Words generally rendered 'true', 'truth', or 'truly' in English occur quite frequently in the biblical literature. While in the majority of cases the Hebrew root *'mn* and its derivative *'emet*, or the Greek *aletheia*, are so translated, this does not imply that the semantic range of these words corresponds precisely, or that their respective meanings may not vary according to context, or have mutated over the centuries. Rather than a simple definition, we need to discern a complex range or cluster of meanings, which reflect the values of the cultures in which the biblical traditions were originally transmitted.

The Western, rationalist, definition of truth, articulated in the linguistic philosophy of Wittgenstein[11] and Ayer,[12] and implicit in the scientific rationalism of Popper[13] and Kuhn,[14] has its foundations in the logic of the European Enlightenment, with its tenuous roots in Hellenistic philosophy. The notion of truth as objective reality, which human scientific and rational endeavours seek to discover and describe, within whatever limitations, is not entirely unconnected with biblical notions, in that both regard truth as in some way ideal and transcendent. Nevertheless, the biblical quest for truth is founded upon rather different principles. However widely the biblical tradition testifies to human endeavours to discover truth, truth is not merely abstract theory or the object of intellectual labour, but a quality of God. Far from being objective knowledge, truth is to be found only in and through divine revelation. Truth can therefore be known only in relationship with God. Furthermore, this would be a very incomplete and inadequate abstraction of the biblical conceptualization of truth, and it is of limited value in addressing the often quite cynical ways in which the rhetoric of truth is manipulated in postmodern discourse.

In order to make some contribution to appreciation of the complexities, and the richness, of the concept of truth reflected, and occasionally articulated, in the Christian Scriptures, I will treat briefly the words used in the Hebrew Bible and the New Testament. It will become clear that the notion is essentially theological, and indeed theocentric, describing a divine attribute reflected in human beings with particular godly qualities, and in the Christian Scriptures, manifested definitively in Jesus. This has implications for ways in which Scripture is read and interpreted, and also illuminates some of the challenges for global Christianity with its competing and often conflicting cultural values.

Truth in the Hebrew Bible

The root *'mn* is attested in no extant ancient near eastern sources earlier than the literature of the Hebrew Bible. This limits certainty as to its origins and the development of its semantic range. The later Aramaic/Syriac and Arabic derivations are essentially consistent with their Hebrew antecedent, and cannot illuminate the development of the notion. It would not be feasible or appropriate within the parameters of this study to treat the technical details of Hebrew grammar, or to explain at length the formation of Hebrew words from (usually) three consonants, and their variation in meaning and function through different vowel combinations (not introduced to the biblical texts until the later Roman period) and occasionally variation of one of the consonants.[15] What is important to note is that significant variations in spelling do not necessarily reflect variations in meaning or usage.

The wide semantic range of the *'mn* root[16] includes connotations of constancy, reliability, and stability (Prov. 25:13; Isa. 8:2), and of endurance (Deut. 28:59; Isa. 33:16; Jer. 15:18), and also of fidelity and honour. The term is used of God (Deut. 7:9; Isa. 49:7; Jer. 42:5), and of the enduring nature of God's promises (2 Sam. 7:16; 1 Kings 8:26; 2 Chr. 1:9; 6:17; Ps. 89:29; Isa. 55:3). Human speech may be so described as reliable (Gen. 42:2), with factual accuracy being a consequence rather than the essence of truthfulness.

Amen is used of Abraham in his relationship to God (Gen. 15:6; Neh. 9:8; Sir. 44:20). This rare usage expresses the righteousness implicit in Abraham's enduring fidelity in response to God's call. *Emet*, a derivative form of *amen* with similar connotations of constancy, permanence, and endurance, is associated with *ḥesed*, steadfast love, and *shalom*, peace, both of which concepts are to be understood more widely than contemporary English usage might suggest. *Emet* concerns not so much factual accuracy as a quality conducive to peace, justice, and human well-being (Ezek. 18:8; Zech. 8:16). *Emet* is attributed to God (Ps. 31:5; 146:6), and to God's word – *dabar* (2 Sam. 7:28; Ps. 132:11; 119; Prov. 8:7). It is expected in and claimed in the proclamations of prophets (Jer. 26:15; Dan. 8:26; 10:1; 11:2), implicit in the utterance *v'atah koh-'amar YHWH* (Isa. 43:1; cf. Jer. 9:23; Ezek. 11:16). The authenticity of the prophetic voice, however, cannot be guaranteed, and false prophets are frequently denounced (1 Kings 22:16; Jer. 23:28). The distinction between true and false prophets is clearly a matter of subjective judgement from alternative bearers of the prophetic voice. Prophets claim to have 'stood' in the heavenly court or divine council (cf. 1 Kings 22), and there to have heard the voice of God.[17] However this experience may be interpreted, those prophets condemned as false cannot simply be dismissed as purveyors of 'fake news' on behalf of the royal and temple establishments.[18] It is important to recognize that prophetic authenticity is not validated by fulfilment in the sense of future events coming about precisely as described, but in acknowledgement of God having spoken. An illustration of this, and of the complexity and subjectivity if not fickleness of such judgements, is Micah's prophecy of the destruction of Jerusalem (Mic. 3:12), the culmination of a passage in which corrupt and misleading prophets are condemned. A century later, this is recalled as authentic despite not yet having been fulfilled in any literal sense (Jer. 26:16–19). On the contrary, it is in having induced repentance in his contemporaries, and thereby having defused the wrath of God, that Micah's prophecy is understood to have been validated. The response of Micah's audience is deemed to be a model for those who heard Jeremiah prophesy judgement and destruction upon Jerusalem a century later. Micah and Jeremiah are acknowledged as faithful, i.e. true, prophets, who evoke the response of repentance which causes God to withhold the judgement of which they had spoken.

Truth in Hellenistic Judaism

It is worth noting briefly that, in Greek translations of the Hebrew Scriptures, *'mn* and its derivatives are usually rendered as *aletheia* or a related word. In some cases, however, *pistis* (usually translated faith or faithfulness) and *dikaiosune* (usually righteousness) are used. This illustrates something of the breadth of meanings associated with *'mn* as well perhaps as reflecting aspects of the cultural and philosophical influences which accompanied the Greek language into the Jewish world, centuries before the dawn of Christianity.

Aletheia is used of integrity of character (Tobit 3:8; 4:6), the truth of statements, and of true teaching (Dan. 8:12; Judith 10:13; Philo, *de Spec. Leg.* 4.178), in continuity as much with Greek as with Hebrew usage (cf. Epictetus, *Diss.* 1.4.31; 3.24.40; Plutarch, *de Iside & Osiride* 1–11.35). The adjective *alethes* denotes such moral characteristics as constancy (*Sibylline Oracles* 5.499; Josephus, *Antiquities* 8.337; 10.263) and sincerity (Josephus, *Antiquities* 13.191), and affirms the truth of statements (Josephus, *Jewish War* 1.254).

In Platonism *aletheia* is used of ultimate reality, also known as the world of ideas, as opposed to the reflection or material appearance thereof, often described as *eidolon* (Plato, *Symp.* 211b–212a; *Resp.* 596a–605c).[19] Jewish thought was expounded, and the Hebrew Scriptures interpreted, within an essentially Platonist paradigm most notably by Philo of Alexandria.[20] While Philo had no known contact with the nascent Christian movement, influences at the very least similar to his writings may be discerned in the New Testament, particularly in correlations between his portrayal of Moses (*de Vita Mosis*) and the Christology of the Gospel of John.[21] The notion that truth is a spiritual quality, which may be reflected in human values and behaviour, but cannot be present in any absolute sense within the created order, is important for understanding much of the biblical material.

Truth in the New Testament

In the New Testament, *aletheia* is closely associated with the gospel and with Jesus. This is expressed differently in the various traditions.

For Paul *aletheia* is a divine attribute, closely associated with God's righteousness and faithfulness (Rom. 3:3–7). The Gospel of Christ definitively reflects the truth of God (cf. 2 Cor. 11:10), to which the law of Moses is at best relegated to a subordinate status, if not a potential deception (Rom. 2:20; Gal. 2:5, 14). *Aletheia* is equated with the gospel (2 Cor. 4:2; 2 Thess. 2:10–12; cf. 2 Pet. 1:12), and with sound teaching (1 Tim. 6:5; Tit. 1:14; cf. Ignatius, *Eph* 6.2; *Polycarp* 7.3), tendencies found in traditions influenced by Paul during the second and third generations of Christianity.[22]

The Johannine tradition provides a distinctive association of ideas, not unlike that of Philo, whereby Jesus, as the incarnate *logos*, manifests light, truth, righteousness, and other divine qualities and attributes revealed in creation. Reception of revealed truth realizes freedom from sin, and, by implication, emancipation from slavery and attainment of the status of children in God's household (John 8:32–36), an image conspicuously similar to that which Paul uses of baptism as a rite of adoption in Galatians (3:15–4:7).[23] Christian living reflects the light and truth manifest in Jesus, which inhabit the Christian (2 John 1; 3 John 1), and are realized in righteousness (John 3:21; 1 John 1:6; 2 John 4; 3 John 3).

Aletheia is associated with *dikaiosune* more widely in the early Christian tradition (James 3:14; 5:19; cf. *Didache* 16:6; *1 Clement* 31:2; 35:5; 60:2; Hermas, *Vis.* 3.7.3; *Sim.* 9.19.2). The related adjective *alethes* is widely used of moral characteristics such as constancy (1 Pet. 5:2), uprightness (Phil. 4:8), trustworthiness (Rom. 3:4; *1 Clement* 45:2), sincerity and honesty (Mark 12:4; John 3:33; 2 Cor. 6:8; *Didache* 15:1; Ignatius, *Polycarp* 1:1; Hermas, *Mand.* 3.3; 11.3). It is used also to affirm the reality of related events (John 10:41; Acts 12:9) and abstract principles which may be equated with the gospel (1 John 2:27; cf. John 5:31; 3 John 12), or with alleged common knowledge (Tit. 1:13; 2 Pet. 2:22).

Truth as understood in Scripture

The concept of truth reflected in the Hebrew Bible, Greek Jewish traditions, and the New Testament is broader than is denoted by the word in contemporary English. Notwithstanding differences between the Hebrew and Greek cultures, and the philosophical systems which evolved in each, the biblical tradition reflects common human values as understood and expressed in the ancient societies of the eastern Mediterranean world. Truth cannot be reduced to the sense of factual accuracy as understood by modern western European logical positivists. Rather, it denotes qualities of honour, sincerity, moral rectitude, trustworthiness, endurance, and reliability. Honesty is an aspect of this, and the accuracy of statements its product but not its essence.

Of particular significance for Christians is that truth is understood as a quality of the divine *Logos*, definitively revealed in the world in Jesus. The gospel, in testifying to the life, death, and resurrection of Jesus, articulates truth as manifested in a particular context at a particular time, but with universal significance. The explicit and repeated denunciation in Scripture of ancient near eastern polytheism and its idolatrous worship is founded upon the premise that divine truth has been uniquely revealed to Abraham, Moses, and the prophets, and, for Christians, ultimately in and through Jesus. While the personification of truth as a divine manifestation in Jesus Christ, the *Logos* incarnate, has been exploited to articulate doctrines of Christian exclusivism, there may also be discerned within Scripture, and in the church fathers, a recognition that people of other faiths, without benefit of the revelation on which the Judaeo-Christian tradition is founded, have sought God and truth within the parameters of their own beliefs and observations. This is articulated most clearly in Acts, where Paul on the Areopagus in Athens refers to an altar dedicated to 'an unknown god', whom he proceeds to identify as the creator of the world and the one whom he proclaims (17:22–31).[24]

While truth as a universal principle may be definitively identified with Jesus, there remain both theological and ethical problems. Interpreting Jesus is a complex and contentious matter, not only of Christology[25] but also of historical reconstruction[26] and enculturation,[27] with the former academic quest engaging scholars from beyond confessional Christianity and the latter becoming increasingly diverse as indigenous theologies are developed throughout global Christianity. Significant as these scholarly and theological endeavours will undoubtedly be for the future of Christianity, and indirectly relevant to humanity and the human quest for truth, we are at present concerned with the written rather than the incarnate Word, and it is with the discernment of truth in Scripture in Christian history and in particular in Anglicanism that the remainder of this chapter will be concerned.

Discerning truth in Scripture

Anglicanism emerged from a series of interrelated cultural movements in western Europe over a period of centuries, from the Renaissance through the Reformation to the Enlightenment and beyond.[28] As Anglican and other forms of western European Christianity were exported to other parts of the world, the issues these movements generated for the interpretation of Scripture have also been disseminated to other continents, where they have mutated and become a significant factor in the conflicts which beset global Christianity and the Anglican Communion in particular.[29]

A central principle of the Reformation was that the Bible should be made available in the vernacular languages of all Christian people, and, in theory at least, that individuals reading the Bible would be able to interpret Scripture rightly without recourse to any ecclesiastical authority.[30] However, all the ecclesiastical bodies which emerged at the Reformation were of course concerned to direct and control the interpretation of Scripture and to entrench their own dogmatic and social authority, whether by intellectual argument, moral persuasion, or political and judicial coercion. Nevertheless, where conformity was not enforced repressively, popular movements emerged which were led by people of limited literacy and no theological competence, but who nonetheless were able to read the Bible in their vernacular languages and to find therein messages for themselves and the world. Their interest in seeing, and if possible precipitating, the return of Christ drew their interest to Revelation and other apocalyptic texts, read without any critical tools.[31] It was in this context, from the early seventeenth century, that millennialist and dispensationalist ideas, including the origins of Christian Zionism, emerged.[32] As those who adhered to such lines of interpretation migrated to North America and gained social mobility, these views became powerful tools in right-wing politics and religion, which they remain to this day.[33]

The Anglican settlement – in England and Ireland at least – was rather more nuanced in its approach to Scripture than was often the case with dissenting groups. Article VI of the Articles of Religion, promulgated in 1573 and thereafter printed in successive editions of the Book of Common Prayer,[34] states:

> Holy Scripture containeth all things necessary to salvation: whatsoever is not read therein, nor may be proved thereby, is not to be required of any man, that it should be believed as an article of the Faith, or be thought requisite or necessary to salvation.

Two points in particular are significant in this, irrespective of what merits or otherwise are attributed to the rest of the Articles. The liberty of individual Christians to follow their consciences in matters on which Scripture provides no unequivocal direction rests upon a recognition that Scripture is neither comprehensive nor always unambiguous in its directions for Christian life. Furthermore, in using the word 'containeth' (*continet* in Latin), the article implies that there is material within the canon of Scripture which is not 'necessary to salvation'.[35] This is entirely in continuity with the first Christians, not least the apostle Paul, in their quest to discern which aspects of Torah were of enduring authority, and which had become obsolete in Christ.[36]

What pertains to 'article[s] of the Faith' pertains also to truth. Just as we have noted the Christocentric nature of truth in the New Testament, so also the enduring value of *torah* is measured by its testimony to Christ and its relevance to the life and mission of the church. This is not to suggest that all truth which Christians might wish to discover is either overtly theological in nature or to be found in the pages of the Bible. Rather, just as truth needs to be discerned within Scripture, and cannot be derived from superficial, uncritically literal, or selective reading of the text, so too any quest for truth in the created order requires a God-centred and rigorous discipline, and a willingness to test the moral value of alternative truth claims in the light of the Christian experience of God in Jesus – the incarnation of divine truth to which Scripture testifies, however incompletely or inadequately.

It may appear that passages in Scripture are amenable to an almost infinite variety of interpretation, at the popular level as well as at the hands of theologians and biblical scholars. This may have merit and value in revealing the richness, diversity, and complexity of the Christian heritage. Nevertheless, when the quest for truth leads to attempts at prescribing laws to govern the lives of individuals and communities, or to absolute and exclusive claims to knowledge or authority, then it would seem that there are at least two prerequisites to any claim to sound interpretation.

The first is to recognize that the vernacular translations and paraphrases all too frequently used to expound 'the clear meaning of Scripture' are dependent on a complex process of reconstructing words and sentences in extinct languages. The methods used to determine how words and phrases are to be rendered in modern languages are not immune to subjective choices influenced more by the theological predisposition of the translator than by such knowledge as may be reconstructed of the ancient language in its social and cultural context. A simple example would be translating *episkopos* in Acts 20:28; Philippians 1:1; 1 Timothy 3:2; Titus 1:7. The evangelical Protestant New International Version of the Bible uses 'overseer', the Roman Catholic Jerusalem Bible uses 'bishop', as does the less theologically partisan Revised Standard Version. Translation is influenced by whether or not the translators believe, on historical or theological grounds, that there were bishops in the church at the time that these documents were written; the text is evidence that the word subsequently translated 'bishop' was in use of church leaders during the New Testament period, but the degree to which those so described can be compared with modern bearers of the title is a very much more uncertain and subjective question.[37] Even without taking into account the fluidity of the manuscript tradition, the process of translation does not allow for absolute certainty when working with extinct languages. This is particularly true of the prescriptions and prohibitions regarding sexual conduct in the Pentateuch, where rare and obscure words, and euphemistic, circumlocutory, and allusive expressions are used, so that neither the physical acts nor the relationships between the parties are at all certain.[38]

The second prerequisite is to recognize the genre of the texts to which appeal is made. It would be something of a truism to observe that the creation narratives in Genesis do not emanate from the intellectual and cultural context in which Stephen Hawking wrote *A Brief History of Time*.[39] Nor were they ever thought to be a literal account of the creation of the universe[40] until Darwin's findings were published[41] in an industrial capitalist society that was, it might be thought, largely incapable of thinking of any value other than profit, or of appreciating any text more polyvalent than a ledger. Darwin published his findings at the end of the decade in which the School of Natural Sciences had been founded at Oxford University, reflecting the emergence of these academic disciplines, independent alike of Divinity and of Medicine.[42] Away from elitist academic circles, that any figurative or poetic meaning might be discerned in the biblical accounts of the creation was anathema to fundamentalists and flat-earthers who compensated for limited literacy with an over-abundance of literalism. The demand for certainty in interpreting Revelation on the end of the world required equal certainty as to the testimony of Genesis to its creation. It was the emerging 'science' of 'creationism' that could countenance no notion of myth in Scripture, not the academic sciences.[43] While racism and fundamentalism often go together,[44] Darwin was also found to be conveniently amenable to racist taxonomies.[45] Despite his recorded opposition to slavery and the slave trade,[46] Darwin's theories were incorporated into literal readings of Scripture to justify trading in and keeping slaves, while overlooking passages which prescribed humane treatment and timely manumission thereof.[47]

This brief and selective review of the pitfalls of reading Scripture without regard for the complexities of translation and of literary genre has drawn attention both to the dangers of facile and ignorant readings of Scripture and to the cynical manipulation of the biblical texts in the service of vested interests. These abuses cannot be corrected, and truth discerned, on the basis of ecclesiastical traditions of interpretation alone. Theological engagement with the texts, taking full account of the insights of critical scholarship, is essential, and neither an expendable luxury nor an elitist and irrelevant academic distraction.[48] This does not imply that academic studies alone guarantee the discernment of truth. Rather, it requires that Christians find ways of integrating an increasingly secular discipline of Biblical Studies in their theological quest for the truth of God, as revealed in Scripture.

Concluding reflections

It is a well established, if nowhere explicitly articulated, Anglican principle that doctrine is articulated in the liturgy of the church, rather than in confessional statements or dogmatic tomes.[49] This implies that Scripture is definitively received in the context of worship. The reading of Scripture is God-centred, and the truth heard and inwardly digested with the body of Christ, so that it may be lived in the power of God's Spirit. This requires that those whose office it is to preach within the liturgy, and to teach in other contexts in the life of the Church, be adequately equipped and spiritually disciplined to lead their communities in discerning the truth of God. While the ordered reading of passages from the Bible is integral to Anglican worship, its exposition is dependent on rigorous extra-liturgical study and reflection. This is a theological process requiring intellectual discipline, integrating academic biblical scholarship with due reverence for the heritage of faith and an openness to fresh insights for the church of today. Where God's presence is experienced in the liturgy, and God's people fed with the body and blood of Christ, the truth of God that is discerned in Scripture and expounded to the community must by the power of God's Spirit guide the lives of God's people, equipping each not merely to receive truth in worship but to seek truth in their own calling in the world.

Questions for discussion

1 In what ways have you been challenged through Christian preaching to understand the Bible differently? Has this had any effect on your lifestyle?
2 If you find a passage in the Bible difficult to reconcile with your understanding of the Gospel, how do you go about resolving this?
3 Part of the Christian Bible is Scripture for others, viz. Jews. In what ways would you expect their discernment of God's truth to differ from yours?

Further reading

A. K. M. Adam, *Faithful Interpretation: Reading the Bible in a Postmodern World* (Minneapolis: Fortress, 2006).
A. A. Bartlett, *A Passionate Balance: The Anglican Tradition* (London: DLT, 2007).
W. Brueggeman, *Truth Speaks to Power: The Countercultural Nature of Scripture* (Louisville KY: Westminster John Knox Press, 2013).
L. W. Countryman, *Interpreting the Truth: Changing the Paradigm of Biblical Studies* (Harrisburg: TPI, 2003).
J. D. G. Dunn, *The Living Word* (London: SCM Press, 1987).
R. A. Greer, *Anglican Approaches to Scripture: From the Reformation to the Present* (New York: Crossroad, 2006).

L. T. Johnson, *Scripture and Discernment: Decision Making in the Church* (Nashville: Abingdon, 1983).

Adam and Countryman are Anglican/Episcopal priests and New Testament scholars. Bartlett is an Anglican priest and pastoral theologian. Greer was an Episcopal priest and church historian. Brueggeman is a Protestant Old Testament scholar who has found his home in the Episcopal Church. Dunn is a Protestant New Testament scholar who has found his home in the Church of England. Johnson is a Roman Catholic New Testament scholar. Their books reflect the contexts in which their professional and Christian lives connect.

Notes

1 A. A. Fischer, *The Text of the Old Testament* (Grand Rapids: Eerdmans, 2014); P. Walters, *The Text of the Septuagint* (Cambridge: CUP, 1973).

2 M. McNamara, *Targum and Testament* (Grand Rapids: Eerdmans, 2010).

3 M. P. Weitzman, *From Judaism to Christianity* (Oxford: Oxford University Press, 2000); J. Joosten, *Language and Textual History of the Syriac Bible* (Piscataway NJ: Gorgias, 2013).

4 J. M. Lieu, *Marcion and the Making of a Heretic* (Cambridge: CUP, 2017).

5 J. D. G. Dunn, *Unity and Diversity in the New Testament* (London: SCM Press, 1977); *The Partings of the Ways* (London: SCM Press, 1991); E. P. Sanders, *Paul and Palestinian Judaism* (London: SCM Press, 1977); D. C. Sim, *The Gospel of Matthew and Christian Judaism* (Edinburgh: T & T Clark, 1998); J. T. Lienhard, *The Bible, the Church and Authority* (Collegeville: Liturgical, 1995); L. M. McDonald, *Formation of the Bible* (Peabody: Hendrickson, 2012).

6 D. C. Parker, *Manuscripts, Texts, Theology* (Berlin: De Gruyter, 2009); *Textual Scholarship and the Making of the New Testament* (Oxford: Oxford University Press, 2014).

7 B. D. Ehrman, *Lost Christianities* (Oxford: Oxford University Press, 2005); *Lost Scriptures* (New York: Oxford University Press, 2005); H. Y. Gamble, *The New Testament Canon* (Eugene OR: Wipf & Stock, 2002).

8 R. A. Pritz, *Nazarene Jewish Christianity* (Skokie IL: Varda, 2006); A. Y. Reed, *Jewish-Christianity and the History of Judaism* (Tübingen: Mohr-Siebeck, 2018).

9 B. Layton, *The Gnostic Scriptures* (London: SCM, 2012); E. Pagels, *The Gnostic Gospels* (New York: Random House, 2004).

10 R. F. Collins, *Letters that Paul did not Write* (Eugene OR: Wipf & Stock, 2006); B. D. Ehrman, *Forged* (New York: HarperCollins, 2011).

11 L. Wittgenstein, *On Certainty* (Oxford: Blackwell, 1975); *Philosophical Investigations* (Chichester: Wiley-Blackwell, 2009); *Tractatus Logico-Philosophicus* (London: Routledge, 2001). For further discussion, see Chapter 3 (Robertson), below.

12 A. J. Ayer, *Language, Truth, and Logic* (London: Penguin, 1990); *The Central Questions of Philosophy* (London: Penguin, 1991).

13 K. R. Popper, *The Logic of Scientific Discovery* (London: Routledge, 2002); *Objective Knowledge* (Oxford: Oxford University Press, 1979).

14 T. S. Kuhn, *The Structure of Scientific Revolutions* (Chicago: University of Chicago Press, 2012).

15 E. Bons et al. (eds), *Biblical Lexicology* (Berlin: De Gruyter, 2015); K. Peters, *Hebrew Lexical Semantics and Daily Life in Ancient Israel* (Leiden: Brill, 2016).

16 For more detailed treatment of the material condensed in this and the subsequent paragraphs, see A. Jepsen, *['mn]*, *Theological Dictionary of the Old Testament. I* (Grand Rapids: Eerdmans, 1977) 292–323. This dictionary, translated from a German original, first published in 1970, is methodologically dated but nonetheless reflects thorough study of the primary sources.

17 For discussion, E. T. Mullen, *The Assembly of the Gods* (Missoula: Scholars, 1982).

18 S. J. de Vries, *Prophet against Prophet* (Grand Rapids: Eerdmans, 1978).

19 For a useful corrective to popular idealization of Plato and his thought, K. R. Popper, *The Open Society and its Enemies I* (London: Routledge, 1945).

20 M. R. Niehoff, *Philo of Alexandria* (New Haven CT: Yale University Press, 2018); T. Seland (ed), *Reading Philo* (Grand Rapids: Eerdmans, 2014).

21 P. Borgen, *Logos was the True Light* (Trondheim: Tapir, 1983); *The Gospel of John* (Leiden: Brill, 2014).

22 For a treatment of Paul's theology, J. D. G. Dunn, *The Theology of Paul the Apostle* (Grand Rapids: Eerdmans, 1998).

23 Cf. N. H. Taylor, *Paul on Baptism* (London: SCM Press, 2016).

24 Justin Martyr (mid-second century) similarly spoke of pagan philosophers as "Christians before Christ", *1 Apologia* 46. This motif has been employed by Christian missionaries to relate the gospel to the religious and philosophical systems of those whom they have sought to convert.

25 Cf. J. H. Hick, *The Metaphor of God Incarnate* (London: SCM Press, 2005); J. Macquarrie, *Christology Revisited* (London: SCM Press, 2010); J. Moltmann, *The Crucified God* (London: SCM Press, 1974); G. O'Collins, *Christology* (Oxford: Oxford University Press, 2009); T. G. Weinandy, *Jesus* (Washington DC: CUA Press, 2014); R. D. Williams, *Christ the Heart of Creation* (London: Bloomsbury, 2018); R. K. Wüstenberg, *Christology* (Eugene OR: Wipf & Stock, 2014).

26 P. M. Casey, *Jesus of Nazareth* (London: T & T Clark, 2010); J. D. Crossan, *The Historical Jesus* (San Francisco: Harper Collins, 1991); D. Flusser, *The Sage from Galilee* (Grand Rapids: Eerdmans, 2007); J. P. Meier, *A Marginal Jew* (New York: Doubleday; New Haven: Yale University Press, 1996–2016); E. P. Sanders, *The Historical Figure of Jesus* (London: Penguin, 1995).

27 Cf. L. Boff, *Jesus Christ Liberator* (London: SPCK, 1979); T. Bohache, *Christology from the Margins* (London: SCM, 2008); L. Isherwood, *Introducing Feminist Christologies* (Sheffield: Sheffield Academic Press, 2002); N. Nassar, *the Culture of God* (London: Hodder & Stoughton, 2018); C. Nyamiti, *Christ our Ancestor* (Harare: Mambo, 1984); J. Sobrino, *Christology at the Crossroads* (London: SCM Press, 2012); D. B. Stinton, *Jesus of Africa* (Maryknoll: Orbis, 2004); R. S. Sugirtharajah, *Jesus in Asia* (Cambridge MA: Harvard University Press, 2018).

28 M. D. Chapman, *Anglican Theology* (London: T & T Clark, 2012); E. Duffy, *The Stripping of the Altars* (New Haven CT: Yale University Press, 1992); C. A. Haigh, *English Reformations* (Oxford: Oxford University Press, 1993).

29 I. T. Douglas & Kwok P.-L. (eds), *Beyond Colonial Anglicanism* (New York: Church Publishing, 2001); R. Strong, *Anglicanism and the British Empire*,

c. *1700–1850* (Oxford: Oxford University Press, 2007); R. Strong (ed.), *The Oxford History of Anglicanism. III. Partisan Anglicanism and Its Global Expansion, 1829–1914* (Oxford: Oxford University Press, 2016); W. E. Sachs (ed.), *The Oxford History of Anglicanism. V. Global Anglicanism, c. 1910–2000* (Oxford: Oxford University Press, 2017); K. Ward, *A History of Global Anglicanism* (Cambridge: CUP, 2006).

30 H. Freedman, *The Murderous History of Bible Translations* (London: Bloomsbury, 2016); J. P. McNutt & D. Lauber (eds), *The People's Book* (Westmont IL: IVP, 2017); P. A. Noss, *A History of Bible Translation* (Rome: Edizioni Di Storia E Letteratura, 2007).

31 This reformation tendency was not without ancient and mediaeval precedent, cf. N. Cohn, *The Pursuit of the Millennium* (London: Pimlico, 1993); J. M. Court, *Approaching the Apocalypse* (London: Tauris, 2008); J. C. Laursen & R. H. Popkin (eds), *Continental Millenarians* (Dordrecht: Kluwer, 2001); C. C. Rowland, *Radical Prophet* (London: Tauris, 2017).

32 A. Crome, *Christian Zionism and English National Identity, 1600–1850* (London: Palgrave Macmillan, 2018); D. M. Lewis, *The Origins of Christian Zionism* (Cambridge: CUP, 2014); R. O. Smith, *More to be Desired than Our Owne Salvation* (New York: Oxford University Press, 2013); N. H. Taylor, 'Christianity, Scripture, and the State of Israel', *SEIJ* 2.2 (2018) 7–34.

33 The North American 'religious right' has its origins in such movements, the progenitors of the Southern Baptist Convention and other conservative evangelical denominations, which have in recent years considered it expedient to endorse the political aspirations of Donald Trump: P. Adorf, *How the South was Won and the Nation Lost* (Bonn: Bonn University Press, 2016); E. Sandoz, *Republicanism, Religion, and the Soul of America* (Columbia: University of Missouri Press, 2006).

34 E. J. Bicknell, *A Theological Introduction to the Thirty-Nine Articles of the Church of England* (London: Longman, 1955); O. M. T. O'Donovan, *On the Thirty-Nine Articles* (Exeter: Paternoster, 1986).

35 Cf. A. K. M. Adam, *Faithful Interpretation* (Minneapolis: Fortress, 2006); A. A. Bartlett, *A Passionate Balance* (London: DLT, 2007); L. W. Countryman, *Interpreting the Truth* (Harrisburg: TPI, 2003); R. A. Greer, *Anglican Approaches to Scripture* (New York: Crossroad, 2006).

36 Dunn, *Theology of Paul*; H. Räisänen, *Paul and the Law* (Philadelphia: Fortress, 1986); E. P. Sanders, *Paul, the Law, and the Jewish People* (London: SCM Press, 1983); N. H. Taylor, 'Paul for Today: Race, Class, and Gender in Light of Cognitive Dissonance Theory', in N. H. Taylor (ed.), *Sociology of Early Christianity and Contemporary Christian Life*, a special issue of *Listening: Journal of Religion and Culture* 32.1 (1997) 22–38; 'Paul, Pharisee and Christian: Israel, the Gentiles, and the Law of Moses in Light of Cognitive Dissonance Theory', *Theologia Viatorum* 24 (1997) 45–65; 'The Contextualization of Christianity in the early Church', pp. 41–54 in E. R. Johnson (ed), *Reflections on Christian Faith: An African Context* (Mutare: Africa University Press, 2002).

37 R. E. Brown, *Priest and Bishop* (New York: Paulist, 1970); A. C. Stewart, *The Original Bishops* (Grand Rapids: Baker, 2014).

38 D. L. Balch (ed.), *Homosexuality, Science, and the 'Plain Sense' of Scripture* (Grand Rapids: Eerdmans, 1999); J. V. Brownson, *Bible, Gender, Sexuality* (Grand Rapids: Eerdmans, 2013); I. Himbaza, A. Schenker, & J.-B. Edart, *The Bible and the Question of Homosexuality* (Washington: Catholic University of America, 2012); J. B. Rogers, *Jesus, the Bible and Homosexuality* (Louisville:

Westminster John Knox Press, 2009); D. O. Via & R. A. J. Gagnon, *Homosexuality and the Bible* (Minneapolis: Fortress, 2003).

39 London: Bantam, 1988.

40 E.g. Augustine, *De Genesi ad Litteram*.

41 C. Darwin, *The Origin of Species* (London: Murray, 1859).

42 The importance of this development should not be overemphasized. There had been a Chair of Botany at Cambridge since 1574, and the Regius Chairs of Zoology and Botany were established in Glasgow University in 1807 and 1818 respectively. Nevertheless, their inclusion in the undergraduate curriculum in the ancient universities represented a departure from the traditional academic curriculum.

43 M. J. Fuller, *Science and Religion* (Glasgow: Scottish Episcopal Church, Diocese of Glasgow & Galloway, 2016); A. E. McGrath, *Darwinism and the Divine* (Chichester: Wiley-Blackwell, 2011); *Inventing the Universe* (London: Hodder & Stoughton, 2015). See also below Chapter 10 (Priest) and Chapter 11 (Fuller).

44 J. D. Lavoie, *Segregation and the Baptist Bible Fellowship* (Palo Alta CA: Academica, 2013); J. A. Loubser, *A Critical Review of Racial Theology in South Africa* (Lewiston NY: Edward Mellen, 1990).

45 A. Pichot, *The Pure Society: From Darwin to Hitler* (London: Verso, 2009); R. Weikart, *From Darwin to Hitler* (London: Palgrave Macmillan, 2006).

46 A. Desmond & J. Moore, *Darwin's Sacred Cause* (London: Allen Lane, 2009).

47 Cf. H. Avalos, *Slavery, Abolitionism, and the Ethics of Biblical Scholarship* (Sheffield: Sheffield Phoenix Press, 2013); D. M. Goldenberg, *Black and Slave* (Berlin: De Gruyter, 2013).

48 N. H. Taylor, 'Some Observations on Theological Method, Biblical Interpretation, and Ecclesiastical Politics in Current Disputes in the Anglican Communion', *Theology* 111 (2008) 51–58.

49 See further below Chapter 6 (Davies).

2

The Origins of Truth in Philosophy, Theology and Theory

DAVID JASPER

The following chapter is offered as a preliminary exploration of ideas concerning the origins of truth in Western philosophy and theology. They are presented for further discussion and debate but they will serve, I hope, to add some complexity to a situation concerning the notion of 'post-truth' that is in danger of over-simplification. If they do no more than provoke us into *thinking* about truth and post-truth a little more carefully and with better information, then something will have been achieved. Such ideas may or may not be 'true' – that is they may even be wrong for various reasons – but, offered in proper humility, they may serve the end of truth or 'righteousness', and that may be in itself a good thing. An indulgence in simplicity, at least in the first instance, is not necessarily a good thing.

Some contemporary discussions of truth and post-truth

One of the more interesting studies of the currently fashionable, though actually very ancient, idea of 'post-truth' is the philosopher Lee McIntyre's short book entitled *Post-Truth* (2018). Although it is a great deal more perceptive than another brief contribution by another writer of popular philosophy, Julian Baggini's *A Short History of Truth* (2017), McIntyre's work is nevertheless somewhat lacking in serious philosophical understanding of the complex concept and history of truth in Western thought and culture, and repeatedly falls into the trap of reading difficult and complex books as though they were actually very straightforward. One obvious example is George Orwell's much quoted novel *Nineteen Eighty-Four* (1949), forgetting its embeddedness in a venerable and subtle literary tradition of satire and irony that looks back to such works as Jonathan Swift's *A Modest Proposal* (1729), and much further, and then forward to Milan Kundera's *The Art of the Novel* (1986) and its literary idea, born of an old Jewish proverb, of the laughter of God: 'But why does God laugh at the sight of man thinking? Because man thinks and the truth escapes him.'[1] Yet just because God laughs at us should we stop *trying* to think? The consequences of not doing so may be even more painful and dangerous.

Let us then return for a moment to Lee McIntyre. He works upon a very basic premise which identifies a 'fact' quite simply with the idea of truth. We have already seen in Nicholas Taylor's chapter that in the biblical tradition this simple equation is quite inadequate. However, a post-truth era replaces actual facts with 'alternative facts', and the results of clear evidence with mere feelings. That seems simple enough. It is clear that for President Trump to claim that his inauguration as President of the United States attracted a greater crowd than that of President Obama simply flies in the face of photographic evidence. Even his own staff at the time have now admitted this. What is more interesting lies in the roots of such a patently false statement by President Trump. What impels us towards telling lies or post-truths, which are not at all the same thing since presumably you know when you are lying? This may not be the case with a post-truth. You do not have to look very far in the ancient history of Western thought to recall that Plato distrusted the rhetoricians, whose concern was with persuasion rather than with the truth, and to find Plato's insistence in the *Phaedrus* that a 'true rhetoric' must rest upon a knowledge of eternal verities.[2] The problem begins, of course, when issues of truth and power become mixed up. Torture me enough and I will no doubt tell you that two and two make five just to make you stop hurting me. It is not true but it just might as well be so as truth no longer matters under extreme forms of constraint, except in the unlikely event that you are a saint and martyr. But if we abandon the ethical and moral bases of truth and they cease to matter in the brute exercise of power, we descend into a purely utilitarian world of success or failure, or of 'truth' being the prerogative of whoever is the strongest or most powerful.

Christianity and truth

But Christianity has a great deal to say about truth and power (and indeed the nature of success and failure). We may begin with the chiasmic statements by Jesus in the Gospels about, for example, worldly profit made at the cost of your eternal soul. We will return to the question of power shortly. And then there is Blaise Pascal who, a generation after Descartes, was asserting in the *Pensées* that the truth is known not only through the reason but also through the heart,[3] and further noting that:

> If [the Christian religion] boasted of having a clear view of God, and of possessing it open and unveiled, it would be attacking it to say that we see nothing in the world which shows it with this clearness. But, on the contrary, it says that men are in darkness and estranged from God, that He has hidden Himself from their knowledge, that this is in fact the name which He gives Himself in the Scriptures. *Deus absconditus.*[4]

It is worth reflecting, with this matter of the hiddenness of God (and truth) in mind as a kind of proto-existentialism, and before we return to begin again with Pontius Pilate's despairing, dismissive question (returning not only to Scripture but to Roger Caillois' mind-bending novel *Pontius Pilate* (1961)), at least for those of my generation, how much we enjoyed ourselves in the 1980s and 1990s in the apparent freedoms granted by the turn to postmodernism after the writings of Jean-François Lyotard and Jacques Derrida. But were they freedoms subsequent upon what Lyotard famously described as 'incredulity toward metanarratives'[5] (Christianity being one of them), or an escape from what Terry Eagleton calls those religious and political 'tyrannical schemes [that] ride roughshod over the complexity and multiplicity of actual history, brutally eradicate difference, reduce all otherness to the drearily selfsame, and issue often enough in a totalitarian politics'?[6] Is that how we saw Christianity's singular demand for orthodoxy – or was postmodernism just an excuse to ride roughshod over the opinions of others without inconveniencing ourselves with having any of our own beyond those of deconstruction itself? Postmodernism, it may be in some sense, opened the door to the world of President Trump and to a revisiting of post-truth. As good postmoderns in those days we were faced with the perfectly legitimate student question as famously recorded by Stanley Fish, 'Is there a text in this class ... I mean in this class do we believe in poems and things, or is it just us?'[7] Is it all just pure subjectivism, just us thinking, and where does *belief* in anything apart from ourselves come into this? And before we finally move on from those heady days at the end of the last century, going back even further to the 1960s, what of the legitimacy of what the once widely-read Theodore Roszak examined in the 'counter-culture' of the youthful opposition to the technocratic society? It seemed an easy, post-Romantic idea to meet the dull predictability of the 'experts' with faint after-tones of Pascalian, or more exactly, perhaps, Rousseau-esque, feeling without the inconvenience of intellectual rigour. The legitimacy, indeed the truth, of Jacques Ellul's words seemed then perfectly obvious:

Technique requires predictability and, no less, exactness of prediction. It is necessary, then, that technique prevail over the human being. For technique, this is a matter of life and death. Technique must reduce man to a technical animal, the king of slaves of technique. Human caprice crumbles before this necessity; there can be no human autonomy in the face of technical autonomy.[8]

So – we all rushed to re-read the fictions of *Nineteen Eighty-Four* and *Brave New World*, and the answer seemed simple. But what we actually got was post-truth and the unpredictability of President Trump. And this oddly appears to work – at least for the time being. The cynics and the opportunists seem to get away with it. But, in the end, what of truth?

Pilate's weary, cynical question is a little different; 'What is truth?' (John 18:38). Pilate was, after all, the supreme pragmatist. But Pilate made what a philosopher would call a category mistake in asking such a question of Jesus in this context, though he was by no means a stupid man. Caillois' extraordinary novel explores Pilate's predicament as he faced the constraints upon the exercise of Roman imperial power in the face of local religious zeal. The truth and the honesty of our decisions can never be realized outside such contextual boundaries. Truth is always to be found in context. The Pilate of Caillois's novel explores the possibilities open to him, and their consequences, in this fictional case, end in his exile and suicide. Honesty is a hard master and history can be unkind.

Truth and philosophy

The designation 'Jesting Pilate' originates from the opening of Francis Bacon's 1625 essay 'Of Truth'. Pilate's question implies an intellectualist understanding of the nature of truth from the Greek philosophical tradition. Its biblical sense, however, is rather different. In the Hebrew Bible, as has been seen in Nicholas Taylor's chapter, truth is grasped not by detached contemplation but rather through commitment to God and God's covenant. In the words of the philosopher Herbert Dreyfus:

> For the Greeks, truth is open to all people since they all have universal, rational souls; for the Hebrews, truth is not universal. It is local and historical, revealed at a specific time and place to a particular people and preserved in a particular tradition.[9]

As a statement about truth this has enough truth in it to be useful. The Christian tradition, its theology an amalgam of biblical commitments and late Greek philosophy, awkwardly combines the two, propelling us into precisely the kind of arguments that we are engaged with here. We will try and draw them together at the end of the chapter.

Philosophers in the Western tradition have, at the same time, provided us with many 'theories' of truth. The *correspondence theory* argues that something is true only if it corresponds to a fact – though the fact itself is dependent upon verification in terms of truth, making that argument finally circular. The *coherence theory* suggests that truth 'consists in a relation which truth-bearers have to one another – such as a relation of mutual support among the beliefs of an individual or a community.'[10] The danger of this is that it disintegrates into chaotic relativism. There are idealist theories of truth and there are Jamesian pragmatic theories. Truth may be seen as either constitutive or regulative, the latter understood in its ultimately Kantian sense. Or truth may be functional, as, arguably, is the case in Derridean deconstruction, Jacques Derrida retorting to the accusation that his thought dwindles into decentred confusion:

> I didn't say there was no centre, that we could get along without the centre. I believe that the centre is a function, not a being – a reality, but a function. And this function is absolutely indispensable. The subject is absolutely indispensable. I don't destroy the subject; I situate it.[11]

For Derrida there is, of course, no 'outside-text' (*hors texte*), no transcendental signifier to guarantee truth: and the centre has a tendency to shift.

The trouble with most theories of truth, and arguments about it, is that they tend very quickly to fall into polar opposites – and it is highly problematic to see truth and falsity, as implied by the principle of bivalence, simply in terms of polarity. One of the most consistent claims for truth is that it is a 'property', but the problem is to decide what exactly it is a property *of*. Religion might claim that it is a property of God, but even as early as the Second Prayer Book of Edward VI (1552), Reformation theology on Holy Communion was rather strangely anticipating scientific literalism in its understanding of the property of Christ's body:

> For it is against the trueth of Christes true natural bodye, to be in moe places then in one, at one tyme.[12]

But we should not abandon too quickly the sense of truth as a property. The philosopher Simon Blackburn has deftly described how Friedrich Nietzsche, 'supremely sensitive to the cultural and political aspect of ideas,'[13] energetically sought to dissolve metaphysical truths as perceived by Plato, and he had a point, though this was, in Nietzsche, a supreme example, perhaps, of throwing the baby out with the bathwater. Moving into the twentieth century, Nietzsche, writes Blackburn, 'would have pre-empted the possibility of standing anywhere near the position that Heidegger or similar other-worldly metaphysicians wish to occupy.'[14]

Why, you might ask, should we bring Martin Heidegger into the discussion in our attempt to rescue the 'idea' of truth? Quite simply, Heidegger is valuable for us inasmuch as he does not deny that 'truth exists' but he does relentlessly attack the fantasy of what Timothy Clark has described as 'our achieving a truth which would be ahistorical and self-grounding, [and this] means that no interpretation, including his own, can or should be called final.'[15] We can see where the later Derrida was coming from. For Heidegger, truth in the sense of correctness is secondary to truth as *aletheia*, which in the Greek means literally something like 'uncoveredness',[16] truth revealed within a practice or system of life. Such unconcealment takes place where we find ourselves (and we need Aristotle here as well as Plato), Heidegger asserting that:

> It is not we who presuppose the unconcealedness of beings; rather, the unconcealedness of beings (Being) puts us into such a condition of being that in our representation we always remain installed within and in attendance upon unconcealedness.[17]

At the same time, Heidegger continues to argue that all theories of truth are only possible by a 'pre-theoretical relation to being that must always be assumed but which could never be fully conceptualized'.[18]

Heidegger keeps his distance from theology, but he does lay a philosophical groundwork upon which theologians must, if they are wise, tread, though warily, having been warned about claiming too much too quickly, a peculiar weakness of theologians. Heidegger offers us the possibility, indeed the necessity of truth but unstructured by any systematic theory of the world. Pilate, then, in addition to his category mistake, quite simply asked the *wrong* question. The question is not *what* (τί) but rather *where* is truth to be found and *how* do we find it? For most of the rest of this chapter I will situate the discussion very largely within the particular realm of ethics and morality.

Truth and power

In his writings on the relationship between truth and power, the philosopher Michel Foucault searches within the historical context for continuities that are capable of resisting the immediate demands of 'power'. Such demands are far more sinister than merely the simplicities of utilitarianism. The great enemy of truth is *discontinuity* – a destabilizing of discourse when relations of power replace relations of meaning.[19] Foucault is quite clear about the limits of his argument, seeking:

> A form of history which can account for the constitution of knowledges, discourses, domains of objects etc., without having to make references to a subject which is either transcendental in relation to the field of events or runs in its empty sameness throughout the course of history.[20]

It is, perhaps, no accident that at the end of his life Foucault was working on lectures concerned with the history of 'regimes of truth', concentrating on early Christian thinkers like Tertullian and Cassian and 'truth acts' in the early practice of baptism, penance and so on.[21]

In his analysis of truth and power, Foucault examines the example of the attitude towards infantile sexuality in bourgeois society in the eighteenth century. Countless manuals of the time convinced parents that sex was a problem, and equally convinced children that their bodies were the problem – so that the attempted evasion of sexuality resulted in both parents and children being sex obsessed.[22] Foucault's point is that all of this actually has nothing to do with sexuality at all, but that it is about relations of power, not relations of meaning. And the point is not so much that it is all 'not true', but that its destructiveness lies in its profound *destabilizing* of social situations. It means that parents (usually the father) are always seen to be right. (The situation continues in the early twentieth century – and there we need only read such works as Vera Brittain's *Testament of Youth*.)

Foucault insists that truth does not lie outside power, nor is it lacking in power. But inasmuch as power has a tendency to corrupt, its *continuities* have to be continually examined, re-articulated and preserved in changing contexts. Truth is a *quality* (perhaps even a property), but not an object, and that is a lesson that religious professionals seem to find it very hard to grasp. The sociologist Bruno Latour ends his book *Rejoicing: or, the Torments of Religious Speech* (2013) with a searing indictment of the fixedness of clerics who nail themselves to 'the truth' and end up hating everything 'idols, materialism, the market, modernism, the masses, sex, democracy – everything has horrified them'. On the other hand this gentle unbeliever, Latour, states more persuasively and wisely:

> Catholicity does not consist in spreading the good word right to the ends of the universe, but in producing from start to finish and in all places, just through talk that is risky every time, the future demands of a universe still to be negotiated.[23]

Continuity properly involves the abandoning of specific certainties of the kind indulged in by, on the one hand, self-appointed defenders of science such as Richard Dawkins, another category-mistake man with a vengeance, though without Pilate's tragic honesty, or, on the other hand, defenders of a particular kind of religious identity against the perceived threat of modernity and the rising tide of secularism.

So what then of the place of the ethical in the matter of truth?[24] Here I am quite prepared to enlist a variety of intellectual colleagues to my aid in pursuit of what we might call truth and the continuances of virtue.[25] It is still worthwhile going back to Iris Murdoch's essay *The Sovereignty of Good* (1970), written before the days of postmodernity, and examining the Kantian assumptions which lie underneath so much of our moral philosophy. Anthony Quinton wrote of Murdoch's theme as being 'the inadequacy of the account of human nature and value provided by contemporary, academic, analytic philosophy.'[26] And so where does Murdoch seek for help? In her essay 'On "God" and "Good"' she writes:

> I shall suggest that God was (or is) a *single perfect transcendent non-representable and necessarily real object of attention*; and I shall go on to suggest that moral philosophy should attempt to retain a central concept which has all these characteristics.[27]

Now I readily admit that this opens up any number of questions for both philosophy and theology. But let us stay with it for a moment in our pursuit of truth.

Though some of us who are clerical might at least wring our hands somewhat nervously at this definition of God, it probably is not all that far from the deity that is assumed in our acts of public worship and even private prayer. Murdoch, though no Christian herself, helps us to soften it a bit by describing prayer as 'simply an attention to God which is a form of love'. Philosophers might tell us what is going on here as we begin to relax from the language of 'objectivity'.

Talking about truth as perceived within a relationship allows it that vulnerability that so much of our theology seems to resist, if we are honest. Martha Nussbaum identifies this in Greek tragedy and philosophy as the fragility of goodness and the vulnerability of the good human life.[28] Perhaps luck comes into it also. So was Job just unlucky? No, an adequate discourse had to be built around his condition, and so we are back to different theories of truth as Job argues it out with his 'comforters'.

Any responsible discussion of truth in the Western tradition can hardly avoid, in the end, attention to the idea of *eudaimonia* or the ethical discourse of Aristotle in the *Nichomachean Ethics*. Ignorance of such is, as we are seeing in our current political and social dilemmas, profoundly dangerous. Truth and goodness must be intrinsically linked, as we must endlessly seek for markers along the way. And it is never easy. Martha Nussbaum concludes her book, *The Fragility of Goodness*, with these words:

> We have discovered that we live in the world that Aristotle describes; that we share, at the same time, a deep longing for another simpler or purer world. But the Aristotelian argument, which continues and refines the insights of tragedy, reminds us that we do not achieve purity or simplicity without a loss in richness and fullness of life – a loss, it is claimed, in intrinsic value.[29]

We must never give up on the complexity of the pursuit of truth and fool ourselves into thinking it is simple. Nussbaum leaves us with an image from Euripides' *Hecuba*:

> In place of the story of salvation through new arts, in place of the stratagems of the hunter and the solitary joy of the godlike philosopher, we are left with a new (but also very old) picture of deliberation and writing. We see a group of sailors voyaging unsafely. They consult with one another and take their bearings from that rock, which casts (under the liquid sky) its shadow on the sea.[30]

In an age that is obsessed by matters of safety and risk assessments designed to minimize risk as inherently a bad thing, it may seem paradoxical that the pursuit of truth is very much a matter of voyaging unsafely and riskily. Just as the Jesus of the gospels, and then Paul after him, have a habit of turning things around – life/death; wealth/poverty; weakness/strength; wisdom/foolishness – so we might turn the notion of the pursuit of truth around, making it rather the idea of allowing ourselves to be pursued by truth. Here, I think, we are on the edge between philosophy and theology – a place to which Heidegger almost, but not quite, takes us. One thinker whom we meet here is the Italian radical Catholic philosopher Gianni Vattimo and his idea of 'weak thought'.[31] His disciple Santiago Zabala describes weak thought very succinctly.

> Weak thought is by no means a weakness of thinking as such, but since thinking is no longer demonstrative but rather edifying, it has become weaker.[32]

One senses everywhere in Vattimo's writing the presence of Heidegger, on the edge of a particular kind of non-foundationalist theology but deeply hostile to any hint of ontotheology or the God of philosophical theology.

Gianni Vattimo

One of Vattimo's most creative and, at first glance, most seemingly unlikely, cooperations is with the pragmatist Richard Rorty in a small book entitled *The Future of Religion* (2004). Rorty has written extensively on the subject of truth, not least on the work of the philosopher Donald Davidson. In the end Rorty is more at home in a world of historical contingencies, less interested in ideas of 'truth', but rather, as he sees of science, the development of habits that enable us to cope with the realities given to us. Actually Rorty and Vattimo have a great deal in common through their (rather different) critiques of metaphysics in the future of religion. But I want to suggest that there is a fundamental coherence (perhaps a better word is honesty) in Vattimo and his 'weak thought'.

Rorty finally wants to have it both ways. Simon Blackburn illustrates the way in which, for Rorty, we seek legitimately to justify ourselves. Rorty states that he fails to see 'how anything can be relevant to deciding whether a sentence *is* true except the outcome of actual or possible practices of justification to our fellows'.[33] When pressed as to who he means by 'our fellows', he would appeal to 'better informed or more enlightened practitioners' – whoever they might be. In the context of a Rortian debunking of truth, Blackburn writes:

> This is fairly astonishing: how can Rorty deny and debunk truth, but keep notions such as 'better informed' or 'more enlightened' which are obviously inextricably entangled with it? We can see the cul-de-sac that lies this way …[34]

ORIGINS OF TRUTH IN PHILOSOPHY, THEOLOGY, AND THEORY

But what now of Vattimo? Actually he begins by returning to biblical categories and commitment, employing a reading of kenosis as 'the incarnation as God's renunciation of his own sovereign transcendence.'[35] This enables him to assert that:

> Postmodern nihilism (the end of metanarratives) is the truth of Christianity. Which is to say that Christianity's truth appears to be the dissolution of the (metaphysical) truth concept itself.[36]

This re-reading of kenotic theology enables Vattimo, as one of the founding members of the European Parliament and shapers of the European constitution, to reach the astonishing conclusion that 'the force of the Gospels and of Jesus' teaching provides the foundation of the secularity of a democratic state today.'[37]

If this seems hard to grasp, let me try and draw to a conclusion with a brief outline of the complex necessity and possibility of truth in this post-truth age that might help us to understand Vattimo's seeming paradox. We have seen the odd phenomenon of the non-believer Iris Murdoch appealing to the idea or concept of God as the basis of moral philosophy: a regulative rather than a constitutive principle. At the same time, we find the Catholic Vattimo speaking of the 'truth' of Christianity in terms of the end of metanarratives and as the foundation of secularity. In each there is an acknowledgement of the idea of truth found between the tradition of the Bible and the tradition of Greek philosophy. If you wish to find the truth, you must abandon any hint of the absolutist and metaphysical sense of 'the truth'. The Romantic poet and thinker Samuel Taylor Coleridge realized this long ago in his experience of reading the Bible in which

> there is more that *finds* me than I have experienced in all other books put together ... the words of the Bible find me at greater depths of my being ...[38]

The truth that is inherent in Coleridge's discovery is very far removed from the abstracted conception of the world that is demanded by correspondence theories of truth. Rather, truth is revealed within particular and actual modes of existence that acknowledge that some interpretations are more valid than others in the encounter with the Other, either in the moral demands upon me of the other person or in that Otherness that may be assumed but is beyond conceptualization. Iris Murdoch is prepared to acknowledge this – and some of us, though probably not Murdoch herself, might call such Otherness God. Attention to truth demands discipline, consistency and thoughtful attention beyond the final amorality of a pure pragmatics that may serve a number of highly questionable ends subject to the temptations of power.

Truth, Jesus, and Pontius Pilate

Allow me finally to return to John 18:33–38 and the dialogue between Jesus and Pontius Pilate that concludes with his famous (or infamous) question, 'What is truth?' The literary critic A. D. Nuttall, who is anxious to confirm to his reader that he is *not* a Christian believer, described this conversation as an example of what literary critics call discontinuous dialogue,[39] a mode more usually attributed to the Russian playwright Anton Chekhov (though we can find it in Shakespeare as well). Questions are not answered but responded to by other questions or answered with gaps in the logic. The conversation then lacks any 'logical fit' on the principle of discontinuity. But being discontinuous does not mean that logic is abandoned. Rather, either steps in the exchange are omitted or else the questions are answered not in the order that they are put in the first place – the discontinuities are quite deliberate and assume an underlying continuity, and in this case the control of the conversation is reversed from Pilate (who should be wholly in command) to Jesus who seems to be shifting the 'mode of existence' in what Nuttall calls 'a technique of deliberate transcendence'.[40] In other words, we, after Pilate, begin to suspect that we are thinking on the wrong plane. We could take it as an infuriating verbal game (it is a literary mechanism that is actually quite easy to indulge in), dismiss it, like Pilate, with weary cynicism, or else finally pursue the possibility that we are in the presence of *aletheia* – a new, for us, unconcealing of the truth. Theologians might call it a revelation. Scientists also make their own claim upon this idea, as we will see in the chapters by Priest and Fuller (10 and 11). But if this latter is the case, we have to be prepared for the consequences. Nuttall, the unbeliever, weighs up the possibilities.

1 'John, for political or missionary reasons, produced the claim to be divine on Jesus' behalf.' That, he suggests, is just bad faith.
2 'John was repeating, in good faith, a tradition about Jesus which he believed to be true.' That, of course, does not *make* it true. The tradition may have been based upon a lie or misunderstanding and John was just taken in by it.
3 *Aut deus aut malus homo.* 'Either God or a wicked man.' Jesus was just a clever rogue, or worse, though it did not do him much good if that is all there is to it.

4 Jesus was mad. This is the possibility that Nuttall, who describes himself as an unbeliever in an unbelieving culture, finds most convincing. He admits that natural explanations must be exhausted before we have recourse to the supernatural. But the natural turns out to be far from simple.

Let us unpick the madness possibility a little further. First, we have to abandon the lingering (and common) presumptions that a) madness is the opposite of intelligence, and b) madness is incompatible with goodness. So-called 'mad' people may be highly intelligent and deeply charitable. Actually, Nuttall admits, to the unbeliever Jesus is very far from being a poor, if mad, candidate for being God. Many others, like the Emperor Caligula, have claimed divinity and Caligula was certainly not, unlike Jesus, 'the best of men'.

So – where is all this leading us? Nuttall's point is that John's Gospel stands on a knife-edge between belief and unbelief, an astounding truth or a downright lie. And on that knife-edge 'truth' itself resides, demanding our full attention and dangerous when simply dismissed. Nuttall concludes his book:

> This barbarous reader took no belief to his reading of the Gospel. But the first thing he encountered was a frontal challenge to that unbelief.[41]

Truth, then, matters, and the sceptical reader is shaken by its claims. Philosophers, theologians, and others, have their own forms of attention to it, their own theories and attempted consistencies. 'Post-truth' is nothing new but is as old as the hills, even if it was only in November 2016 that the *Oxford English Dictionary* named it as the word of the year. It was not invented by or on behalf of President Donald Trump. In Plato's *Gorgias* and *Phaedrus* there is the dark suspicion that the evil lies in the art of rhetoric – speeches used to whip up the crowd usually based on immediate and simplistic claims designed to attract the unwary for purposes of gain or self-aggrandizement. Rhetoric is, of course, a deception, indifferent to either truth or morality, and Plato's antidote is 'dialectic, whose province is definition and division in the ceaseless search for truth.'[42]

The danger of post-truth is not only that we are all capable of believing it, but that actually it fascinates us as a debased form of enchantment even when we know (or think we know) we are being hoodwinked. And once it has us in its grip it seduces us away from the demands of ethics and morality and the inconveniences and worse that accompany any commitment to truth and its continuances. It allows us to shift and change when it suits us to do so and within its grip we can have no proper relationship with the Other – be that another person, an idea or principle, or indeed God. Post-truth thrives on the abuse of power and, like alcohol or nicotine, it is highly addictive. When post-truth begins to flourish one should fear for more than one's goods and prosperity. 'For what shall it profit a man, if he shall gain the whole world, and lose his own soul (ψυχη)?' (Mark 8.36, AV).

Questions for discussion

1 Why is the principle of truth so essential to the preservation of our humanity?
2 How do we keep a proper balance between power, authority and truth?
3 A post-truth world is amoral rather than immoral. What is the significance in this distinction, and does it matter?

Further reading

J. Baggini, *A Short History of Truth: Consolations for a Post-Truth World* (London: Quercus, 2017). A readable example of one of the many current brief books on truth and post-truth.
S. Blackburn, *Truth: A Guide for the Perplexed* (Harmondsworth: Penguin, 2005). A clear and helpful philosophical introduction written in an accessible style by a leading philosopher.
S. Blackburn and K. Simmons (eds), *Truth* (Oxford: OUP, 1999). Essays on theories of truth by major philosophers. Some are difficult but repay close reading.
M. Kakutani, *The Death of Truth* (London: William Collins, 2018). Widely reviewed, this is a relentless exposure of current politics, with some sense of the way out.

Notes

1 M. Kundera, *The Art of the Novel*. Trans. Linda Asher (ET London: Faber and Faber, 1988), p. 158.
2 Plato, *Phaedrus*. Trans. Walter Hamilton (Harmondsworth: Penguin, 1973), p. 79.
3 See also below, Chapter 9 (Gillies).
4 B. Pascal, *Pensées* (1660). Trans. W. F. Trotter (New York: Dutton, 1958), p. 53.

5 J.-F. Lyotard, *The Postmodern Condition: A Report on Knowledge*. Trans. Geoff Bennington and Brian Massumi (Manchester: Manchester University Press, 1984), p. xxiv.

6 T. Eagleton, *Literary Theory: An Introduction*. 2nd edn. (Oxford: Blackwell, 1996), p. 200.

7 S. Fish, *Is There a Text in This Class?* (Cambridge MA: Harvard University Press, 1980), p. 305.

8 J. Ellul, *The Technological Society*. Trans. John W. Wilkinson (New York: A. A. Knopf, 1964), p. 138. See also Theodore Roszak, *The Making of a Counter Culture: Reflections on the Technocratic Society and Its Youthful Opposition*. (London: Faber and Faber, 1970).

9 H. L. Dreyfus, 'The Roots of Existentialism', in Herbert L. Dreyfus and Mark A. Wrathhall (eds), *A Companion to Phenomenology and Existentialism* (Oxford: Blackwell, 2006), p. 138.

10 E. J. Lowe, 'Truth', in Ted Honderich (ed.), *The Oxford Companion to Philosophy*. New edn. (Oxford: OUP, 2005), p. 926.

11 J. Derrida, *Writing and Difference*. Trans. Alan Bass (London: Routledge & Kegan Paul, 1981), p. 279. Also, Frank Lentricchia, *After the New Criticism* (London: Methuen, 1983), p. 174.

12 *The First and Second Prayer Books of King Edward VI* (London: J. M. Dent, 1913), p. 393.

13 S. Blackburn, *Truth: A Guide for the Perplexed* (Harmondsworth: Penguin, 2006), p. 82. This book has its origins in the Gifford Lectures delivered in the University of Glasgow, 2004.

14 Ibid.

15 T. Clark, *Martin Heidegger* (London: Routledge, 2002), p. 24.

16 On *aletheia* see also Chapter 1 (Taylor) and Chapter 9 (Gillies).

17 M. Heidegger, *Poetry, Language, Thought*. Trans. Albert Hofstadter (New York: Harper & Row, 1971), p. 52.

18 T. Clark, op. cit. p. 24.

19 M. Foucault, *Power/Knowledge: Selected Interviews and Others Writings, 1972-1977*. Ed. Colin Gordon (New York: Pantheon Books, 1980), p. 114.

20 Ibid. p. 117.

21 See M. Foucault, *On the Government of the Living*. Ed. Michel Senellart. Trans. Graham Burchell (New York: Picador, 2012).

22 Foucault, *Power/Knowledge*, p 120.

23 B. Latour, *Rejoicing: or, the Torments of Religious Speech*. Trans. Julie Rose (Cambridge: Polity Press, 2013), pp. 172-3.

24 See Chapter 10 (Priest) for a discussion of the role of beauty in science.

25 See W. Berthoff, *Literature and the Continuances of Virtue* (Princeton: Princeton University Press, 1986).

26 Review in the *Sunday Telegraph*.

27 Iris Murdoch, *The Sovereignty of Good* (London: Routledge & Kegan Paul, 1970), p. 55.

28 M. C. Nussbaum, *The Fragility of Goodness: Luck and Ethics in Greek Tragedy and Philosophy* (Cambridge: Cambridge University Press, 1986).

29 Ibid. p. 421.

30 Ibid.

31 This might be related in some sense to Dietrich Bonhoeffer's earlier idea of 'religionless Christianity'.

32 Santiago Zabala, 'Gianni Vattimo and Weak Philosophy', in Zabala (ed.), *Weakening Philosophy: Essays in Honour of Gianni Vattimo* (Montreal: McGill-Queen's University Press: 2007), p. 19.

33 R. Rorty, 'Response to John McDowell', in Robert B. Brandom (ed.), *Rorty and His Critics* (Oxford: Blackwell, 2000), p. 125. Simon Blackburn, *Truth: A Guide for the Perplexed*, p. 161.

34 Blackburn, op. cit. p. 161.

35 G. Vattimo, 'The Age of Interpretation', in Santiago Zabala (ed), *The Future of Religion* (New York: Columbia University Press, 2005), p. 51.

36 Ibid.

37 Zabala, 'Gianni Vattimo and Weak Philosophy', p. 28.

38 S. T. Coleridge, *Confessions of an Inquiring Spirit* (London: William Pickering, 1840), p. 13. (Reprinted as facsimile, Scolar Press, 1971).

39 A. D. Nuttall, *Overheard By God: Fiction and Prayer in Herbert, Milton, Dante and St. John* (London: Methuen, 1980), pp. 128–43.

40 Ibid. p. 131.

41 Ibid. p. 143.

42 See D. Jasper, *Rhetoric, Power and Community: An Exercise in Reserve* (London: Macmillan, 1993), pp. 17–18.

3

Seeing As: Wittgenstein's Approach to Truth

SCOTT ROBERTSON

And the LORD said ..., 'Come, let us go down, and confuse their language there, so that they will not understand one another's speech.' So the LORD scattered them abroad from there over the face of all the earth, and they left off building the city. (Gen. 11:6–8)

... and after the fire a sound of sheer silence. (1 Kings 19:12)

As we saw in the previous chapter, the perennial goal of philosophy has widely been perceived to be the pursuit of wisdom or truth. The unsaid but by no means universal assumption behind this quest was that there existed an objective known as 'wisdom' or 'truth' waiting to be discovered.[1] Truth understood as such held some distinctive shape or form which human beings could reach toward and somehow appropriate. In other words, many philosophers held to what is known as a realistic or ontological view of truth. An obvious example here can be discerned in the system of René Descartes (1596–1650), who sought to provide a secure footing for knowledge or truth. Writing in an environment where religious wars were not a distant memory but a very present reality, Descartes strove to offer an unassailable account of truth as a means of potentially alleviating the monstrous consequences of internecine religious conflict which were largely fuelled by division over the specific nature of religious truth.[2] Descartes' famous dictum, *Cogito ergo sum* (I think therefore I am), though starting from an inward place of radical doubt about the world, nevertheless presumed an essence 'out there' to be discovered. Indeed, for Descartes, it was God's own existence which guaranteed such confidence. Both Kant and Hume were later fatally to damage Descartes' metaphysical assumption that one can move seamlessly from an idea to a reality, but nonetheless, it illustrates for us that Descartes becomes a touchstone between a pre-modern and modern conception of truth.

The great irony in this is that, while the notion of God for Descartes was secured (developing, as he did, Anselm's ontological argument: 'that than which nothing more perfect could be conceived'[3]), a cultural sea change had taken place in so far as the measure of judgement was no longer in God's control but lay with humanity itself. In Descartes, we are unwittingly returned to Protagoras' understanding of 'man [sic] as the measure of all things', with all the concomitant implications for the discernment of truth. Truth, then, in the modern period, appears to hold within itself an instability, freed as it is from any metaphysical anchor and yet, as we shall see, remaining in large part the objective focus of philosophical enquiry.

The development of what has become known as analytic philosophy in the early twentieth century was to radically augment this initial Enlightenment critique of theocentrism. As we have noted, Descartes chose to delve inwards to find the foundation for knowledge, but he allied this radical scepticism with the safety net of a God whose existence he could not possibly doubt. However, analytical philosophers like Bertrand Russell (1872–1970) and G. E. Moore (1873–1958) placed the emphasis, not on any assumed metaphysical system, but on the very building blocks used to communicate truth in the first place, namely language. This may appear somewhat pedantic and in a certain sense even obvious. The reality is very different. To place the emphasis upon our use of language was as radical as René Descartes' desire to doubt everything apart from his own ability to think. One further and supremely significant figure in this 'linguistic turn' was the Austrian-British philosopher Ludwig Wittgenstein (1889–1951), who is the particular focus of this chapter.

Ludwig Wittgenstein is almost universally acknowledged to be the foremost philosopher of the twentieth century.[4] Certainly, there has been no other philosopher in the modern period who has exerted such a cultural influence and this despite the notoriously dense, tortuous and even mystical nature of his writing. Notwithstanding the formidable character of his intellectual endeavour, particularly in the field of logic, and the associated massive secondary literature that his thought has generated within the philosophical and broader academic community – Wittgenstein's idiosyncratic demeanour, his frequent depressions and suicidal thoughts (two of his brothers committed suicide), coupled with an unwavering intensity of moral purpose (he gave away his inheritance, which would have made him one of the richest men in Europe) – Wittgenstein has attracted the attention of not only other philosophers but filmmakers, writers, poets and painters.[5] This has (inadvertently no doubt) led to an unhealthy separation of the man Wittgenstein from his thinking. Such a pathology reveals not simply a lack of contextual grounding but, more significantly, runs counter to Wittgenstein's own broad philosophical vision which, despite its admittedly arcane presentation, is intended to be deeply holistic.[6] This chapter seeks to re-forge the link between Wittgenstein the man, and his philosophical endeavour. As well as examining the key themes from his major works, I will also reflect upon Wittgenstein's experience and understanding of religion, with a particular emphasis upon the practice of confession. In so doing I hope to present in an accessible and clear way the implications of Wittgenstein's thinking for our understanding of the nature of truth.

The description of Wittgenstein as the greatest philosopher of the twentieth century is remarkable for a number of reasons. In his lifetime, Wittgenstein published only one slim volume, the *Tractatus Logico-Philosophicus* (1921).[7] In that work, which is by turns scientific, logical, and mystical, Wittgenstein claimed to have provided 'the final solution' to all the problems of philosophy.[8] This grand claim was made despite the fact that, by the time the *Tractatus* was published, Wittgenstein, by then a decorated war hero, had read next to no philosophy. Indeed, throughout his life he would regard the professional practice of philosophy with some disdain. He specifically reacted against the prevailing notion of philosophy as a branch of science, preferring it to be regarded as '*a poetic composition*'.[9] Having, as he believed, solved 'all the problems of philosophy', Wittgenstein gave up philosophy altogether and worked in various roles as a teacher, an architect (memorably co-designing, in 1925, a house for his sister, Margaret), as a gardener in a monastery, and later during the Second World War as a hospital porter. It is also fair to say that Wittgenstein's writing style as well as content are challenging, if not stretching us to the bounds of comprehension.[10] As Ray Monk has written, 'Wittgenstein did indeed believe that one could *show* deep truths, either by remaining silent about them or by saying things that, strictly speaking, were nonsensical.'[11] Wittgenstein, himself, says in the *Tractatus*:

> My propositions serve as elucidations in the following way: anyone who understands me eventually recognizes them as nonsensical, when he's used them – as steps – to climb up beyond them. (He must, so to speak, throw away the ladder after he has climbed up it.)[12]

So, Wittgenstein, a philosopher who profoundly stood against the professional practice of philosophy; someone who published little; someone who taught sporadically; someone whose writing is often arcane – how does this person achieve the accolade of the greatest philosopher of the twentieth century? And, for our immediate purpose, what does this mean for the pursuit of truth? The answer may lie in those dense, terse and, at times, mystical statements in his two major works the *Tractatus Logico-Philosophicus* and the *Philosophical Investigations* (published posthumously in 1953). It is therefore important, for our understanding of truth, to sketch out the aims of Wittgenstein and the tools he uses to reach towards those aims.

The first epigraph which opens this chapter offers us a way into Wittgenstein's early thought. The biblical story of the Tower of Babel is one of language confusion. It is just such language confusion which thinkers like Bertrand Russell, Wittgenstein's mentor and, at times, counsellor, had sought to overcome. Russell's goal was to discover what he called a perfect language which would correspond more or less exactly to the way things are in the world. The so-called ordinary language of everyday use was, for Russell, an impediment to such a desired clarity. Russell's theory about the nature of logical facts – 'logical atomism' – implied that if you dig down deep enough to the 'atomic level' of logic, one can be more sure of the philosophical ground one will be standing upon. This most basic level Wittgenstein was later to call 'states of affairs'. Thinkers like Russell claimed that

> Modern analytical empiricism ... differs from that of Locke, Berkeley, and Hume by its incorporation of mathematics and its development of a powerful logical technique. It is thus able, in regard to certain problems, to achieve definite answers, which have the quality of science rather than of philosophy. It has the advantage, in comparison with the philosophies of the system-builders, of being able to tackle its problems one at a time, instead of having to invent at one stroke a block theory of the whole universe. Its methods, in this respect, resemble those of science.[13]

Russell thus argued for what is known as a theory of correspondence in order to establish the truth of a given statement.[14] In other words, he claimed that the words we use have meaning if and only if they correspond to the nature of things in our world. So, for example, the phrase 'the cat sat on the mat' only has meaning if there is indeed a cat in the world who at that moment is seated on a mat. This, once again, may sound more than a little pedantic, but it is crucial in differentiating between a realist or foundationalist understanding of truth and a non-realist or, as some postmodern thinkers put it, pragmatic understanding.[15] This 'logically idealized language', as Hans-Georg Gadamer was later to describe it, was, for Wittgenstein, the means by which we overcome what he called the senselessness of philosophy. As Wittgenstein put it, 'most questions and propositions of the philosophers result from the fact that we do not understand the logic of our language.'[16]

Following in the wake of Russell, Wittgenstein believed that in his *Tractatus Logico-Philosophicus* he had overcome Babel – that he had finally resolved the problems of philosophy through making propositions and thoughts clear. As he put it in his later work, he was condensing what he called 'the whole cloud of philosophy into a drop of grammar'.[17] We can, therefore, describe Wittgenstein's approach as therapeutic, designed as it is to unravel the confusion brought about by the misuse of language. Wittgenstein summed it up in his celebrated phrase, 'Philosophy is a battle against the bewitchment of our intelligence by means of our language.'[18] A good example here might be found in the asking of the not insignificant question: 'What is the meaning of life?' Wittgenstein argues we are mistaken if, by asking such a question, we assume that we are speaking of meaning as a *thing*. This would constitute a failure 'to give a meaning to certain signs in [the] propositions.'[19] James Klagge helpfully amplifies Wittgenstein's point when he writes:

> Once we realize that 'meaning' is not functioning here as a name of *something*, we can consider other possibilities. Perhaps what we really want to know is: 'What things or activities make life *meaningful?*' This seems much more answerable, if not quite so mysterious and profound. In a sense, we have offered a critique of language by noting that what appeared to be a name, really functions as an adjective.[20]

Like Russell, Wittgenstein regarded logic as the therapeutic agent which would encourage this healing process.[21] Such therapy, however, extends to the point of seeking to discern the very limit of language itself, which means that, for Wittgenstein, unlike Russell, there are areas of human experience which transcend language. We shall follow the implications of this for Wittgenstein's understanding of truth in due course.

Returning to the *Tractatus* we discover that, for Wittgenstein, there is a hierarchical relationship between the world as it is, the thoughts we think and the words we use to express those thoughts. As Norman Malcolm puts it: 'The sentences one utters, just like the thought it expresses, will be a model of the situation that is being described. Both a proposition and a thought *reproduce*, in a sense, the situation they describe.'[22] This leads us to what has become known as Wittgenstein's celebrated Picture Theory of language.[23] It is important to notice at this point that, for Wittgenstein, the world is not made up of 'things' but of 'facts'.[24] By this he means that things are simple, while facts are articulate, which is to say that, like machinery which can move and so fulfil a specific function, they tell us something, and this is achieved through picturing. Wittgenstein thus concludes that a logical picture of facts is a thought.[25] We are confronted here with Wittgenstein's initial understanding of how language and thought are a kind of seeing. At this point Wittgenstein assumes that there can be a logical correspondence between the picture and the fact. As we shall shortly see, however, this was to be radically modified in Wittgenstein's later thinking.

Although Wittgenstein initially shared with Russell the belief that one can by sheer force of logic overcome language confusion and provide a definitive sphere of clarity, he later came to recognize (as Russell had not) that the assumption that philosophy, with science, shared the responsibility of providing answers to philosophical problems was simply a mirage created once again by a misunderstanding of language. As he once put it, the difficulty is 'not (as) the intellectual difficulty of the sciences, but the difficulty of a change of attitude'.[26] Wittgenstein goes on to make the astounding claim that philosophy does not result in philosophical propositions.[27] This, at first sight, seems paradoxical but in reality it follows from what has been suggested above. The notion that there are such things as 'philosophical propositions' implies that there is therefore a goal, a target to which philosophy is aiming. Wittgenstein says this is again the result of confusion over language. Philosophy's task is not to provide propositions or answers, but to clear the ground so that there can be a better way of seeing the world.

Having said this, Wittgenstein recognized the limits (indeed the meaninglessness) of his own position, and this is expressed most clearly in his notion of seeing and showing. In the *Tractatus*, Wittgenstein famously writes 'There are, indeed, things that cannot be put into words. They *make themselves manifest.*'[28] We come here to the part of the *Tractatus* that Wittgenstein's teacher, Russell, had most difficulty in comprehending, coming at it as he did from a strictly logical point of view. This was very close, Russell believed, to mysticism. Russell was, of course, correct. It illustrates Wittgenstein's point that philosophy is less a science than it is a poetic composition. As Ray Monk has put it:

> If philosophical understanding is to be conveyed, then it cannot be conveyed in the same way that scientific knowledge is conveyed – i.e. stated directly in literal language – it must be through something more analogous to poetry. The philosopher has to bear in mind always that what he or she really wants to say cannot be said, and therefore, it has to be conveyed another way: it has to be *shown*.[29]

Philosophy, then, is not so much an exercise in providing answers to specific problems, which Wittgenstein considered a philosophical mistake, and instead is more of 'a way of seeing'. This way of seeing Wittgenstein describes as 'perspicuous representation'[30] a means by which a clear view of the way we use words can be found. Wittgenstein, as we have noted, criticized the pretenses of philosophy to regard itself as a science. He regarded those who saw philosophy in this way as 'not equipped with the right visual organs'.[31] The same sentiment is found in Wittgenstein's prayer: 'God grant the philosopher insight into what lies in front of everyone's eyes.'[32] In this one phrase Wittgenstein is criticizing the temptation to scientistic elitism which he believes can infect philosophy. He is suggesting that philosophy is less a discipline like mathematics, and more a way of viewing the world which is open to all. The purpose of philosophy in this sense is not to provide answers but to result in a change of perspective.[33] And this is where the breach between the 'early' and the 'later' Wittgenstein is made most evident, namely in his notion of 'meaning as use'.[34]

It would be to misunderstand Wittgenstein if one were to equate 'meaning as use' with an unthinking relativism. Equally, while it is clear that Wittgenstein emphasizes the linguistic confusion which can surround any metaphysical sense of truth, this does not imply that truth finds itself diluted to the point of simple 'opinion' or, as the Vienna Circle assumed, confined to empirically verifiable statements. Truth, for Wittgenstein, is not to be determined on the basis of either a crude relativism or an equally crude prescriptivism. Rather, what we are confronted with (somewhat paradoxically given Wittgenstein's association with logic) is the vital recognition that truth moves beyond explanation and indeed objectivity. At this point we can detect Wittgenstein's debt to existential philosophers like Kierkegaard and his notion of 'truth as subjectivity', which has little to do with relativism and more to do with what Edward Mooney calls an emphasis upon 'the worth and inescapability of personal immersion in life.'[35] Wittgenstein would surely find himself assenting when Kierkegaard describes the truth of God in this way: '[a]n objective uncertainty held fast in an appropriation-process of the most passionate inwardness is the truth, the highest truth for an existing individual.'[36] Truth, in this sense, cannot be equated with objective fact as evinced in the correspondence approach in the *Tractatus*, but is rather linked more to Wittgenstein's notion of 'family resemblances' in the *Philosophical Investigations*, where we discover tentatively, and sometimes painfully through our immersion in life, where the truth at any given moment lies.

Such immersion in life involves looking at the world differently. This is achieved by reorganizing how we use language. Wittgenstein describes this basic principle in his *Philosophical Investigations* as an awareness of what he calls 'language games',[37] 'the *speaking* of which, is part of an activity, or of a life-form'.[38] This contrasts sharply with Wittgenstein's view of language in the *Tractatus*, where the fundamental argument was that language did indeed correspond to a given reality. In that work, as we noted, Wittgenstein believed that he had provided the 'final solution' to the problems of philosophy.[39] However, in *Philosophical Investigations*, Wittgenstein recognized that such definitive understanding was not actually possible, or even desirable. Indeed, his insight is that we use language very differently. Wittgenstein argued that:

> Our clear and simple language-games are not preparatory studies for a future regimentation of language ... The language-games are rather set up as *objects of comparison* which are meant to throw light on the facts of our language by way not only of similarities, but also of dissimilarities.[40]

An example of forms of life would be the playing of a game like chess or football. Any individual game or pursuit can hold within it its own specific language which delimits and contextualizes that particular form of life. And these forms of life are, by definition, limitless. In this changed, expanded understanding, to assume that language itself is in a sense systematic or precise is an illusion. We cannot have any definitive order in our knowledge or use of language.[41] That is one of the reasons why Wittgenstein chooses to offer a number of concrete cases to illustrate how we use our language and deploy concepts in different contexts. As a result, we are confronted with the conclusion that, for Wittgenstein, there is no conclusion, there is no end point as such. Instead we are exposed in the numerous examples Wittgenstein gives of 'language games' to a multiplicity of possibilities.[42] He makes the point thus: 'If someone were to advance *theses* in philosophy, it would never be possible to debate them, because everyone would agree to them.'[43] His point being that philosophy's task is an open-ended one, bounded only by the infinitely variegated nature of human experience itself.

All of this is, paradoxically, to suggest that there is a limit to the power of explanation. For Wittgenstein, the task of philosophy is not to explain but simply to become aware of what lies before it. Philosophy cannot explain, and it cannot effect change. It can only describe and, in Wittgenstein's memorable phrase, 'It leaves everything as it is.'[44] Marie McGinn helpfully summarizes Wittgenstein's approach here when she writes:

> This understanding is expressed, not in doctrines, but in a change of attitude which is connected with the emergence of a concern with

what lies open to view in the concrete details of our practice of using expressions, and with the abandonment of the attempt to construct elucidations or speculative accounts.[45]

The desire to avoid definition ironically makes it difficult for Wittgenstein himself to be definitive about his task. Nowhere does he specifically say: 'I want to change your way of seeing things.'

How we see is hugely variegated. We can look at the same object and see different things at different moments. Wittgenstein tells us that this 'noticing an aspect' is the experience of seeing the same thing in a different way.[46] The thing itself – a face, for example, hasn't changed, but a comparison with another face (or a different context) brings about this experience of seeing the face differently. It is the active engagement with reality which reveals how things actually are. In other words, 'neither objectivity, nor subjectivity solves philosophical problems; rather activity alone dissolves them.'[47]

The famous image of the duck/rabbit (above) graphically symbolizes this engagement with the immediate task at hand which is to simply 'see'. This has paradoxical implications for our appreciation or understanding of truth. For, as Wittgenstein asks us, when we look at the picture and see at one moment a rabbit and the next a duck:

> [W]hat is different? my impression? my point of view? – Can I say? I *describe* the alteration like a perception; quite as if the object had altered before my eyes. 'Now I am seeing *this*', I might say. This has the form of a report of a new perception. The expression of a change of aspect is the expression of a *new* perception and at the same time of the perception's being unchanged.[48]

One significant contrast between the *Tractatus* and the *Philosophical Investigations* is that in the former Wittgenstein sought for an overview of the world 'in the light of eternity'[49] whereas, in the *Philosophical Investigations*, Wittgenstein recognized that such an overview was impossible and that a perspicuous representation of life as it is encountered in its various forms is all that can be hoped for. As Genova puts it: 'Perspicuous representation eliminates all super views.'[50] In so saying we discover that Wittgenstein is pragmatic but not a pragmatist. He does not assume that he has discovered a framework for how the world works for all time.[51] Instead, his pragmatism extends to the acknowledgement of the importance of context and use for the determination of meaning. Thus, the meaning or truth of religious practice, for example, cannot be determined by those who, for whatever reason, have become estranged from the practices and contexts of religion.[52]

It can be suggested that Wittgenstein saw his role as a purifier of thinking – not in any moralistic sense but in his persistent awareness of the pitfalls of clouded thinking, that is, thinking which seeks to prescribe too closely – the kind of reductionist thinking which can adversely affect not only religious circles but also scientific ones. The notion of pure reason is regarded by Wittgenstein as a chimera, indeed an idol to be avoided at all costs. 'There is', he argues, 'no religious denomination in which the misuse of metaphysical expressions has been responsible for so much sin as it has in mathematics.'[53] In so saying, Wittgenstein was seeking to press home the point that what is commonly called 'a mathematical discovery had much better be called a mathematical invention.'[54] A proof in mathematics does not, he argues, establish the truth of a conclusion but rather the meaning of the terms involved. He amplifies this when he writes, 'To deny that two plus two equals four is not to disagree with a widely held view about a matter of fact; it is to show ignorance of the meaning of the terms involved.'[55] For Wittgenstein, a proof is nothing so sacred but is instead, 'a record of connection, nothing more'.[56] To describe such a state of affairs as 'true' is therefore, in a certain sense, superfluous.

This has led some to describe Wittgenstein's approach as a 'deflationary' account of truth.[57] This approach implies that there is no property of truth 'out there' which can be applied to statements of fact. It is certainly arguable as to whether Wittgenstein would accept this interpretation of his approach. It is, to my mind, more likely that Wittgenstein, while seeking to clarify our linguistic confusion, would demur from any attempt to diminish the importance of the encounter with truth. This is not because he wished to delineate too closely the term 'truth', but that he was more concerned about the pursuit of a clear vision of the human encounter with the world as it is. Clearing away our language confusion reveals to us that concepts such as 'truth' can, if used injudiciously, lead us away from the world as we encounter it. But that does not mean that the 'experience' of truth in our lives becomes somehow of secondary importance. This would be to ignore

Wittgenstein's sense of philosophy's place in the world as a means to clearing the ground that we can see more clearly.

To illustrate this, Wittgenstein, early in his *Philosophical Investigations*, quotes St Augustine's discussion in his *Confessions* on the nature of time.[58] This question and others like them, e.g. 'What is meaning?' 'What is thought?', as St Augustine himself knew, are not questions to which one can give a definitive explanation or answer. And the danger, for Wittgenstein, is that if we seek to try to reach an explanation in the scientific sense, we will actually find ourselves in a worse epistemic situation than before. Wittgenstein describes the difficulties we get ourselves into by adopting scientific principles to explain philosophical problems as akin to 'trying to repair a torn spider's web with our fingers'.[59] Wittgenstein argues that the philosophical temptation is to think that the solutions to problems of philosophy are presumed to be deep and hidden (like buried treasure). Instead he suggests they are hidden in plain sight.[60] This is counterintuitive.[61] Wittgenstein goes out of his way not to replace one philosophical 'system' with another. He has no system. He simply (or not so simply!) wants us to change our way of looking at philosophical questions. This is a radical departure from more traditional ways of thinking about thinking.

Having looked at Wittgenstein's broad philosophical approach, it is now the time for us to try to connect this with his own personal experience and particularly as this relates to religion and the nature of truth. On his deathbed it is believed that Wittgenstein's last remarks were, 'Tell them I've had a wonderful life.'[62] On the face of it, this may appear inconsistent with how many encountered Wittgenstein. For example, he was, in the words of one close friend, 'intolerant, irascible, idiosyncratic'.[63] He was a man driven by an almost puritanical desire for perfection. He was tortured in many ways by his own unrealistic standards and his inability to make allowances for those who could not even begin to look at life the way he did. It would appear that, in the final analysis, he was 'a tragic character'.[64] However, if we reflect upon Wittgenstein's determined desire to see the world with greater clarity then we can maybe begin to understand this remark a little better. In *Culture and Value*, we hear Wittgenstein say, 'Man has to awaken to wonder.'[65] What Wittgenstein means by this is referenced in the *Tractatus* when he proclaims, 'It is not how things are in the world that is mystical, but *that* it exists.'[66] Wittgenstein appears to be suggesting that there is a fundamental unity between the world and our experience of truth. That the world exists is the interface between our reflection and our action. Truth must *do* something. It must impinge upon the experience of the individual in order to have any meaning. In other words, the word 'truth' is meaningless if it has no concrete connection with us and our commitment to the world as we perceive it. But it is important to recognize that such a concrete connection may, paradoxically, exceed the capacity of language. And it is at this point where we are exposed to Wittgenstein's notion of religion. For it is clear that two critical dimensions of Wittgenstein's understanding of truth as it connects with his experience of religion are commitment and silence.

Wittgenstein once remarked, 'I'm not a religious man but I cannot help seeing every problem from a religious point of view.'[67] Religion, for Wittgenstein, was tied less to any dogmatically confessional approach and more allied to the commitment of the individual to the world and to the service of others. In the light of this, to remain within the religious sphere was, for Wittgenstein, 'to struggle'.[68] In other words, religion for Wittgenstein is less about doctrinal correctness or philosophical speculation than it is about action. Wittgenstein, in a conversation with a close friend once said:

> Christianity is not a matter of saying a lot of prayers; in fact we are told not to do that. If you and I are to live religious lives, it mustn't be that we talk a lot about religion, but that our manner of life is different. It is my belief that only if you try to be helpful to other people will you in the end find your way to God.[69]

This is not to be confused with any casual understanding of 'salvation by works'; rather it is to place the individual in the world where life has its true and only meaning. The importance of Tolstoy, whom Wittgenstein discovered during his army service, cannot be underestimated here.[70] The notion of commitment, of having purpose, remained critical for Wittgenstein throughout his life. An early instance of this is found in a wartime conversation Wittgenstein had with his friend Paul Engelmann, when he exclaimed: 'How can I be a good philosopher when I can't manage to be a good man?'[71] For Wittgenstein there was a profound link between his commitment to philosophical endeavour and his moral struggle. A critical expression of this sense of commitment is that of confession. Indeed, we can detect a confessional tone in the *Tractatus* when Wittgenstein writes in the Preface, 'Perhaps this book will be understood only by someone who has himself already had the thoughts expressed in it – or at least similar thoughts. So it is not a textbook.'[72] In *Culture and Value*, we read,

> Christianity is not a doctrine, not, I mean, a theory about what has happened and will happen to the human soul, but a description of something that actually takes place in human life. For 'consciousness

of sin' is a real event and so are despair and salvation through faith. Those who speak of such things (Bunyan for instance) are simply describing what has happened to them, whatever gloss anyone would want to put on it.[73]

Wittgenstein's own experience of the need for confession forms a graphic illustration of his commitment to truth as a need of the soul. One cannot underestimate this word as far as Wittgenstein is concerned. What we are dealing with here is a sense of the inner life and the drive to live fully. In this sense, truth is less associated with the understanding than it is with the will and the desire to fully engage with the world. This sense of yearning is found in Wittgenstein's revealing comment to his friend, Maurice Drury, about religion: 'I think it seems to me that your religion will always take the form of desiring something you haven't yet found.'[74]

Such yearning mirrors Jasper's suggestion in the previous chapter of being pursued by truth, and we can witness Wittgenstein's personal experience of this in his own visceral need for confession. Confession, for Wittgenstein, becomes a vehicle for truth determination. In the *Philosophical Investigations,* Wittgenstein outlines his understanding thus:

> The criteria for the truth of the *confession* that I thought such-and-such are not the criteria for a true *description* of a process. And the importance of the true confession does not reside in its being a correct and certain report of a process. It resides rather in the special conclusions which can be drawn from a confession whose truth is guaranteed by the special criteria of *truthfulness*.[75]

What does this mean? It would appear that to confess is, in a certain sense, 'to change an aspect'. It is to reorient oneself to the truth in a manner of complete commitment. Confession, by definition, cannot be a casual affair. It implies that sense of engagement which allows the truth to *become* true, however uncomfortable that experience may be. Truth, for Wittgenstein must be confronted. Truthfulness, in this sense, is more than simply an awareness of a state of affairs but of being impacted by the truth. As a young man, Wittgenstein, when in a state of heightened anxiety (which affected him on numerous occasions throughout his life) was once asked by Russell, 'Are you thinking about logic or about your sins?' 'Both,' Wittgenstein replied.[76]

In his remarkable biography of Wittgenstein, Ray Monk tells us that Wittgenstein's earliest recorded reflection was on the nature of truth: 'Why should one tell the truth', he asked, 'if it is to one's advantage to tell a lie?'[77] This early foray into the realm of moral philosophy was to dominate not only Wittgenstein's philosophical endeavour but his own moral development. If one allies this initial question with what later became known as the Haidbauer incident, which took place while Wittgenstein was teaching in April 1926, one can immediately detect an autobiographical resonance. Having taken a post as an elementary school teacher, Wittgenstein, who had little patience for slow learners, struck an 11-year-old boy, Joseph Haidbauer, several times causing him to lose consciousness. This was not an isolated incident of assault. He had earlier hit a girl in his class and subsequently denied that it had taken place. The Haidbauer incident was the last straw and, though Wittgenstein avoided judicial punishment, he left the town in some disgrace. What is crucial, though, for our purposes is that he later returned to apologize profusely to the families concerned. It was an incident that was to haunt him for the rest of his life.[78]

This juxtaposition of Wittgenstein's desire to explore the nature of truth, with his later bitter experience of denying the truth, however painful, of his own culpability, serves to show us the biographical and psychological context within which Wittgenstein's philosophy operated. It graphically illustrates what Monk has described as the inability of some scholars to discern 'what his work has to do with him – what the connections are between the spiritual and ethical preoccupations that dominate his life, and the seemingly remote philosophical questions that dominate his work.'[79]

It is certainly clear that for Wittgenstein truthfulness is found not in adherence to any set of secular or sacred propositions (what Genova calls 'the knowledge game' where truth becomes an object).[80] Instead one must look to the commitment one makes in the pursuit of truth (which, as we have noted, can be the experience of being pursued *by* the truth), and how this pursuit works its way out in the vicissitudes of life. Wittgenstein asserts his belief that one of the things Christianity says is that sound doctrines are all useless. That you have to change your *life*. (Or the *direction* of your life.)[81] In this sense, for Wittgenstein, the notion of post-truth would, in all probability, have seemed incoherent, given that the governing directive of truth-telling, namely passion, is absent and is, in the exercise of post-truth, replaced by a driving expediency.

And this measure of commitment ultimately brings us to silence, to the awareness that to live religiously or committedly implies 'the renunciation of a very powerful desire in our nature', as Fergus Kerr puts it.[82] And this powerful desire is to say too much. In a beautiful turn of phrase, Kerr goes on to describe Wittgenstein's work as a 'discipline of reticence'.[83] Indeed, Kerr points to the connection between the religious point of view as understood by Wittgenstein in his later writings, and the ethical/mystical dimension discerned at the conclusion of the *Tractatus*.[84] The dramatic and enigmatic phrase with which the *Tractatus* ends: 'What we cannot speak about we must pass over in silence'[85] can be misinterpreted as a call to regard the pursuit of metaphysical concepts such as religion, ethics or, indeed, truth as, at best, fruitless or, worse, positively harmful. A more measured understanding of Wittgenstein's call to silence is to see it as another example of exercising an awareness of what lies before us, and to respond accordingly. Indeed, it can be suggested that the *expression* of silence is to treat metaphysical concepts such as truth with the utmost seriousness.

In his personal life, Wittgenstein often sought solitude and silence. This desire was no doubt influenced by his own volatile temperament, which he sought, in some small way, to contain. However, beyond the undeniably significant biographical and psychological arenas, one can detect more broadly a fundamental connection between Wittgenstein's thought and silence. His confessional rather than apologetic approach indicates a desire for a holistic vision. Such a 'metaphilosophy', as Paul Horwich puts it, has, at its core, the aim of quieting the philosophical noise which threatens to drown out the opportunity each of us has to experience the reality of the world – a reality which goes beyond language.[86] Silence then does not simply serve a therapeutic purpose, it is the essential focus for the recovery of a clearer vision of the way things are. Silence by no means shares the negative connotations of meaninglessness or contradiction, which form the accusation of the logical positivists and other empirical rationalists. Rather silence is the resonating background and the chiming focus of all human reflection.

For, as the story of the solitary Elijah in 1 Kings reminds us, it is in the silence that truth so often speaks most clearly. And like Elijah emerging from the cave on becoming aware of that silence, and though so often surrounded by the reverberations of Babel, we are encouraged by Wittgenstein to awaken to the wonder of the world as it is and to live more fully in the light of that deep truth.

Questions for discussion

1 In what way can Wittgenstein's understanding of 'forms of life' be applied to the practice of religion?
2 Can commitment and silence as a combined approach to religious truth be compatible with one another?

Further reading

R. Monk, *The Duty of Genius* (London: Vintage, 1991). Monk performs a remarkable feat in being able to combine Wittgenstein's philosophical work with a deeply researched biographical account. In my view, the place to start.

L. Wittgenstein, *Culture and Value* ed. by G. H. von Wright (Chicago: The University of Chicago Press, 1984). While this is not one of Wittgenstein's key texts, it nonetheless offers a way into his aphoristic approach particularly as it relates to theology and truth.

Notes

1 As a counter to this perceived notion, Socrates, for example, saw his task as revealing just how little knowledge he had. See Plato, *Defence of Socrates* 23b (Oxford: Oxford World's Classics, 1999), p. 34. In addition, it is important to acknowledge the moral dimension of ancient philosophical endeavour which sought above all things, even truth, to understand what it meant to live a good life. This extended into the Renaissance period where we discover humanists such as Petrarch writing: 'It is more important to want the good than it is to know the truth.' See P. Hadot, *What is Ancient Philosophy?* (Cambridge MA: Harvard University Press, 2004).

2 The European wars of religion in the sixteenth and seventeenth centuries devastated the continent, killing over 10 million people. Descartes' *Discourse on Method* (1637) was published in the midst of the 30 Years War (1618–48), one of the bloodiest conflicts on the continent.

3 St Anselm, 'Proslogion' in *The Major Works* (Oxford: OUP, 2008), pp. 87f.

4 At one point, Wittgenstein was described by his close friend, the economist John Maynard Keynes, as 'God'. See R. Monk, *The Duty of Genius* (London: Vintage, 1991), p. 255.

5 See, for example, *Wittgenstein* (1993). [DVD] Directed by D. Jarman. London: Channel 4 Films; T. Eagleton, *Saints and Scholars* (London: Verso, 1987); D. Markson, *Wittgenstein's Mistress* (London: Dalkey Archive Press, 1988).

6 It is illustrative of what Ray Monk pointed out in his excellent biography of Wittgenstein, namely the 'unfortunate polarity between those who study his work in isolation from his life and those who find his life fascinating but his work unintelligible.' *The Duty of Genius*, pp. xvii-xviii.

7 Other works have been published posthumously by editors who were former students or colleagues of Wittgenstein. The most significant of these, as we shall see, is *Philosophical Investigations*, published in 1953.

8 L. Wittgenstein, *Tractatus Logico-Philosophicus* (London: Routledge, 2001), p. 4.

9 L. Wittgenstein, *Culture and Value* ed. by G. H. von Wright (Chicago: The University of Chicago Press, 1984) p.24. See also *Tractatus* 4.111.

10 Bertrand Russell and G. E. Moore examined Wittgenstein's PhD thesis (the *Tractatus* in essence) and following the viva Wittgenstein memorably clapped each of them on the shoulder, saying: 'Don't worry, I know you will never understand it.' *The Duty of Genius*, p. 271.

SEEING AS: WITTGENSTEIN'S APPROACH TO TRUTH

11 R. Monk, *How to Read Wittgenstein* (London: Granta Books, 2005), p. 21. Wittgenstein graphically described his writing as 'stuttering', see *Culture and Value*, p. 18.

12 *Tractatus* 6.54.

13 B. Russell, *The History of Western Philosophy* (London: Routledge, 1995), p. 788.

14 On correspondence theory see previous chapter.

15 A more radical (and ultimately doomed) approach was that adopted by the so-called Logical Positivists who courted Wittgenstein and who argued for what is known as the Verificationist Principle. This means that for any given statement to be true it has to be empirically verifiable. If it cannot be shown to be so, it must perforce be rejected as nonsense. One can see clearly here that many if not most theological statements, under this definition of truth, would not qualify.

16 *Tractatus* 4.003.

17 *Philosophical Investigations*, p. 189.

18 *Philosophical Investigations* 109. It can also be suggested that Wittgenstein follows in the tradition of Socrates here, insofar as he sought to clarify our philosophical confusions rather than offering solutions as such.

19 *Tractatus* 6.53.

20 J. C. Klagge, *Simply Wittgenstein* (New York: Simply Charly, 2016), p. 22.

21 His indebtedness to Russell (and Russell's colleague, G. E. Moore) is clear at this point, and the notion of logical atomism was to encourage the Vienna Circle (a specific group of logical positivists) to seek out Wittgenstein as a philosophical ally. That Wittgenstein felt he could not remain with the Vienna Circle says something about the fact that one can discover, even in his early work, a resistance to any kind of overarching system which 'explained' all of reality. Wittgenstein, though he adopted the language of logic, remained open to 'what cannot be said'.

22 *Wittgenstein: A Religious Point of View?* (London: Routledge, 1997), p. 33.

23 'A picture is a model of reality' *Tractatus* 2.12. Echoing note 17 above, Wittgenstein would, however, demur from the notion of 'theory'.

24 *Tractatus* 1.1.

25 *Tractatus* 3.

26 Quoted in M. McGinn, *Wittgenstein's Philosophical Investigations* (London: Routledge, 2013), p. 14.

27 *Tractatus* 4.112.

28 *Tractatus* 6.522.

29 *How to Read Wittgenstein*, p. 27.

30 *Philosophical Investigations* 122, p. 42.

31 *Culture and Value*, p. 29.

32 *Culture and Value*, p. 63. See also *Philosophical Investigations* 126, p. 43.

33 *Philosophical Investigations* 144, p. 49.

34 *Philosophical Investigations* 138, p. 46.

35 E. Mooney, *Excursions with Kierkegaard* (London: Bloomsbury, 2013), p. 4. See also R. Gaita, *A Common Humanity: Thinking about love and truth and justice* (London: Routledge, 2002), and M. Midgley, *What is Philosophy For?* (London: Bloomsbury, 2018) both of whom argue for the importance of the recovery of the subjective as a therapeutic means of living.

36 S. Kierkegaard, *Concluding Unscientific Postscript*, trans. D. Swenson and W. Lowrie (Princeton: Princeton University Press, 1941), p. 182.

37 *Philosophical Investigations* 7, p. 4.
38 *Philosophical Investigations* 23, p.10.
39 *Tractatus*, p. 4.
40 *Philosophical Investigations* 130, p. 43.
41 *Philosophical Investigations* 132, pp. 43–4.
42 Judith Genova writes: 'Knowledge is not a matter of guessing meanings, offering explanations, or other kinds of summaries that take law like form, but of listening to and observing the connections that obtain without interpreting. Perspicuous representation produces a synthesis, not an analysis.' J. Genova, *Wittgenstein: A Way of Seeing* (London: Routledge, 1995), p. 35.
43 *Philosophical Investigations* 128, p. 43.
44 *Philosophical Investigations*, 124.
45 M. McGinn, *Wittgenstein's Philosophical Investigations* (London: Routledge, 2013), p. 33. There is a close link here between this philosophical approach and Wittgenstein's understanding of religion.
46 *Philosophical Investigations*, p. 165.
47 Genova, p. 26.
48 *Philosophical Investigations*, p. 167.
49 *Tractatus*, 6.45.
50 Genova, p. 32.
51 Genova, p. 36.
52 This particular insight has led some scholars, such as Kai Nielsen, to describe Wittgenstein as a fideist. This, I believe, is to say too much and relies on a very blunt view of religion as a language game, whereas Wittgenstein is simply saying that it is the surroundings and circumstances of the particular language game which enables a person to come to an understanding of its truth or meaning.
53 *Culture and Value*, p. 1.
54 *The Duty of Genius*, p. 418.
55 Ibid.
56 Genova, p. 37.
57 See particularly P. Horwich, *Truth, Meaning, Reality* (Oxford: OUP, 2010).
58 St Augustine, *Confessions* XI.14. (London: Penguin, 1984), pp. 263ff.
59 *Philosophical Investigations* 106, p. 39.
60 *Philosophical Investigations*, 126 & 129, p. 43.
61 *Culture and Value*, p. 42.
62 R. Monk, *Wittgenstein: The Duty of Genius*, p. 579.
63 F. Pascal, 'Wittgenstein: A Personal Memoir' in *Wittgenstein: Sources and Perspectives*, ed. by C. G. Luckhardt (Ithaca, New York: Cornell University Press, 1979), p. 44.
64 Pascal, p. 60.
65 *Culture and Value*, p. 5.
66 *Tractatus* 6.44.
67 M. O'C. Drury, 'Some Notes on Conversations with Wittgenstein' in Rush Rhees, *Ludwig Wittgenstein: Personal Reflections* (Oxford: Basil Blackwell, 1981), p. 94.
68 *Culture and Value*, p. 86.
69 M. O'C. Drury, 'Conversations with Wittgenstein', p. 129.
70 Wittgenstein discovered Tolstoy's *The Gospel in Brief* quite by accident in a small bookshop near where he was stationed during the war. So attached

was he to this slim volume that his fellow soldiers called him 'the one with the Gospels'. See Brian McGuinness, *Young Ludwig: Wittgenstein's Life 1889–1921* (Oxford: OUP, 2005).

71 Brian McGuinness, p. 227.

72 *Tractatus*, p. 3. Anthony Kenny suggests that for Wittgenstein grammatical confusions infest the world like 'original sin' and that the proper purpose of philosophy is to fortify the will 'to resist certain temptations'.

73 *Culture and Value*, p. 28.

74 M. O'C. Drury, 'Conversations with Wittgenstein', p. 179.

75 *Philosophical Investigations*, p. 189.

76 B. Russell, *The Autobiography of Bertrand Russell* (London: Routledge, 2000), p. 330.

77 Ray Monk, *The Duty of Genius*, pp. 232–3.

78 Fania Pascal recounts Wittgenstein's deep desire to confess the incident to her in her memories of Wittgenstein, see Luckhardt, pp. 45–50.

79 *The Duty of Genius*, p. xviii.

80 See *On Certainty*, 153.

81 *Culture and Value*, p. 53.

82 F. Kerr, *Theology after Wittgenstein*, 2nd edn (London: SPCK, 1997), p. 37.

83 Ibid.

84 Ibid., p. 38.

85 *Tractatus* 7.

86 P. Horwich, *Metaphilosophy* (Oxford: OUP, 2012).

4

Truth and Public Theology

JENNY WRIGHT

One cannot help but wonder if talking about truth in a post-truth world is somewhat oversimplifying the world in which we find ourselves. When talking about post-truth we are talking about politics, economics, media (and the rapid changes occurring here) and, for the purpose of this essay, Christian theology. If we find ourselves in a post-truth world, does this call into question democratic governance – literally, the rule of the people which, for better or worse in our current political system, is delegated to an elected official, and the associated liberties. Closely connected to post-truth is the concept of alternative truth and 'fake news'. Here is the platform where people are swayed by their emotions and will be drip-fed news content which plays into their specific circumstances, sympathies and weaknesses. Given how this appears to play on the right of people to protect what is theirs, their nation, their freedom, their way of life, their liberties, then perhaps it is time to revisit and reframe Alisdair MacIntyre's now oft paraphrased question: 'Whose Justice? Which Rationality?'[1] – 'Whose Truth? Which Agenda?' or perhaps 'Whose Freedom? Which Theology?'

Talking about truth and theology, truth in theology and theology as truth is a daunting task. Theological truth as a theological or even philosophical concept allows itself to debate within the confines of its own discipline, or in an interdisciplinary platform within the academy. Truth in theology recognizes too, of course, that what theology assumes as Christian truth, that which is at the heart of Christian doctrine – God's work in creation and human life, the eschatological nature of our existence and the divine ordering of the world – is not accepted as truthful or relevant by the majority of people for whom debates as to the very *existence* of God and the *relevance* of Christ form the foundation of discussions rather than, for example, debates about the *nature* of God. Theology as truth might broaden its audience somewhat, inviting interaction with a plurality of voices, offering one way of thinking with regards to political, social, economic and ethical life, while recognizing equally valid yet different voices.

The answer to the question of truth and theology will look different depending on your angle of approach. As is clear from the other chapters in this volume there is no one definition of truth. It is perhaps best that I begin with a disclaimer: I am in no way going to attempt to 'prove' the truth of Christian theology. As a theologian and priest, I work on the faith assumption that what I believe is true. Providing proof for the existence of God is not the primary task of theology in the public sphere and is certainly not my task here. Eloquent arguments have been made in this regard, and for a rigorous study of theology and truth, D. Stephen Long's book *Speaking of God* provides an academically robust starting point.[2]

In a post-truth world, where politicians and the media are distrusted, where mention of faith in the public sphere is often in a negative context, be it related to violence, sectarianism, sexism or abuse, it is important for us to ask not only what the nature of theological truth may be, as other chapters do, but perhaps even more *why* Christian truth matters. Answering this question may help us to formulate a theological response to truth and its relationship to public life in politics, economics, religion and media. Why does what we believe and hold as true matter not only for the church but for society as a whole? I want to suggest that the answer to this question lies not only in asserting the nature of Christian truth in relation to philosophy, science, biblical interpretation and theological tradition, but in the relevance of what we, as Christians, believe to be true for theology in the public sphere. This chapter concerns itself with how theology is expressed in the public sphere in tumultuous times, when information in the media must often be regarded with suspicion and adherence to truth, particularly where politics and religion are concerned, is frequently based on emotional and uninformed personal belief. However, this is not always the case and I would argue that as much as the response to politics by evangelical religion might often look and sound emotional and uninformed, it actually is deeply and historically rooted in a response to injustice by one side and the desire to protect the status quo by the other.

I begin by looking at truth, apologetics (that is the defence or justification of Christian beliefs in the public sphere) and pluralism. This is then followed by a discussion of the contribution of North American theologian Reinhold Niebuhr to theological truth, particularly in relation to politics, in his social theological contribution in the mid-twentieth century. I turn finally to the relevance of the search for theological truth in public dialogue, drawing on the wisdom of contextual theology, where churches have formulated responses to gross injustice.

Truth, apologetics and pluralism

The *Oxford English Dictionary* defines post-truth, its word of the year in 2016, as 'relating to or denoting circumstances in which objective facts are less influential in shaping political debate and public opinion than appeals to emotion and personal belief'. An interesting dichotomy is drawn here between facts on the one hand and emotion and personal belief on the other. While religion is caught up in the emotional response to political situations, it is not so much religion that is referenced here as it is personal belief in terms of what is politically owed to one as an individual. Caught up here is a claim to individual human rights and political freedom and liberty, not only belief as in faith and spirituality.

There is some justification for truth being related to emotion and personal belief, because our particular circumstances will influence our worldview. An impersonal response to politics is difficult to achieve, as desirable as it may sometimes be. Contextual influence is true too for our faith response to the world in which we live, for our interpretation of our religion, for who God is and how that relates to our political lives is dependent upon our context and the place of religion in our society. Truth, as is repeated throughout this volume, is always contextual.

Given the religious starting point of this book, the existence of God is assumed by its authors as a given. However, it quickly becomes apparent that the truth claims of theology across theological disciplines and within Christian denominations and traditions, are actually fairly limited, although when one attempts to clarify what is *meant* by the fundamental truths of our faith rooted in the truth of Christ, it is easy to lose your way in a tangled maze. This exercise is further complicated by several other factors: the religiously motivated fake-truths which are often parochial and fundamentalist but nonetheless find their way into the public sphere and gain credibility; the knowledge of religious correspondents of traditional media is not always to an adequate level, thus perpetuating fake-truths and weakening the religious position in society; social media means that there is opportunity for anyone to say anything about God, blurring the line between personal opinion and rigorous research. There are many ways in which the relationship between faith and life, including economics and politics, never mind goodness and salvation, relating to race, nationality, sexuality and gender orientation, can be misunderstood and unfortunately become representative of religion as a whole rather than simply a very small, fundamentalist part of religion.

Apologetics are necessary in a world where religion broadly speaking is misunderstood and misrepresented. A robust Christian apologetics should be advanced because this can help clarify the difference between 'truth' and 'justification of belief'. It can be argued that the intention of apologetics is not to convert unbelievers, but rather to offer a lucid defence of the Christian faith in an increasingly hostile world and sometimes also as a response to unreasonable and divisive Christian rhetoric. Indeed, this should be true not just of Christianity but of all religions, for lack of understanding about religion is fuel to the fires of sectarianism and secularism. Apologetics is not only about practicing faith in public and educating about doctrine, but also about justifying the public role of *all* faiths.

It is in the space called apologetics that Christianity can take a truth stance in society because apologetics seeks to create a space for understanding between all people by speaking, in the words of the theologian Elaine Graham,

> in ways that can be grasped by those who doubt or do not share their faith. It thus tests the reasonableness and morality of the faith and those who hold it by engaging those who are not already convinced. It acknowledges that if it is in principle impossible to make a case for the truth or justice of theology, others are under no obligation to take it seriously.[3]

Graham argues that apologetics need to be reclaimed as more than a declaration of personal belief or 'the scholarly reflection on Christian apologetic witness and dialogue as the intellectual justification of the truth and relevance of the Christian faith',[4] and need further to be directed at political authority, 'encouraging Christian engagement in or commentary upon matters such as economics, civil society, media or politics.'[5]

Asking how my belief in the existence of God impacts the relationship between theological truth and the world or between my existence and that of my neighbour, can be a helpful starting point. Our faith impacts the emotion and personal belief we bring to our political situations, and we cannot consider our engagement in society without first considering what our faith requires of us. Living in a pluralist society asks of us to interpret our belief, and this is where it becomes important to speak of truth. We need to ask how believing in God relates to the truth and how that truth relates to the way in which we live. Put differently, we might ask how our faith is connected to the way in which we read the news, how we reflect upon it and ultimately how we act in response to this news.

While a pluralist society necessitates apologetics, pluralism is not only a question of living well together with those belonging to other religions, but of living well together with other members of the Christian tradition. Robin Gill, an Anglican priest and ethicist, argues that 'if Christianity is seen as a form of religion founded upon an elusive relationship to God in Christ, then pluralism resulting from a myriad of socio-political contexts would be readily expected. And the consequent pluralism of Christian theology will also be readily expected.'[6] This pluralism within Christianity indicates that when speaking about truth it is not primarily with the expectation that there will be clear empirical proof and rationale for what we believe, thus uniting all denominations doctrinally. However, rather than viewing this as a weakness as some proponents of a secular society would argue, this is part of the very strength of theology. Robust dialogue between different points of view may help to point us towards the elusive God and to understand God as God is revealed to us. Furthermore we need to recognize that although 'Christianity has a strong tendency to pluralism and could soon become fragmented and thoroughly relativized', it is in its very diversity that seemingly 'incompatible Christian movements are able to express the fullness of the Christian faith'.[7] The unity is precisely in the diversity which helps to keep extreme fundamentalist views in check.

Pluralism within Christianity, often viewed as binary opposites such as Protestant and Catholic, liberal and conservative, and so on, highlights how difficult it is even to begin to talk meaningfully of 'Christian truth' and how unhelpful it is to try to quantify or qualify Christian belief within any realm of truth that can be measured by empirical standards. Once we move beyond theological discussion of the triune God, there is possibly very little unity to be found, at least when one begins to dig deeper. We may think, for example of the endless and divisive debates which rage around same-sex marriage, the ordination of women and who may be allowed to preach a sermon.[8]

The Canadian philosopher Charles Taylor in his book *A Secular Age* highlights the difficult choices that people see themselves having to make when faced with 'the unacceptable faces of orthodoxy: the authoritarianism, the placing conformity before well-being, the sense of human guilt and evil, damnation, and so on,' and the equally unacceptable alternative of 'a sense of malaise, emptiness, a need for meaning'. 'In the face of opposition between orthodoxy and unbelief,' says Taylor, 'many, and among them the best and most sensitive minds, [are] cross-pressured, looking for a third way.' Most people will find a solution somewhere between 'the extreme ones of authoritarian orthodoxy and materialist atheism.'[9] This gives some idea of the scope of the complexity of what is meant when we talk about God and theology and truth. The pluralism within the Christian faith and the generosity needed when participating in the public sphere need to guard against private interpretation, protecting the 'public character of the truth', trying to represent a 'consensus of a covenant community which lives upon the basis of common convictions and commitments.'[10]

I would hope that a vigorous renewal of Christian apologetics can help foster unity in the face of the division found in society as we search to find our common convictions and commitments. This begins, I maintain, with the recognition that we need to be open to recognizing other truth claims, and in doing so allow ourselves to be able to make a clear stand for that which we cannot support. In the face of divisive political rhetoric, fake news and increasingly polarized economic spheres which are both fuelled by and offer kindling to political and media divisiveness, we cannot shut ourselves off by claiming that we have the only truth or shut ourselves out of the public sphere, essentially leaving our neighbours (both nationally and internationally) to care for themselves, concerning ourselves only with matters of spirituality.

Truth, human nature and the will to power

Reinhold Niebuhr (1892–1971) was an American theologian and Lutheran pastor who still carries much weight for the engagement of theology in the public sphere nearly 60 years after his death. For Niebuhr, theology was inseparable from a desire for justice in society, a desire closely linked to his sociological interpretation of the particular society in which he lived. While he wrote very much for his specific context – a white, middle-class, North American audience in the early- to mid- twentieth century – his analysis of the human condition and biblical interpretation continues to provide a lens through which we may engage with our own struggles in this age of globalization, pluralism, mass media and political upheaval.

While much of his work was focused on social justice,[11] Niebuhr remains relevant to our current discussions about truth in that his perceptive analysis of what he called 'the human condition' is closely linked to a specific, personal view of what is considered the only truth. In his book *The Nature and Destiny of Man* (1941–43),[12] Niebuhr writes of the sin of pride as one of the great stumbling blocks in our being unable to accurately interpret the world in which we live. In speaking of truth pride can be seen as encouraging the need to create and cling to a truth to sustain a particular lifestyle or worldview, so that *a* truth ultimately becomes what seems to be, immovably, *the only* truth.

In thinking about the way truth functions in our culture, particularly in politics and the media, we can see how closely linked it is to our own insecurity and our need to protect what is ours. It is not too difficult to construct our truth to represent the world in which we would wish to live. In so doing, we forget that

> Every form of modern secularism contains an implicit or explicit self-glorification and deification. Humanistic rationalism, forgetting that human reason as well as human physical existence is a derived, dependent, created, and finite reality, makes it into a principle of interpretation of the meaning of life; and believes that its gradual extension is the guarantee of the ultimate destruction of evil in history. It mistakes the image of God in man for God Himself.[13]

Our insecurity with our finitude and the constant attempt to overcome this supposed weakness to control our own destiny means that we become ever more creative in the ways in which we try to establish control over our destiny; the more we appear to be in control of the political and economic climate, the more we need to convince ourselves that our actions are justified.

While, in Niebuhr's words, we do not 'envisage reality widely enough to comprehend the actual center of life' we also 'protest against [our] finiteness by seeking to make [ourselves] infinite'.[14] We might say that the way in which truth becomes malleable could be what Niebuhr speaks of in theological language as sin. Just as power results in pride and injustice because it tempts us to forget that we are finite and do not control our destiny, so truth needs to be twisted to support the narrative of power, pride and injustice with which we attempt to control our reality. With his rather pessimistic view of human nature, in opposition to the 'romantic overestimate of human virtue and moral capacity', Niebuhr saw it as inevitable that many people would be unable to interpret and analyse 'the contemporary situation'.[15] A lack of interpretation and analysis certainly creates a culture in which fake news and alternative truths can flourish.

If pride leads to the oppression, suppression and abuse of others in the attempt to save the self from becoming finite by protecting that which a group holds most dear at all costs, it becomes relevant for our argument here in that pride, and its quest for superiority of power, knowledge and virtue is inseparable from some form of deceit. Our pride, which develops from our self-love, generates the need to deceive itself about the affirmation and attention and reward which it deserves. Self-deception precedes the deceit of others and we need first to convince ourselves of our importance, over and against our finitude, before we can convince others of our superiority. But the self in isolation never quite believes this deception. If others accept the deception it becomes easier for the self to obscure the truth and deny the insecurity which causes the self-deception in the first place. The proliferation of fake news on social media offers a platform from which deception can be practised. Because others are liking, sharing and posting 'news items' it is easier to believe it for yourself.

In a world where there is a proliferation of fake news, credibility given to so-called 'alternative truths' and false political promises where lies are paraded as truth, the question of the deception of the self and others is one which we cannot ignore. When we, and our community, our nation, our people, become the centre of our news, our stories, our politics, to the exclusion of all others unless they serve a purpose in making our point, it becomes easy to obscure our self-deception, becoming blind to other, better truths in the face of our superiority. This situation is exacerbated by being unable to recognize the insecurity which caused the self-deception in the first place. In speaking about truth, we have to speak about pride, because relative truth is only successful in so far as it appeals to our weakness with regard to the promise of salvation. When there is no space for an eschatological hope for the future outside of our current reality, it becomes increasingly important to ensure our own future here and now, creating and sustaining economic and political security for ourselves and our communities at whatever cost. Living in fear of what the future holds allows lies and fake news to flourish in an attempt to avoid the insecurity which is created by the lack of control of human life.

Belief in ourselves to secure and overcome our finitude is linked to what Niebuhr calls 'intellectual pride', a form of self-deception by which we believe we have arrived at the final truth. Progress is of course always possible and indeed to be welcomed, but we never actually discover *the* truth; rather, what we believe to be truth can and probably will be ever-changing, whether we are talking about politics, economics or science. Our quest for scientific truth,[16] the disenchantment of the world, the secular rejection of religion and religious fanaticism all draw, to a certain extent, on intellectual pride which refers to human knowledge that always 'pretends to be more true than it is'.[17] Our knowledge can never be final and ultimate since it is always tainted by our particular perspective and experience. We need to realize this so that we can always search for a better way of living for all people. It is only by recognizing and admitting imperfection that *our* truth will never be mistaken for *the* truth and it is only then that we can actually make progress and remain humble at the same time. There is much to be learnt from the wisdom and humility of Scripture and the Christian tradition, where it has been rightly practised.

In accepting that our truth is never the only truth, we open ourselves to the possibility of dialogue which in turn will give us the opportunity to find the elements of truth in other positions and philosophies. Niebuhr says that

> there is an element of truth in each position which becomes falsehood, precisely when it is carried through too consistently. The element of truth in each creed is required to do full justice to [our] real situation. For [we] transcend the social and historical process sufficiently to make it possible and necessary deliberately to contrive common ends of life, particularly the end of justice.[18]

We always only know part of the truth and we must guard against accepting our part as the whole truth. It is in the search for truth that 'intellectual intercourse' is one of our best defences against moral superiority, leading instead to a more tolerant point of view.[19] Toleration does not mean admitting defeat, giving up and losing hope in our own answers. Rather, toleration is 'an expression of the spirit of forgiveness in the realm of culture'.[20] There is a fine line between knowing that we do not know and continuously searching for the truth on one hand, and falling into either scepticism, thinking that there is no answer, or fanaticism on the other.

Our faith should always call us to question our actions because our responsibility and our striving for justice lie within our faith, which has at its centre 'the paradox of grace, the "I, yet not I, but Christ," and of a having and yet not having'.[21] For Niebuhr, it is Christianity which has stood the test of time and which can give guidance in the struggles of life, particularly as it reclaims its prophetic origin and holds the moral and social structure of society accountable, pointing *'to a source of meaning which transcends all the little universes of value and meaning* which "have their day and cease to be" and yet not seek refuge in an eternal world where all history ceases to be significant'.[22] When we cannot accept at face value that which we encounter in the world, we need to be ready to engage in rigorous debate, questioning why we are being presented with such information as we are, whose perspective are we seeing and which stories of what are we unaware.

Our longing for truth and justice will remain a hope because our knowledge of God is always only in part. When we are aware of our own inadequacies, we can attempt to improve on previous mistakes and seek to think better, for we must never deceive ourselves that our work is done. While motivation for social action can be found in our faith and our religious communities, this faith needs to be complemented by a wise understanding and a social intelligence which can adequately translate the Christian ethic into a suitable social ethic. As Niebuhr goes to great length to point out, and as we are all too aware from current polarizing Christian rhetoric facing the particular crisis of migration, 'the Christlike life is not accompanied with sufficient social intelligence to know what the Christlike ethic is.'[23] While formation may occur within the liturgy of daily worship, we need to read the Bible with the newspaper in our other hand.

It is all too easy for our own desires to influence our faith and for our religious views to masquerade as the ultimate truth that will allow our worldview to flourish, while seemingly blissfully ignorant of the suffering, marginalization and isolation this may cause. If we think of renewed 'religious regeneration', following Niebuhr, it must be accompanied by social education which offers a lens through which to critique the situations we encounter. While some would argue that religious regeneration has no place in a pluralist society and religion is best kept out of public life, we perhaps need to 'begin at home', and within the church need to find a way of thinking better than what is currently presented to us by society. This also needs to take seriously our own shortcomings, allowing us to become more self-aware and indeed self-critical, so that we do not fall into complacency with our own faith. How do we, as people of the way, answer the pressing issues of our day, weighing up the truths presented to us about our world? The only way to engage with inflammatory post-truth rhetoric is to educate ourselves to what it is that our faith allows us to offer as an alternative, engaging with the flourishing of all people and denying that which is not life-giving.

Theology, truth and the public sphere

Part of discipleship is relating our faith life to our daily life – social, economic, political, personal. It is perhaps too easy and glib to say that theology must speak truth to power. Yes, good theology does indeed speak truth to power.[24] But part of this is the acceptance that theology is one of many voices, and allowing a space for dialogue to take place is more important than our assertion that we hold the only truth. Theologically we bring a unique perspective, adding to the exchanges between scientists, economists, politicians, educators and other religions who participate in the public sphere, attempting to hold those with power to account and encourage citizens to responsible, informed living.

In our appropriation of biblical truth, we can often take as timeless those attitudes which are, in fact, contextual, particularly when this may suit our political agenda. It is only through realizing that our own view of tradition and culture needs to be critiqued that we can begin to understand how Jesus challenged the power systems of his day and how we are invited to do the same. Through increased self-awareness we become better able to detect 'inconsistencies between claims and actions, between theory and practice, and between beliefs and behaviour'.[25] The philosopher and theologian Nicholas Wolterstorff writes about looking beyond 'evidences for the truth of Christianity, arguments for the inspiration of Scripture, proofs for the resurrection of Jesus [and] best explanation accounts of Christian faith', allowing our theology to 'interpret the world, culture, and society in the light of Scripture'.[26] This is where theology speaks truth to power and we can learn to speak this language, allowing us to shine the light of the gospel in the spheres of the world.

One way in which this has been done historically is in the long line of confessions in the Protestant tradition as a response to the specific social contexts, sometimes referred to as *status confessionis*.[27] While the confession itself is rooted in a specific social, political and church context, at the same time it is firmly grounded in asking whether the Bible is being correctly heard – in other words, the truth of the confession is not in the truth of the historical context, but in the truth of the gospel for the historical situation.[28] Eberhard Busch described (Reformed) confessions as 'banners in the battlefield'. They are part of the ongoing search for how to live theological truth as a response to the political and social situation in which we find ourselves.[29]

In the last century, the Confessing Church in Germany and the Barmen Declaration (1934) attempted to hold those in power to account. The Belhar Confession (1986) in South Africa in the 1980s similarly asked those in power to recognize the heresy of what they upheld as biblical truth. Of course, the reputation of theology is often held to account for this. The instances of the churches' abuse of power, collusion with the government and support and justification of unbiblical political policies are called into question. The response of the church in Germany to the rise of Nazism and the tangled web of church and politics in apartheid South Africa certainly show the need for a better truth to be developed and the necessity of confessing our faith in public. This is particularly in the face of a faith which buys into the narrative of post-truth.[30]

The German theologian and Lutheran pastor Dietrich Bonhoeffer wrote that a confession like Barmen is 'the decision of the church based upon its entire doctrine, to take up the struggle at a particular place.'[31] The Belhar Confession was similarly an attempt by South African theologians to hold the church to account by stating again Christian truths as found in Scripture and tradition. Dirk Smit, the influential South African theologian, who was involved in the drafting of the Belhar Confession, described it as developing in a time when

> free debate and discussion is over and the church, if it is going to be the church, has to take a stand. It rests on a claim to what is essential to Christian existence: it appeals to the Church's entire doctrine. And it addresses a particular crisis. In the light of Jesus Christ we are to ask anew from situation to situation: What is commanded of us now in this setting?[32]

A confession might represent a rejection of the current political, economic or social situation but ultimately 'its merit will be based not upon its main message being a No to something wrong but rather upon its Yes to the truth of the divine gospel.'[33]

To truly challenge the place of religion in the public sphere,[34] we need to be able to offer opinion and truth that is timely, relevant and open to comment, dialogue, and argument. Theology needs to be critical enough of itself and aware of its own context and biases to bear witness in broader society in a way that is firmly grounded in our Christian truth, yet allows room for all others to encounter the moral/ethical/political viewpoint from outwith the Christian tradition. Public theology 'claims that the most profound presumptions of the faith are, and can be shown to be, as reasonable, as ethical, and as viable for authentic, warranted commitment as any other known religion or philosophy and indeed indispensable to other modes of public discourse'.[35] In a culture of suspicion, in Peter Crumpler's words,

> the power of the Christian narrative, an ability to bring diverse groups together, and commitments to both the local and the long-term will not alone solve the pervasive issue of mistrust in our society. But together they provide a vital resource to help the Church play its part in countering the destructive culture of post-truth.[36]

Perhaps part of what is missing in our discussion both about theological truth and truth in society in general, particularly in relation to politics and media, is the question about whether it is true simply because I think it or say it; whether it is universally true simply because I believe it. In an individualistic society where the rights of the individual are upheld almost above all else, do 'my' feelings and 'my' thoughts and 'my' right to express myself in any way I choose, with few limitations for not infringing on the rights of others, become confused with what is truth?

So we continue with our search for truth, reassessing our own opinions and values and worldviews, critiquing the assumptions that underpin these, the traditions that inform them and the interpretation we employ, as we seek to maintain our integrity in our faith and hope while not allowing our judgement to become clouded by holding fast to one truth which alienates others. The search for truth is both intensely personal and unavoidably communal.

Questions for discussion

1 How important do you consider religious truth (as traditionally found in the Bible, church tradition, and theology) to be in relation to your faith?
2 What role should religion play in critiquing society, both by engaging in public dialogue and helping worshipping communities to better understand the relationship between their faith and the world?
3 Have any persons of faith challenged your understanding of truth in politics, economics and civil society?

Further reading

R. Niebuhr, *Moral Man and Immoral Society. A Study in Ethics and Politics* (Louisville KY: Westminster John Knox Press, 2001 (1932)). Although written in the first half of the previous century, offers valuable insights into religious critique of civil society and the relationship between the individual and the collective society.

R. Gill, *Theology Shaped by Society* (Surrey, UK: Ashgate Publishing, 2012). The second book of three in sociological theology, which looks at how theology responds to culture.

W. Brueggeman, *Truth Speaks to Power: The Countercultural Nature of Scripture* (Louisville KY: Westminster John Knox Press, 2013). With reference to Old Testament examples, Brueggeman examines the prophetic role of religion in contemporary culture.

T. Gorringe, 'Climate Change: A Confessional Issue for the Churches?', *Operation Noah Lecture 2011*, accessed 23 October 2018. An accessible article, based on a lecture, that argues for the necessity of theological engagement in environmental crises.

Notes

1 A. MacIntyre, *Whose Justice? Which Rationality?* (Notre Dame IN: University of Notre Dame Press, 1988).

2 For anyone interested in a more philosophical discussion of truth and theology, D. Stephen Long's book, *Speaking of God: Theology, Language and Truth* (Grand Rapids MI: Eerdmans, 2009) offers an in-depth, analytical study of language and God, particularly in relation to philosophy and theology. Long draws on a wealth of sources, entering into critical engagement with diverse arguments.

3 E. Graham, *Between a Rock and a Hard Place* (London: SCM Press, 2006), p. 183.

4 Van den Toren, quoted in Graham, *Between a Rock and a Hard Place*, p. 181.

5 Ibid., p. 182.

6 R. Gill, *Theology Shaped by Society* (Surrey, UK: Ashgate Publishing, 2012), p. 89.

7 Ibid., pp. 81–2.

8 T. Eagleton, *Culture and the Death of God* (New Haven CT: Yale University Press, 2014).

9 C. Taylor, *A Secular Age* (Cambridge MA: Harvard University Press, 2007), p. 302.

10 R. Niebuhr, *Leaves from the Notebook of a Tamed Cynic* (New York: Living Age, 1957 (1929)), p. 59.

11 Niebuhr was particularly critical of the Ford motor industry and the impact that had on the Detroit community. Human imperfection (the fallibility of human nature) and the dangers of power (the will to power and the resulting sin, including the sin of pride) meant that while he was pessimistic of people and their ability to live good lives, he believed that faith and religion could encourage a greater good, even if people would never fully attain freedom from sin and vice.

12 R. Niebuhr, *The Nature and Destiny of Man. Volume 1. Human Nature* (New York: Charles Scribner's Sons, 1941) and R. Niebuhr, *The Nature and Destiny of Man. Volume 2. Human Destiny* (New York: Charles Scribner's Sons, 1943).

13 *The Essential Reinhold Niebuhr*, ed. Robert McAfee Brown (New Haven CT: Yale University Press, 1986) pp. 80–1.

14 R. Niebuhr, *An Interpretation of Christian Ethics* (London: Harper and Brothers Publishers, 1935), p. 87.

15 R. Niebuhr, *Moral Man and Immoral Society. A Study in Ethics and Politics* (Louisville KY: Westminster John Knox Press, 2001 (1932)), p. xx.

16 See Chapter 10 below (Priest).

17 R. Niebuhr, *Moral Man and Immoral Society*, pp. 194.

18 R. Niebuhr, *The Irony of American History* (Chicago: University of Chicago Press, 2007 (1952)), pp. 107–8.

19 R. Niebuhr, *Moral Man and Immoral Society*, Ch. VIII §III.

20 R. Niebuhr, *The Nature and Destiny of Man. Volume 2. Human Destiny*, p. 243.

21 L. Gilkey, *On Niebuhr. Theological Study* (Chicago: The University of Chicago Press, 2001), p. 192.

22 R. Niebuhr, *An Interpretation of Christian Ethics*, p. 34.

23 R. Niebuhr, *Man's Nature and His Communities* (New York: Charles Scribner's Sons, 1965), p. 76.

24 W. Brueggeman, *Truth Speaks to Power. The Countercultural Nature of Scripture* (Louisville KY: Westminster John Knox Press, 2013).

25 Gill, *Theology*, p. 69.

26 N. Wolterstorff, *Hearing the Call: Liturgy, Justice, Church, and World* (Grand Rapids MI: Eerdmans, 2011), p. 10.

27 T. Gorringe, 'Climate Change: A Confessional Issue for the Churches?', *Operation Noah Lecture 2011*, accessed 23 October 2018.

28 D. J. Smit, 'Oor die Teologiese inhoud van die Belydenis van Belhar', *Acta Theologica* 2012 32(2): 184–202, p. 184.

29 Ibid., p. 194.

30 It is difficult to determine how far this is appropriate for the Scottish context, but I contend that to be a part of global movements, we need to determine how much influence the church (broadly speaking) has in the public sphere.

31 Bonhoeffer, 'Zur Frage nach der Kirchengemeninschaft' in *Gesammelte Schriften* (Munich: Ch Kaiser Verlag, 1965 vol 2), p. 226; ET in *The Way to Freedom* (London: Collins, 1966), p. 83. My italics.

32 D. J. Smit, 'Oor die Teologiese', p. 184. My translation.

33 E. Busch, *The Barmen Theses Then and Now* (Grand Rapids MI: Eerdmans, 2010), p. 9.

34 R. Putnam, *American Grace: How Religion Divides and Unites Us* (New York: Simon and Schuster, 2010).

35 M. Stackhouse quoted in Graham, *Between a Rock and a Hard Place*, p. 186.

36 P. Crumpler, 'We have to face up to the threat of fake news,' *Church Times*, 19 October 2018.

5

Tangling the Fibres of the Threefold Cord: Truth and the Anglican Tradition

TREVOR HART

'The truth is out there – if only we demand it.' So writes Matthew d'Ancona in an essay aimed at responding to what he takes to be a widespread culture of anti-intellectualism abroad in our society, manifest everywhere from the popular impatience with 'experts' to increasing political willingness to sideline the 'facts' of the matter (whatever the matter in hand may be) in preference for versions of events conveniently charged with affective or otherwise persuasive force, or even brazenly to supply a set of 'alternative facts', secure in the conviction that, when push comes to shove, no one really cares any more anyway about which is 'true'.[1] What is at stake here, d'Ancona insists, is a difference between two very different orientations, two conflicting ways of approaching 'reality' itself in our dealings with it, one of which is concerned above all with being guided by the world's actual shape and substance, while the other is content wantonly to make reality up as it goes along, and as best fits its purposes and priorities. Demanding truth, his argument suggests, is something we should all be at pains to do, not just as a matter of principled protest against inappropriate whimsy, but lest reality turn around in due course and bite us in ways for which we have become ill-prepared, demanding of us responses we are no longer in any position to make. The truth is out there – if only we demand it.

But is it? Is the truth 'out there', waiting simply to be identified, classified and responded to in an appropriate manner? Clearly, it would be very convenient if this were so. But it is not only Nietzscheans and political spin-doctors who want to insist that, in reality, things are not quite so simple as that. And while we may wish, with those like Matthew d'Ancona, to inhibit the potentially corrosive impact of a wanton disregard for truth and 'the facts', we do have to come to terms with the equal and opposite dangers of a false 'objectivism', which presumes that there are such things as uninterpreted 'facts', neutral nuggets of information divorceable from the particular schemes of value, feeling and other constituents of human 'meaning' which enable us to identify, classify and respond to them at all. 'Facts' of this ideologically virgin sort were, as Alasdair MacIntyre reminds us, like telescopes and wigs for gentlemen, an eighteenth-century invention,[2] born of an optimistic epistemology which may have had considerable influence for some three centuries, but which is now largely discredited and the deconstruction of which has revealed its own politically and morally problematic heritage and potential. That such naïve appeals to 'the facts' continue unabated in certain sorts of populist discourse is no reason whatever to grab them as the nearest blunt instrument lying conveniently to hand with which to bludgeon post-truth into submission.[3] In that direction lies only another form of dangerous loss of one's moorings in reality, just as prone to proffer its own constructions as an account of 'the truth' of things as its devil-may-care relativistic counterpart, and with some equally disastrous potential consequences. The truth is not simply 'out there' to be plucked effortlessly like fruit from the tree. Facts are not things we simply trip over. They are in some measure always the product of frameworks of meaning which grant them significance, and which human beings are responsible for generating in their constructive engagements with the world. A proper concern for 'truth', therefore, needs to proceed by way of a more nuanced account of what is involved in seeking and finding it, one that, rather than polarizing 'facts' on the one hand and emotions, values and imagination on the other, acknowledges the complexity of the search and integrates all these, among other facets of our humanity, in its account of what is involved.

Religious faith, of course, has often fallen victim to the false polarity of 'objective' and 'subjective' that characterizes modernity's way of dealing with questions of knowledge and truth. Marx famously opined that religion was but the 'opiate of the masses', a metaphor finding resonances in d'Ancona's account of much of the post-truth culture as 'narcotic' rather than 'rational'. Others have insisted on reducing the content of religious 'belief' to include only things that can pass muster with 'reason'. But the sharp polarity itself will not bear careful scrutiny in theology or elsewhere. Accounts of 'believing' that begin by endorsing it uncritically tend in practice to suffer, championing one pole needlessly at the expense of the other rather than managing to hold belief's objective and subjective components together in a constructive manner. 'Blind faith' which buries its head in the sand, refusing to engage responsibly with the insights of current human learning and understanding, is unlikely to be taken seriously or make any meaningful contribution to wider intellectual and cultural conversations; while a 'rational' religion drained of imagination, emotion, narrative, and personal commitment in order to exalt the concerns of a dispassionate and disinterested 'reason' is hardly deserving of the term 'faith', whatever concerns may properly also be had for its appropriate 'moorings in reality'.[4]

Theological accounts of how truth (about God, the world, the wider substance of what we take to be 'real') may fruitfully be sought and had, and the sorts of claims that may legitimately be made about it, vary significantly.[5] My concern in this chapter is with what has sometimes been suggested to be a typically Anglican way of approaching such questions (especially questions of faith and order in the church) and which, whatever its faults, acknowledges a variety of different elements in the pattern of human knowing of whatever truth may be had or engaged with. Indeed, while the approach is generally offered as an account of specifically theological knowing, it lends itself helpfully to a wider account of our knowing of things, and much in recent writing on the subject contains echoes of it, whether intentional or otherwise.[6] What I have in mind is sometimes referred to as 'the threefold cord', an approach to questions of theological truth gravitating around three acknowledged 'centres' of authority – Scripture, tradition, and reason (or, as I prefer, 'the present'). It is not uncommon for fairly sweeping appeals to be made to this triad, as though some sort of classic Anglican consensus existed across time and place about these respective authorities and the relationships pertaining between them. In fact, while such an approach (a characteristic Anglican 'method' in theology) has often been held to be identifiable,[7] I am persuaded that it is in large measure a chimera. In other words, appeals to some more or less consistent *application* of the 'threefold cord' since the sixteenth century in reality mask a multitude of quite diverse understandings and practices, not least in the recent past.

At this point it may be useful to clarify the meaning of some key terms as I shall use them. 'Scripture' refers to the canonical books of the Old and New Testaments, configured as they are as a single, carefully ordered book in the text of the Christian Bible. Although there have been and remain differences and disputes about precisely which books ought to be included and where they should arise, these are relatively slight and not relevant for our purposes. In broad terms the 'canon' of Christian Scripture is easily identifiable, and its identification as 'Scripture' at all flags the church's commitment to treating it as authoritative, whatever that may mean in practice.[8] I prefer the phrase 'the present' as a substitute for the more traditional 'reason' (for reasons that will become clear) rather than a reference to the precise temporal juncture at which we happen to find ourselves today. In other words, 'present' refers to the pattern of intellectual and cultural factors which form part of the matrix for Christian reflection in particular times and places, whether our own or some other. By 'tradition' I mean ways in which the church has made and does make sense of things in the light of the gospel, not just in formal pronunciations and authoritative texts of one sort or another, but in a whole range of forms of thought and practice which embody its distinctive take on the truth of things.

In what follows I want to provoke our reflection by identifying some of the more obvious concerns and questions surrounding the so-called threefold cord, especially noting some insights and challenges peculiar to our own historical and cultural present, with a view to addressing the main question that concerns us in this volume: as creatures who naturally crave contact with truth, what different factors are involved in our pursuit and identification of its manifestations in our lives, and our willingness to grant it our assent and practical commitment?

Reconsidering the so-called threefold cord

Quite apart from the diverse (even incompatible) approaches to theological construction which its bare statement permits, there are other manifest inadequacies with appeal to the familiar triad of 'Scripture, tradition, and reason' itself.

The sixteenth-century divine Richard Hooker (c.1554–1600), who lays no claim to originality in his appeal to a threefold set of authoritative voices, is nonetheless usually taken as the *locus classicus*, presenting us with the threads out of which the cord of an 'Anglican way' of asking and answering questions is duly woven.[9] But Hooker can be and often is appealed to too quickly, and in ways which mask the significant discontinuities between his own context and concerns and our own. For instance, he does not use the polysemous term 'tradition' at all, but refers instead to 'the voice of the church', which is at best a very specific *instance* of Christian tradition. And in Hooker's use this category tends naturally in any case to overlap with his appeal to 'reason' – an appeal to the use of 'human authority' within the church, including, among other things, the intelligent ('reasonable') exegesis of Scripture to settle disputed questions of (authoritative) meaning. By way of allusion and response to the teaching of the Roman Catholic Church's Council of Trent (1545–63) Hooker refers to *'traditions'*, i.e. unwritten sources of alleged antiquity (another of his preferred terms) and ultimate apostolic descent. These, he insists, even when they may be supposed authentic, are not 'a part of Supernatural necessary truth'.[10] They are quite distinct and have a quite different role from other possible manifestations of human authority in the life of the church. It is difficult, then, to lump together some coherent conglomerate under the rubric of 'tradition' from Hooker's writing, disentangle it from reason and Scripture, and ascribe to it some consistent theological function. In this complexity his treatment may prove to be more nuanced than some of those who have subsequently attempted to tidy things up.

Hooker's concern in context is not in any case with establishing a general theological method, but with the specific questions arising from what he perceives as the twin errors of the Catholic and Puritan approaches to questions about the 'sufficiency' of Scripture for communicating that which is 'necessary for salvation' (cf. Article 6 of The Thirty-Nine Articles of Religion of 1571). The way one understands or orders the relationships properly pertaining between Scripture, 'reason', and 'the voice of the Church' in wider theological contexts or engagements with questions of truth can therefore hardly be based on his directives without further question or consideration. More needs to be said and done.

The question to which many appeals to the 'threefold cord' appear to offer an answer (what are the relevant sources of authority – or criteria – for Christian truth-seeking, and how are these to be ranked and ordered relative to one another?) may not reflect Hooker's way of thinking about things once we translate it into a different milieu. This need not invalidate it, but we need at least to take stock of the difference. For Hooker the supreme authority of Scripture within the life of the church was an absolute given, and the main concern. The introduction of the subsidiary authorities of reason and 'the voice of the church' was really part of an audit of the process whereby this same authority of Scripture functioned.

This involved, for instance, recognition of the obvious fact that, in order to function authoritatively, the text of Scripture must be read, interpreted, and applied by human beings within the church. In some sense, then, its authority must be held to be contingent upon other sorts of 'authoritative' activity within the community of faith. But these secondary authorities are understood as *functions of, encompassed within and derived from, Scripture's own authority and not independent of it.* The question to be answered was about the nature of the complex contingency. In what sense was it true, and in what senses was it not true, that God's authoritative speaking through Scripture in the church required these other subsidiary phenomena? Only in situations where Scripture was silent was it considered legitimate to treat reason and 'the voice of the church' as having any seemingly free-standing authority. Even here, though, Hooker's assumption is that the exercise of such authorities would be shaped from first to last by what the patristic theologians would have called the 'mind' or the 'scope' of the Scriptures themselves. There could be no serious question of their competing or conflicting with this primary authority. This, I suggest, constitutes a considerable difference from assumptions and priorities often operative in our own context. Here, 'reason' (generally understood in the Post-Enlightenment manner, as a context-transcendent, impartial and universally reliable gauge hard-wired into the human machine) is too often taken as the legitimate measure of all things and thus, in practice, accorded the highest authority.[11]

It is thus important to note that Hooker presupposes what we today generally do not; namely, that the various authorities to which he alludes will work together *in harmony* in order to feed the life of faith. He does not propose some Hegelian emergence of truth out of competitive struggle or conflict. And those who, in his day, saw potential conflict between Scripture and tradition (the Puritans) did not propose some dialectical progress towards higher synthesis, but the wholesale abandonment of tradition in preference for the (illusory) voice of 'Scripture alone'. Before the Enlightenment, of course, the appeal to 'reason' in theology was largely for clarificatory or supplementary rather than critical purposes. Since the middle of the eighteenth century, though, the 'threefold cord' has been rendered rather more prone to spontaneous unravelling, as 'reason' has generally been identified with the significantly reduced canon of credibility permitted by various philosophical commitments masquerading as objective universal prescriptions (as in the dogmatic assertion so often trotted out to preclude rather than precede serious intellectual engagement with some idea or claim: '*nobody* can believe that sort of thing nowadays!') and, as I have said, more often than not granted unchallenged primacy in the triangular relationship. Scripture has been rigorously submitted to its scrutiny, and 'tradition' all but banished as a source of intellectual irresponsibility (childishly relying on what others have thought and believed, rather than thinking for yourself before 'believing' anything). It is all rather more like a working model of 'the survival of the fittest' than the balanced and harmonious intellectual ecology envisaged by Hooker.

At this point, partly on the basis of what we have already seen, and partly by way of anticipation of what is to come, I want to propose that a different question might be formulated. The problems with that posited above are numerous, but include its easy disentanglement of Scripture, tradition, and reason from one another, its tendency to slip into treating them as things of a similar sort or on a similar level to be related to one another, and (perhaps most significantly) its exclusion of all sorts of other elements which, while they may not readily be located under the rubric of 'authorities' or criteria for theologizing, are nonetheless essential parts of the complex process whereby Scripture functions authoritatively within the church and thus (since most Christian communities acknowledge Scripture as their primary authority) how truth is sought and identified there. If, then, we asked a different question (e.g. 'What different factors may be identified in the authorizing of Scripture in the pursuit of truth within the church by the Spirit?') we might get a more satisfying and adequate account than versions of the threefold cord have tended to provide. Answering it, in fact, is likely to require reference to a much more complex and matted bunch of fibres altogether, and to return us to some of the issues of complexity, provisionality, and the need for a broader and more integrated account of knowing.

Imagination and the grammar of assent

In a work surprisingly undervalued in recent years, *An Essay in Aid of a Grammar of Assent* (1870), John Henry Newman provides a penetrating account of what is involved in believing things to be true and how such beliefs (religious or otherwise) arise and flourish. Although Newman can hardly be claimed as an Anglican theologian (the book was published long after his transition to Rome)[12] it contains much that is consistent with and provides a vital complement to any appeal to the triumvirate of Scripture, tradition and reason. In effect Newman furnishes much that is otherwise lacking to point us in the direction of a broader, more complex and integrated account of believing and knowing.

Newman's concern is both with the conditions for and the nature of our granting of assent to various kinds of propositions. To grant assent to something, he notes, is a mental act essential to what we mean when we say that we 'believe' something to be the case. We do not doubt it, and we do not infer it on the strength of other things (though these may be important to our coming to believe it), but hold it unconditionally and are content to assert it as true. But assent, Newman observes, may be granted to two quite distinct sorts of object. We may assent to propositions apprehended as 'notions' (ideas, abstractions, and logical relations of one sort or another which exist in the mind), or we may assent to propositions which 'are apprehended as experiences and images, that is, which stand for things' that we encounter or are presented with in the particular circumstances of concrete reality.[13]

Both sorts of assent may be important in one way or another; but assent which is merely notional, while intellectually stimulating and impressive, lacks much purchase in or hold on reality, and is in itself a purely academic form of 'believing in'. While, for its part, 'real assent' lacks the clarifying and critical force of notional assent, it nonetheless furnishes the living substrate and impulse that earths thought in the realities of human existence. Thought needs something to think about and to make sense of. And believing in something is much more than subscribing to a set of intellectual categories and relations, no matter how fully grasped and articulated.

Newman applies this distinction, of course, to the life of the church, where, he complains, in the English church of his day there is rather too much 'believing' which turns out to be of a mostly notional sort – creedal subscription, scriptural literacy, liturgical propriety of an impressive standard; but all rather remote from evidence of a direct living engagement with the concrete realities of which such ideas are originally and properly intended to speak. Religious truth, he suggests (though not religious truth alone), is of a sort which 'believing' in properly entails living participation and indwelling, and not simply intellectual gymnastics or prowess. And in this sense, the uneducated or theologically unformed 'simple believer' who grasps and assents to the basic propositions called forth by a living engagement with God is more solidly grounded in his or her beliefs than the most learned student of Bible, theology and liturgy whose prayer life has atrophied or whose involvement in the life of the community of faith has grown cold and remote. While Scripture, tradition and reasoning may well be an important part of the pursuit of truth in the church, therefore, on Newman's account they are far from sufficient, and in fact always secondary to the believer's concrete encounters with truth. And one may properly believe in things (and have good, concrete grounds for doing so) without attaining or aspiring to much by way of comprehending their place in the larger intellectual scheme of things.

Newman also anticipates much in recent theory concerning the ways in which beliefs are born, sustained and nurtured in the complex fabric of human living. We do not, he reminds his readers, come to assent to things because we have them all figured out or neatly placed in the 'notional' schemes which reasoning constructs and reconstructs as it proceeds. On the contrary, reasoning is a quite secondary stage in our dealings with reality, and it needs things to think about. These are supplied in various ways, of course, but Newman is particularly helpful in drawing attention to the vital role of imagination in engendering and nurturing the plethora and complex web of 'assents' which any human life in the world is involved in granting daily, and which duly provide the stuff with which our acts of reasoning and reflection seek to get to grips. Humans, he suggests, as well as craving truth also (and perhaps more primally) crave *meaning* – some sense that the bits and pieces of our concrete experience finally hold together and make sense and afford something like a stable world to live in rather than a chaotic flotsam and jetsam of particulars all different from one another.[14] Acts of reasoning (notional and abstract reflection which takes a step back from the world in order to 'think about' it) are obviously concerned to investigate such questions at a high level and offer a verdict. But the fabric of daily life, while not presenting itself to us in the sort of overall orderly, systematic unity to which reasoning aspires, is nonetheless certainly not bereft of meaningfulness. Rather we experience it as already shot through with meaning and value of various sorts, as particulars are tacitly situated and presented to us in patterns that 'make sense' in one way or another, and enable us to navigate through the complexities and endless variety of things. As C. S. Lewis (who may or may not be aware of drawing on Newman's account at this point) reminds us, imagination is the organ of meaningfulness – that which takes the particular bits of our experience of things and works them up already into patterns, configurations and forms which relate them to one another and enable us to grasp them as meaningful.[15] Reasoning may duly apply itself critically to such constructs and test their usefulness, but it is imagination that grants them for our consideration, and our capacity for acts of imagination that thereby engenders a meaningful world for us to indwell. Something similar is explored in the recent writings of Charles Taylor (already mentioned in the previous chapter[16]), who writes of the vital importance of 'social' and 'cosmic imaginaries', imaginative frameworks and narratives that underwrite the sense of reality (and inform the beliefs and assumptions) of any human society.[17] Where religious belief is concerned in particular, Newman argues, the cumulative impact of a host of considerations drawn from such meaningful engagements with and apprehensions of the world is basic to its engendering and sustaining, and a prior condition of any sort of theological reflection or argument designed to articulate or reinforce it.

But imagination plays a further vital role in all this too, for it grants us the capacity to glimpse, apprehend and respond to realities lying deeper than the surface of the material world and to experience certain of them in particular as the vehicles of the approach of God in and through our experience of other things. Newman concentrates in particular on the way in which the voice of conscience functions in this regard – not simply as the basis for a 'moral argument' for the reality of God, but, via imagination's ministry of permitting us to trespass beyond the empirically given, as something which may be *experienced as* the reality of God in our lives, granting us an apprehension of the real to which 'real assent' may properly be given. Recent developments of Newman's thought such as that of Aidan Nichols have emphasized the way in which other features of our meaningful experience of things – including aesthetic and affective responses, and our deep human longing or desire which seemingly finds no satisfaction in the sphere of the immanent – may function in a similar manner.[18] Again, such features of our human experience of the world as a meaningful environment invite the scrutiny, critical accounting and systematic articulation of reason, but assent (believing in the truth they present) need not be and typically is not withheld until reason has done its work. There is something self-evidencing, some glimpse or grasp of reality made available by imagination's extension of the range of our perceptions, that compels response of a more than intellectual sort, and without which acts of mere intellectual assent remain dry and lacking roots in the soil of truth.

Peculiar insights and challenges of our own present

I want in this section briefly to refer to some of the more obvious insights of recent intellectual endeavour which support my attempt to complicate the account of a 'threefold cord'.

Literary theory, studies of translation and semantics have taught us that the notion of objective meanings located 'within' a text 'like wisdom teeth within a gum, waiting patiently to be extracted' by any skilled interpreter is problematic.[19] We have to recognize the vital contributions of what communities of readers and individual readers bring with them to the event in which meaning happens, as well as what the text furnishes.[20] For a text to function with authority for a community there would seem, prima facie, to have to be some level of agreement about its meaning. Fluidity of an unbounded sort seems inevitably to lead to terminal diversity and chaos, and to wreak havoc with any workable notion of 'truth'.[21] But fluidity as such, in dialectic with a responsible recognition of the relatively fixed form of the text and the ethical obligation to listen to what it is saying through established conventions of interpretation, may actually provide a model for Scripture as a living Word spoken afresh to the church in ever new contexts.[22] The alternatives – either a word with sharply fixed semantic boundaries, spoken long ago and once for all, or a word which says no more than we ourselves bring with us to the text – are unattractive.

Studies in the sociology of knowledge have drawn attention to the social and historical particularity of what counts as 'reason'.[23] Reason is thus better construed as an intellectual tool working within the horizons provided by particular sets of assumptions about what is possible, credible, meaningful, etc., than as some transcendent set of truths to be applied with equal validity in any time and place (an intellectual equivalent of Bill Gates' globally dominant Microsoft software, preloaded into the hardware of the human mind). Thus, what has counted for 'reason' in Christian theology has in fact variously meant 'everything from Platonism to Vedantic philosophy or the critical theory of the Frankfurt School'.[24] Again, recognition of this fact need not entail capitulation to utter relativism and its consequences. Total incommensurability between differing intellectual contexts is contradicted by our experience of the capacity to communicate across the boundaries which distinguish them;[25] but significant levels of incommensurability and 'untranslatability'[26] may and do nonetheless exist. Hence Richard Bauckham suggests that we cease to use the term 'reason' and substitute for it the more inclusive and less misleading term 'context'.[27]

The same studies have insisted that the neat distinction between 'reason' and 'tradition' is no longer sustainable. 'Reason' in the sense articulated above is always related directly to some tradition of intellectual and practical endeavour. Tradition is not something over against which it stands in a relationship of potential contradiction, but furnishes the conditions within which alone reason may operate. Rational inquiry is both 'tradition-constituted' and 'tradition-constituting'.[28] Tradition furnishes the standpoint and the place from which all intelligent reflection is attempted and accomplished.

Studies of the role of 'tradition' in human communities also tend nowadays to insist upon a broad rather than a narrowly intellectual definition of the term. Traditions are manifest and expressed not only in intellectual 'creeds', but in all the forms of life: rituals, art, architecture, social and political institutions, codes of dress, hopes and aspirations, and the ways people behave in general.[29] The root metaphor behind the theological notion of 'tradition' (from the Latin verb *tradere*) is that of something being reliably 'handed on' like the baton in a relay race, or 'delivered' like a package in the hands of a courier, from one time and place to another. References to tradition in discussions of Christian theology have mostly had in mind the body of words and ideas (doctrines, sermons, liturgical texts, and the like) in which Scripture has been interpreted and by which it has been supplemented, handing on not just a sacred text but authoritative or official indicators of its authorized meanings too. If, though, we ask what it is that is handed on from one generation to another, one community to another, in such a way that it informs and shapes the understanding, expectations, aspirations, desires and practices of Christian believers, a wide rather than a narrow definition of the term would certainly seem to be warranted or demanded.[30] For in reality our approach to the life of faith is, as Newman properly discerned, only concerned in part with conciliar creeds and confessions and the like; and the assent we grant to these as fitting interpretations of Scripture is likely to be secondary (temporally and logically) to our immersion in the texture and patterns of particular forms of Christian existence. Here, where through hymnody, ways of worshipping and styles of spiritual practice, preaching,[31] experiences of community, involvement in acts of service and ministry to those outside the church, the arts (music, painting, literature, drama, film), the example of 'saints' (those in the calendar and those known to us personally), and, chiefly, our relationships with a local network of other Christians – *anything*, indeed, which might properly be said to constitute a form of faithful 'interpretation', performance, or actualization of the gospel message within the church in the midst of the world[32] – the reality of which creeds and confessions speak is 'known' and responded to in ways that shape our thinking from the bottom up. And again, all this inherited tradition bears significantly upon the way in which Scripture functions authoritatively within the church, as well as being in its turn the product of that functioning.

So, theological appeals to tradition as part of the threefold cord are thus potentially as imprecise as concomitant appeals to 'reason', depending on just how widely the net of definition is cast. And the sharp distinction between 'Scripture' and 'tradition' itself proves to be less easy to draw once we zoom in and ask not just about the physical form of the text (the words on the page) but its range of possible meanings; because meaning is always the product of things that we bring with us to a text as well as what we find waiting for us there. In an important sense, therefore, since it shapes the meanings arising from the Bible as an authoritative text (whether consciously or tacitly impacting upon the ways we read and make sense of biblical texts) this pervasive living tradition is 'Scripture-constituting' as well as 'Scripture-constituted' and, we might even risk saying, 'truth-constituting' as well as 'truth-constituted'. One gain of a broader rather than a narrower definition of tradition is its recognition that even a church which has no peculiar confessional heritage may yet have a distinctive doctrinal standpoint or horizon of interpretation (being reminded of which may serve to make some of its theologians less rather than more comfortable).[33] But the very breadth of the definition brings into sharp focus the question of just where the relevant thresholds of identity lie, and what sorts and levels of diversity may be permitted before they must be held to have been crossed.

Particularity, diversity and continuity – the limits of our claims to 'know the truth'

Traditions, in order to be identifiable as traditions at all, must have characteristic features and boundaries. In order for theological developments within the Christian tradition (in doctrine, ethics, matters of ecclesial order, or whatever) to be identifiably Christian, therefore, there must be the possibility of boundaries being trespassed, and Christian identity being compromised. Diversity cannot be completely unbounded, or else the meaningfulness of tradition as such is compromised. Orthodoxy and heterodoxy must remain meaningful notions, even in an age besotted with pluralism as an ideology and not just an empirical fact. For interpretations or performances of the tradition to be particular to contexts cannot simply mean that 'anything goes'. Even the metaphor of performative improvisation (sometimes appealed to enthusiastically by those making a case for radical novelty and diversity) cannot overlook the basic fact that an improvisation is utterly contingent on apprenticeship in a tradition and faithfulness to the basic harmonic and melodic pattern of a larger piece. Otherwise it is simply an impetuous and arbitrary show of technical dexterity with little to be said for it.

The description of tradition as a set of forms of life constituting a faithful 'interpretation' or 'performance' of Scripture[34] appeals to such levels of continuity, and indicates that some identifiable (if not precisely specifiable) continuity of motif, character or pattern is required. An interpretation of *King Lear* in which Edmund and Goneril do not appear, or in which Kent is portrayed as a scheming malevolent, can easily be adjudged a poor interpretation of Shakespeare's play. In many other respects there is considerable latitude and licence to be enjoyed by director and actors alike in their production. But such licence is not without limits. So too, in the case of Scripture, we may acknowledge the legitimacy and even the vital importance of open-ended trajectories of meaning (rather than precisely bounded sets), while insisting that such trajectories must be able to be traced back identifiably to centres of gravity in the pattern of the objective form of the text of Scripture. (More may yet need to be said, for example, about hermeneutical strategies for reading the text – canon, intertextuality, relations between the testaments, recognition of diversity and dialectic within the text, and so on.) Thus, Oliver O'Donovan urges that the authority and warrant possessed by tradition must lie in its capacity identifiably to illuminate the text (which can and must be returned to again and again in order to ground and refresh our interpretations). Reciprocally, the text verifies or challenges the authority of interpretations of it within the same relationship.[35]

Finally, it needs to be reiterated that we are not engaged in a merely two-dimensional exercise in which disembodied minds seek to relate two distinct sets of texts or ideas to one another meaningfully ('reason' being applied to Scripture and 'tradition' respectively). That would be an exercise of a purely 'notional' sort in Newman's sense, and largely bereft of the contact with concrete realities of which more full-blooded assent aspires to speak, and which draws some sort of halt to the pursuit of endless diversity of interpretation. Diversity of some sort and some level may be an ineradicable feature of our human attempts to grapple with the question of truth in this world. It is not clear that as Christians we are in any position to expect that it is a circumstance attaching to God's own reality or the reality of whatever God has made. That 'truth' is, in so far as we grasp it, always as much a matter of our own making as what is 'out there' need not commit us to the view that Reality itself is some sort of postmodern kaleidoscope of ever-shifting and infinitely malleable options. This being so, even as we acknowledge the shortfall of our knowing and the abiding mystery and depth of what confronts us, the fragility and provisionality of bringing that reality to expression in language, and in the midst of whatever diversity of apprehensions of 'truth' results from all this, we can and should remain committed in principle to the task of pursuing a unitary truth. Such truth lies for now beyond us; for that very reason, though, it calls even our best acts of reasoning and interpreting into question and compels us to act responsibly rather than merely playfully in our pursuit of it.

Claims that 'the truth is out there' need to be carefully handled if we are not to collapse back into a form of modernist fundamentalism. Yet we should not be unduly pessimistic about our capacity to grapple with what is real, and when we believe that reality is broken open for us more fully by one perspective, interpretation or tradition than another, we ought not to be afraid to say so with confidence, thereby risking ourselves and our theologies in what George Steiner dubs with fruitful ambiguity a 'wager on transcendence'.[36] For in some sense reality ought to be allowed to be the final arbiter of our statements about it, and God of our theologies.

Questions for discussion

1 'The distinctions between Scripture, tradition and reason are best drawn lightly rather than with too thick a pencil.' Why?
2 In what sense might a 'simple believer' be held to have an equally secure grip on 'truth' as someone well-versed in theology?
3 'Only those who acknowledge that their claims may turn out to be false can have any rational warrant for asserting their truth.' How would recognizing this affect the way in which we approach (a) those who interpret passages of Scripture very differently from ourselves or (b) the adherents of other religious traditions?

Further reading

B. Drewery and R. Bauckham (eds), *Scripture, Tradition and Reason: A Study in the Criteria of Christian Doctrine* (Edinburgh: T & T Clark, 1988). Essays on aspects of the 'threefold cord' by scholars in a range of philosophical, historical, biblical, and theological disciplines.

T. Hart, *Faith Thinking: The Dynamics of Christian Theology* (London: SPCK, 1995). An accessible and clear introduction to the categories 'Scripture', 'tradition' and 'reason' and their place in Christian theology.

W. Marshall, *Scripture, Tradition and Reason: A View of Anglican Theology through the Centuries* (Dublin: Columba Press, 2010). An informed and informative account of Anglican approaches to theology from the sixteenth to the twenty-first centuries.

S. Wells, *What Anglicans Believe: An Introduction* (Norwich: Canterbury Press, 2011). A helpful and readable overview with a chapter concentrating on the 'threefold cord' or, as the author prefers, the 'three-legged stool'.

Notes

1 M. d'Ancona, *Post Truth: The New War on Truth and How to Fight Back* (London: Ebury Press, 2017), p. 6 *et passim*.

2 A. MacIntyre, *Whose Justice? Which Rationality?* (London: Duckworth, 1988), p. 357.

3 See Chapter 2 (Jasper).

4 See further on this false polarity and alternatives to it: T. Hart, *Faith Thinking: The Dynamics of Christian Theology* (London: SPCK, 1995); J. K. Smith, *Desiring the Kingdom* (Grand Rapids MI: Baker Academic, 2009).

5 See Chapter 1 (Taylor).

6 Accounts resonating significantly with it include those to be found in M. Johnson, *The Meaning of the Body: Aesthetics of Human Understanding* (Chicago: University of Chicago Press, 2007); MacIntyre, op. cit.; M. Polanyi, *Personal Knowledge* (London: Routledge & Kegan Paul, 1958); C. Taylor,

Sources of the Self: The Making of Modern Identity (Cambridge: Cambridge University Press, 1999).

7 See, e.g., M. Ramsey, *The Anglican Spirit* (Boston MA: Cowley Publications, 1991), pp. 23–4; cf. S. W. Sykes, *The Integrity of Anglicanism* (London: Mowbray, 1978), pp. 44–52, 63–75.

8 On the way the biblical text is used as 'Scripture' in the church and its theology see, helpfully, J. Goldingay, *Models for Scripture* (Grand Rapids MI: Eerdmans, 1994); J. Goldingay, *Models for Interpreting Scripture* (Grand Rapids MI: Eerdmans, 1995); D. Kelsey, *The Uses of Scripture in Recent Theology* (London: SCM Press, 1995).

9 See R. Hooker, *The Laws of Ecclesiastical Polity and Other Works* (in 3 vols, ed. Hanbury, London, 1830).

10 Ibid., p. 136.

11 See, e.g., M. Wiles, *What is Theology?* (Oxford: Oxford University Press, 1976). For a more measured modern take on the relationship cf. J. Macquarrie, *Principles of Christian Theology* (London: SCM Press, 1977), p. 17.

12 Newman (1801–90) was an Anglican priest, theologian, and poet who was received into the Roman Catholic Church in 1845. He was ordained as a Catholic priest, and was made a Cardinal in 1879.

13 J. H. Newman, *An Essay in Aid of a Grammar of Assent* (4th edn, London, 1874 [1870]), p. 40.

14 Cf. V. Frankl, *Man's Search for Meaning* (London: Ebury, 2004 (1946)).

15 Meaning, Lewis observes, 'is the antecedent condition both of truth and falsehood, whose antithesis is not error but nonsense'. See 'Bluspels and Falansferes' in C. S. Lewis, *Rehabilitations and Other Essays* (London: OUP, 1939), p. 157.

16 See Chapter 4 (Wright).

17 See C. Taylor, *Modern Social Imaginaries* (Durham NC: Duke University Press, 2004); C. Taylor, *A Secular Age* (Cambridge MA: Harvard University Press, 2007).

18 A. Nichols, *A Grammar of Consent: Existence of God in Christian Tradition* (Edinburgh: T & T Clark, 1991).

19 T. Eagleton, *Literary Theory: An Introduction*. 2nd edn. (Oxford: Blackwell, 1996), p. 89.

20 See further G. Steiner, *After Babel: Aspects of Language and Translation*. 2nd edn. (Oxford: OUP, 1992); A. C. Thiselton, *New Horizons in Hermeneutics: The Theory and Practice of Transforming Biblical Reading* (Grand Rapids MI: Zondervan, 1992).

21 See further Chapter 2 (Jasper).

22 See Hart, op. cit., pp. 135–42.

23 So, e.g, MacIntyre, op. cit.

24 R. Bauckham in B. Drewery and R. Bauckham (eds), *Scripture, Tradition and Reason: A Study in the Criteria of Christian Doctrine* (Edinburgh: T & T Clark, 1988), 140.

25 MacIntyre, op. cit., p. 350.

26 Steiner, op. cit.

27 Drewery and Bauckham, op. cit., p. 140.

28 MacIntyre, op. cit., pp. 349–69.

29 So MacIntyre, op. cit., p. 355.

30 See Smith, op. cit.

31 See also Chapter 6 (Davies), on liturgy, and Chapter 7 (McLuckie), on spirituality.

32 See T. Hart and S. R. Guthrie, *Faithful Performances: Enacting Christian Tradition* (Aldershot: Ashgate, 2007).

33 See Sykes, op. cit., p. 41f.

34 See, e.g., F. Young, *The Art of Performance: Towards a Theology of Holy Scripture* (London: Darton, Longman and Todd, 1990); Hart and Guthrie, op. cit.

35 O. O'Donovan, *On the 39 Articles: A Conversation with Tudor Christianity* (Carlisle: Paternoster, 1986), pp. 113–16.

36 G. Steiner, *Real Presences: Is There Anything in What We Say?* (London: Faber and Faber, 1989).

6

Liturgy as a Repository of Truth

JOHN REUBEN DAVIES

> Sanctify them in the truth; your word is truth. (John 17:17)

> Christianity is a liturgical religion. The Church is first of all a worshipping community. Worship comes first, doctrine and discipline second. (George Florovsky)[1]

The premise of this chapter is that truth is revealed in the person of Jesus Christ, the one who is the incarnate Logos, the Word of God that was made flesh and dwelt among us (John 1:14). This is the same man who, standing before Pilate as the one 'full of grace and truth' that had 'come into the world to bear witness to the truth' (John 1:14, 17), was asked by the Roman prefect, 'What is truth?' (John 18:37–38).

We might begin, then, by returning to the sense that truth, even when it is standing in front of us, is something to be discovered, a question to be answered: it is not self-evident. Pilate might therefore just as well have asked, '*Where* is truth?'.[2] An answer to that question, which I shall propose and outline in this chapter, is that, for the Christian, truth can be found in and through the liturgical worship of the church, in the textual tradition of liturgy as well as in its enactment.

Perceptions of The Most Holy

> In Christ your Son the life of heaven and earth were joined,
> sealing the promise of a new creation, given, yet still to come.
> (Scottish Liturgy 1982)[3]

Psalm 19 provides a most beautiful poetic expression of the relationship between God's creation, God's glory, God's truth (as expressed in the 'law of the Lord'), and the human response.[4] The psalmist articulates how worship is grounded in God's self-revelation and is the response of the creature to that revelation. And following this scriptural pattern, the Christian community is brought through worship from exile into a place where God can truly be known. And so it is through worship that we come to a knowledge of truth. Liturgy is the vehicle by which we worship God and encounter God both communally and individually; it is therefore through liturgy that our human minds are drawn towards and conformed to the truth: conformed, that is, to the Word and mind of God.

Since liturgy takes place within space and time, it is within the specific spatial and temporal coordinates of liturgy that the natural world, through God's grace, comes to reveal the supernatural, that the immanent gives way to the transcendent. Within the context of liturgy, therefore, the order of creation becomes conformed to the order of grace.

Thomas Aquinas offered a useful argument for understanding this process of conformity. For Thomas, creation – understood as the natural world and natural things – is to be seen as a means by which our human minds are conformed to God. For when our intellect engages or interacts with any natural thing, and the two conform or are coordinated, and when the intellect apprehends the natural thing, the human mind comes to know what the mind of God already knew to be true. This, for Thomas, is what truth adds to being: the conformity or equation of a natural thing and our intellect.[5]

It is in the practice of liturgy, however, that we can encounter the supernatural as well as the natural. The liturgy is precisely the place where the natural and the supernatural, the transcendent and the immanent, come to be distinguished. For example, in the natural order and in the contemplation of the Eucharistic host it is not true that the thing in front of us is *just* a piece of bread: in and through the actions of the liturgy it has been supernaturally revealed that what appears to be a piece of bread is in fact – even for the Zwinglian – not mere bread, but (in some sense, whether as a sign or in substance) the body of the Lord.[6] If we did not know that this thing had been liturgically consecrated, we could mistake it for something other than what it truly is.

We know, moreover, that all things are revealed in Christ: all things, that is, both natural and supernatural. In this sense creation is also a sacrament and sign of Christ, since 'all things came into being through him' (John 1:3). And if all natural things are given to us in and through Christ, so too all things are connected with our salvation, both before and after 'the Word became flesh' (John 1:14) in the conception and birth of Jesus of Nazareth. But although we encounter natural things both in and as nature itself – as 'the natural world' – when, on the other hand, we encounter the supernatural things of God, we do so in a specifically liturgical setting. In other words the encounter with God's salvation, the encounter with Christ as the fullness of grace and truth, which God promises us through the sacraments of the church, takes place one way or another in the context of the temple sanctuary. For the Word is both definitively revealed and objectively encountered in the temple, and the Gospels emphasize this relation between the Word and the Jerusalem Temple as that which reveals Jesus to be the divine Son of God. 'Destroy this temple', said Jesus, 'and in three days I will raise it up' (John 2:19). Indeed, when Stephen was brought before the Council, he was accused of saying that 'this Jesus of Nazareth will destroy this place [the Temple] and will change the customs that Moses handed on to us' (Acts 6:14). As John the Evangelist made clear, however, Jesus 'was speaking of the temple of his body. After he was raised from the dead, his disciples remembered that he had said this; and they believed the scripture and the word that Jesus had spoken' (John 2:21–22). Stephen's speech to the Sanhedrin develops this prophecy of Jesus as the new Temple who inaugurates the new worship and, with his sacrifice on the cross, replaces the ancient sacrifices.[7] And so, for the Christian, the temple is wherever the liturgical action is taking place, wherever the body of Christ is assembled for worship.

Liturgy as revelation – a quality of God's presence with us all the time

> Making himself known in the breaking of the bread ...
> he renewed the promise of his presence ...
> (Scottish Liturgy 1982)

The body of Christ, the baptized community assembled for worship – and most especially in the Eucharistic liturgy – therefore embodies the temple, the place where the immanent and the transcendent coincide. Laurence Paul Hemming, from an explicitly (Roman) Catholic perspective, takes us further into this mystery. Liturgy, for Hemming, although it takes place within the created order, is not primarily a human creation, but a natural thing that is natural to God but supernatural to humans. For presiding over the Eucharistic liturgy is the priest (*sacerdos*), and priesthood in its essence, as Hemming understands it, 'is the effecting of divine things at human hands'.[8] Through the administration of the sacraments the priest shows God to the people. (But an Anglican might additionally wish to emphasize that, as a royal priesthood, the whole baptized community also shows God to the world.) The priesthood is, moreover, for Hemming,

> properly exercised in the Holy of Holies, in the Sanctuary of the Lord, where its human signification is essentially different. For the Sanctuary is (ritually and symbolically) outside time and beyond

(earthly, 'humanly natural') place: its time is God's (eternity), and its place is heaven.⁹

The 'sanctuary', the place where the altar or holy table is set, is ritually speaking the 'Holy of Holies': it becomes a midpoint between heaven and earth, between the natural and the supernatural realms. The altar shows how heaven and earth, the supernatural and the natural are related for us; it is made of natural material and yet it intends, and reveals, the supernatural; and, in the context of the Eucharistic liturgy, what is found within the 'Holy of Holies' is nothing of (non-divine) nature. It is in this sense that the altar and its environs are sacred: although made of natural materials, it is a reserved place, such that, through the eyes of faith, only the supernatural is visible and to be encountered within it. And yet, if priesthood is properly exercised in the 'Holy of Holies', then wherever and whenever the priest ministers before the Lord and shows God to the world, that is, wherever the sacraments are administered, then that place must become heaven and that time eternity.

Jean-Yves Lacoste has reminded us, however, that the Eucharistic species also alerts us to the limits of liturgy: for the world draws a veil between God and humankind. Although God may be said to be present in the earthly realities of bread and wine, the believer must acknowledge that 'God's phenomenality [the capability of being known through experience] cannot be understood if we do not understand that God transcends his phenomenality'.¹⁰ God and the presence and experience of God, and God's truth, cannot simply be pinned down to specific things or actions or places. So, the worshipping believer who takes part in the liturgy, while seeking, does not grasp or take hold of what is sought, but only receives. If this is the case, then can we say that what is received must be the truth?

The liturgy, accordingly, is how Christ comes to be known and continues to be revealed both in the midst of as well as through the natural world. The liturgy is how the Word, which is truth, both reveals and brings about the supernatural understanding of salvation to us.

Liturgy: drawing the human together in revelation

O admirabile commercium! (O wonderful exchange!)
(First antiphon, Lauds and Vespers,
In Circumcisione Domini, Divinum Officium)

In Christ your Son our life and yours are brought together in a wonderful exchange.
(Scottish Liturgy 1982)

In Anglicanism, liturgy is the place where doctrine is definitively expounded.[11] A vital task for the people of God, therefore, is to study and understand the liturgical tradition, seeing it as a repository of revealed truth, and understanding how it speaks to us and what it shows us about the coming kingdom. The Christian should be seeking to recognize Christ in the liturgy. What does the liturgy let the worshipper see? To what extent is it revealing or showing or manifesting the oneness of the body of Christ, the unity that is the working of the Holy Spirit which leads us into all the truth? For believers do not just believe, but see: that is, they perceive spiritually, intellectually, and physically. And this seeing is part of the receiving which Lacoste alludes to.

Liturgical rites therefore allow for a liturgically engaged human body, since true worship avoids the largely unconscious tendency to dualism, as if we were only soul; as if worship were only something that happens inwardly.

The Constitution on the Sacred Liturgy, *Sacrosanctum Concilium*, promulgated by Pope Paul VI in 1963, served to remind the whole church that by virtue of our baptism we are full, active and conscious children of God. The fundamental principle of the liturgical reforms that took a firm hold in the 1960s was, then, this 'fully conscious, and active participation in liturgical celebrations' by all the people of God.[12] A shared understanding of the liturgy is therefore important so that we can participate fully and consciously.

We can also say that our external actions express our internal understanding. And these external actions have a further significance, both for those whose intellectual capacities are not mature or highly developed, and for those whose sensory perception is impaired. How do we ensure that the human body as well as the human mind is fully engaged in liturgical worship?

We should remember that there is no 'inner person', as such. Human beings are made in the image of God (Gen. 1:26), irrespective of whether we have physical disabilities or (for the time being) are able-bodied. Therefore a person has meaning in relation to the other and in relation to the world.

Liturgical worship, as we have already said, always takes place within spatial coordinates and that space and the action performed within it is not an expression of an 'inner reality'. The external is just as real as the internal. The link between existence and place is one of essence. And we must be mindful that liturgy takes place in this context.

In the location of the liturgical action – although made of natural materials – we encounter through sight, and touch, and taste and smell, that which is supernatural and transcendent. The whole fabric is required for this sensory perception to be effected: and the essential parts of the fabric also include the practices, the texts and the actions that belong there – that is, the liturgy. Since the Passion of the Lord, since the rending of the Temple veil (Mark 15:38), the supernatural it reveals can be seen and touched and tasted by all the faithful.

For this reason the human body – in every condition – has to be liturgically engaged. Our bodies are engaged in the imposition of ashes, in the Palm Sunday procession, in the washing of the feet in the Maundy, in the physical attitudes of prayer during the Solemn Intercession of Good Friday, and in the veneration of the cross, through varied postures, movements, and sacramental actions of the Easter Vigil – but above all, in baptism and in the reception of Holy Communion.

And so in a context of our human bodies, of word and song, of movement and touch; of wood and stone, silver and glass, paper and ink; with the branches of trees, and ashes; through silk and linen, wax and incense; and above all in the essential matter of the sacraments, bread and water and wine, the liturgy is how Christ comes to be known and continues to be revealed in the midst of, and through, the natural world.

The liturgy is therefore part of a process by which we are conformed to the truth; and in being conformed to the truth, the physical aspects of the liturgy just described – movement, speech, music, architecture, etc. – must conform to the truth also, that is, they must be beautiful and good.[13] For as participants in these liturgies, and in the Eucharist especially, the liturgical action and its physical context should allow – must allow – all worshippers to be active participants in the work of God's saving purpose for all the world, the restoration of all things in Jesus Christ.

Liturgy as a repository of Scripture

> Your word lights up our minds.
> (Scottish Liturgy 1982)

In its liturgy the church therefore experiences God's presence in a special way. Yet the two fundamental categories of experiencing God's presence might still be defined as word and sacrament. Indeed, 'the liturgy is the privileged setting in which God speaks to us in the midst of our lives'.[14] In a well-known passage, Augustine of Hippo taught that we should 'listen to the Gospel just as if to the Lord if he were present ... For the body of the Lord in which he arose can be in one place; but his truth is spread out everywhere'.[15]

There is a sense of the presence of God in the words of Scripture throughout patristic thought and into the Middle Ages. It may be, however, that God's presence in this way gradually became obscured by the special awareness of the somewhat different kind of presence of Christ in the sacrament of the altar. Yet these two kinds of presence were by no means mutually exclusive, and were even intimately interconnected in the minds of the Greek and Latin fathers.

For the ancient Jewish people, meanwhile, the liturgy was the place and situation in which the formative events were told and retold in order to draw out a fitting response in worship and way of life to God, who is faithful to the promises declared beforehand in the prophets in the holy Scriptures (cf. Rom. 1:2). This remains the case for Christians today. The Scriptures, as the place where the original stories were set down, developed, and classically defined, help to further that continuing function of the liturgy.

This understanding of the liturgy has persisted in Israel's religion since the time of the Exodus. The annual Passover liturgy allowed the succeeding generations to relive in ritual form the original deliverance from the bondage in Egypt; and a belief in an experience of the saving power of the Lord who 'brought us out of Egypt with a mighty hand and an outstretched arm' (Deut. 26:8) was transmitted; and the identity of God's chosen people was maintained, 'throughout the generations' (Exod. 12:14, 42). Because of God's true faithfulness, the prophets Isaiah and Jeremiah were later able to point to the Exodus from Egypt as an archetype and assurance of the deliverance from Babylonian captivity that they were hoping for.[16] In the early first century, at the time of Jesus' ministry, when Palestine was under Roman domination, the season of Passover, and the paschal night especially, was a time of heightened messianic expectations among the Jews.[17] For Christians, the suffering, death, and resurrection of Jesus at the time of the Jewish Passover, on the paschal night, did indeed bring about a deliverance with significance for the whole of creation. And among the early Christians, the paschal sense of expectancy was continued at Easter time, and again maintained 'from generation to generation', but now as an awaiting of the final *parousia* of Jesus Christ.

The paschal mystery, the passion, death, and resurrection of Christ, rememoratively celebrated over the Triduum of Maundy Thursday, Good Friday, and Holy Saturday, can be viewed therefore as the source of liturgy. Indeed, for Alexander Schmemann (1921–83), an Orthodox priest and liturgical theologian, the liturgy is the paschal mystery coming to meet us in our lives. But we might also say, with Lizette Larson-Miller, that all of Jesus' life was paschal mystery, and that all of faithful Christian life is paschal mystery, and that salvation is embedded in that union of life and liturgy.[18]

The liturgical element in the New Testament

If the paschal mystery of Christ comes to meet us in the liturgy, then we can also say that the word of God dwells in the prayers, praises, and teaching of the church. Liturgy is therefore also the home of sacred Scripture, its natural environment.[19] The recognition of the deeply embedded place of the Bible in worship was expressed by Bishop Jeremy Taylor, a seventeenth-century Anglican divine. In defending the legitimacy of the Book of Common Prayer, he said: 'Very much of our liturgy is in the very words of Scripture. The Psalms and Lessons and all the Hymns, save one [the *Gloria in excelsis*], are nothing else but Scripture.'[20]

Many of the portions in the Gospels had already been used in the earliest preaching of the church, and we find that the New Testament is broadly liturgical in character.[21]

Some obviously liturgical texts are found at Rev. 4:8, 11 and 5:9–10, 12b, 13b, allowing us a partial view of what bridged the gap between Jewish synagogue worship and later Christian liturgical practice.[22] Rev. 1:4–8 and 22:6–21 can also be seen as forms of liturgical dialogue.[23] Chapter 1:4–8, rather than being attached to a specific occasion, looks like a model of the dialogue that would have taken place every time a lector read John's message to an assembly that recognized itself as part of the church symbolized by the seven churches of Asia.[24]

> *Lector*
> Grace to you and peace
>   from him who is and who was and who is to come,
>   and from the seven spirits who are before his throne,
>   and from Jesus Christ
>   the faithful witness,
>   the first-born of the dead,
>   and the ruler of kings on earth.
>
> *Assembly*
> To him who loves us
> and has freed us from our sins by his blood
> and made us a kingdom, priests to his God and Father,
> to him be glory and dominion for ever and ever. Amen.

Lector
Behold, he is coming with the clouds,
   and every eye will see him,
      every one who pierced him;
   and all tribes of the earth will wail on account of him.

Assembly
Even so. Amen.

Lector
I am the Alpha and the Omega,
   says the Lord God,
who is and who was and who is to come,
the Almighty.

Similarly, 22:6–21 also contains what looks like a concluding liturgical dialogue; and this dialogical form appears to be used throughout the book.[25]

Other types of liturgical material are also embedded throughout the New Testament. There are acclamatory confessions, such as Rom. 10:9–10, 'If you confess with your lips that Jesus is Lord ...'; 1 John 4:15, 'those who confess that Jesus is the Son of God ...' Even the forms in which the evangelists report Peter's confession may also reflect liturgical usage: 'You are the Christ' (Mark 8:29), 'You are the Christ, the Son of the living God' (Matt. 16:16), 'The Christ of God' (Luke 9:20). Then there are longer creedal forms and hymns, such as Phil. 2:5–11.[26]

One can even discern a (Eucharistic) liturgical shape in Gospel pericopes. If we take Luke 7:11–17, for example, where Jesus raises the widow's son at Nain, there is what appears to be a fourfold structure. First there is a crowd that has gathered to follow Jesus (*Gathering*). Second, Jesus speaks (*Proclamation of the Word*). Third, in encountering the weeping mother, Jesus has compassion, and at his word the dead son is raised to life – death is defeated – he sets things right – an encounter with God is recognized by all (*The Priestly Act of Service*). Finally the people go out to spread the news through the whole of Judaea and the surrounding country (*Sending Out*).

We should therefore be aware that liturgy can be as much a source for sacred Scripture as sacred Scripture is a source for liturgy.

The role of the lectionary – the thematic sequence of reading

Geoffrey Wainwright, in his systematic treatment of worship and doctrine, *Doxology* (1980), set out a view of how Scripture relates to liturgy, and how the liturgy can be seen as a hermeneutical continuum for the scriptures.[27] For Wainwright, the liturgy is first of all the most concrete way in which the texts of the Bible have been preserved and transmitted. One might add that the Bible as a codex was not, and still is not, required for the liturgical celebration of the Church's sacraments, since the scriptural lections were – and in most denominations continue to be – an integral part of the liturgical books. Scriptural passages often survived, moreover, in modified and adapted forms within the liturgy, as they still do today. The principal liturgical purpose of a Bible was, and remains, for the continuous reading of Scripture that forms part of the daily office. Otherwise a Bible's purpose was essentially scholarly.[28]

For Wainwright, the use of Scripture in the liturgy is also the proper context for exegesis and interpretation, since the fundamental motivation of exegesis and hermeneutics should be the praise of God. The liturgy moreover supplies thematic guidelines for the exegete and interpreter. The liturgical calendar and lectionary compose the varied motifs of the scriptures into a coherent vision. In fact, Wainwright has viewed the liturgy as the pre-eminent place in which the Church ponders and enacts the scriptures: 'it thus contributes creatively to the development of doctrine'.[29]

The liturgy can also act as a control on the 'untoward development' of the Church's teaching and belief:

> since official liturgies are generally slow to change, they allow a breathing space while new popular or intellectual tendencies can be tried out unofficially without immediately affecting the authorised worship and doctrine of the Church.[30]

But how does the contemporary effective loss of stability in the liturgy since the time Wainwright was writing, with the internet, one-off printed service sheets, and the consequent temptations to bend liturgical discipline, affect the development of doctrine? For Wainwright is surely correct in saying that 'Where doubtful developments have made their way into the worship and doctrine of the Church, the liturgy is the place from which doctrinal reform can radiate into the wider thinking of the Church'.[31] The case of gender-neutral marriage rites in the Scottish Episcopal Church being used as an argument for the marriage of couples of the same sex in church is, perhaps, one of the most recent examples of this.³² It would also be possible to cite use of the Book of Common Prayer and the Ordinal against any change, including ordination of women, as in the Anglican diocese of Sydney, Australia.³³

Finally, for Wainwright, liturgy can contribute to the 'surmounting of the historico-cultural gulf between the ancient writings and the present community'.³⁴ Drawing on quotations from James Barr and C. F. Evans, he highlights the idea that liturgical and devotional use of the Bible demonstrates its reapplicability to new situations. As 'a treasury of imagery usable again and again, a sort of divinely-given poetry', the Bible provides the church throughout the ages with the means to express itself and understand itself.³⁵ But where he reiterates C. F. Evans' observation that the effects of cultural relativism are 'commonly mitigated by the use of the Bible in the liturgy', Wainwright's note that the bridging of the historico-cultural gap demands serious interpretative work in theology and preaching may have a particular resonance for a postmodern, post-truth age, where the use of once-uncontroversial categories in both secular life and liturgical language has become difficult and controversial.³⁶

Liturgical language as a bearer of truth

> The Spirit of truth lead you into all truth,
> give you grace to confess that Jesus Christ is Lord,
> and to proclaim the word and works of God.
> (Scottish Liturgy 1982)

A live debate in the second decade of the twenty-first century – and which has been going on for a lot longer – concerns the use of gendered language in relation to God.³⁷ While it ought to be an uncontroversial proposition that God does not have a sex in the human sense, the problematization of the male identity of Father and Son in the Holy Trinity, and the masculine associations of divine epithets such as Lord, King, Almighty, and so on, will no doubt be a matter of debate in liturgical theology for some time.

In addition to the gendered representation of God in Scripture and liturgy, however, there has emerged an equally complex issue in relation to human gender-identity and the liturgy. As an example, a prominent cleric in the Scottish Episcopal Church has raised the issue of gender-binary categories in worship, through posts on his widely-read web blog.

> Addressing an assembly of people as 'brothers and sisters' or (better)

'sisters and brothers' has for a long time seemed to me to be inclusive and capable of drawing people in.
I've recently learnt that it can leave some people feeling very much excluded and left out of the circle of faith.
If you identify as non-binary then you are not going to feel included by sisters and brothers language at all.
And remember that God is distinctly non-binary in Scripture.
This affects how we develop liturgy in the future. It's a good thing I think to write and speak in ways that don't leave people feeling left out.[38]

'Brethren' (best known in 'Dearly beloved brethren' from the Prayer Book services of Morning and Evening Prayer) as a technically unisex but archaic term, translating *adelphoi*, is altered to 'brothers and sisters' in modern translations of the Bible ('brothers' coming first for stylistic reasons: cf. 'Ladies and Gentlemen'). But clearly this kind of superficial change will not do in a society where gender has been problematized and complicated. The Holy Trinity, with Son interceding with Father, or the Spirit proceeding from the Father (and the Son) can be viewed as hierarchical and somehow expressive of dominant masculine imagery. Cally Hammond reminds us not only that 'there are three aspects to the use of words that require constant care to interpret: how they act as signs; how they express meaning; and how they affect worshippers and effect things'; but also that there has been a failure to go beyond words in the countering of traditional gender-norms.[39] She points out that there are differences between the sexes in terms of posture and body language in interpersonal communication, and that this has uncomfortable implications for the training of clergy in their liturgical, preaching and teaching roles.[40]

Some with pastoral responsibility in the Scottish Episcopal Church, even some in an otherwise conservative evangelical tradition, have told me that they do not like to use the language of family in case it alienates those whose experience of family life has been traumatic. Is it not possible, however, for church and liturgy to compensate for what is lacking in earthly family life?

In a faith, the imagery of whose scriptures and creeds centres around the categories and relationships of Father and Son, Virgin and Mother, we are therefore bound to ask what truth we lose by circumventing this kind of language of family relationship and implied gender, and what might be gained by it.

In answering such a question we need to think carefully about whether we are sacrificing truth on the altar of subjective preferences. If we accept that liturgy, as a bearer and repository of Scripture – of truth – helps us to see the world accurately, how do we go about seeing the world through the lens of the liturgy? Or to what extent might we make the liturgy – in all its aspects, performative, textual, physical, material – reflect the kind of world we want to see?

Here I return to the arguments made earlier in this chapter, that the church's task is more about understanding the liturgical tradition than shaping it anew in our own image; seeing it as a repository of truth, and interpreting what it says to us, rather than making it say what we want to hear. N. T. Wright has tackled the question in a forthright and uncompromising way:

> the existentialist movements of the twentieth century have taken us back to gnosticism. Each of us has inside ourselves a true self which, though long buried, is now to be discovered and enabled to flourish. This, ironically, is actually a form of Pelagianism: what you need, if you are an existentialist or a gnostic, is not to be confronted by the gospel and redeemed from your present state, but to be helped to discover 'who you really are.' Huge swathes of our contemporary culture are built on this premise, and churches both liberal and conservative have bought it hook line and sinker. (Perhaps I might add as an aside that one of the great triumphs of the film *The Lord of the Rings* is that it takes precisely the opposite line, urging us to find our true selves by following and staying loyal to the vocation that comes from outside, challenging us to do and be what otherwise we would not have.) But the snare of existentialism is that, as in the theology of Rudolf Bultmann, it appears before us wearing the robes of a sixteenth-century Reformer, telling us that all pressures from the outside are 'Law,' which must be abolished if we are to attain authentic existence.[41]

All this seems to mean that we have to be careful about using the liturgy as a vehicle to develop subjective theological views or visions, especially those based on individual or group identities. We find our identity in Jesus Christ: our community is defined by him, in him, and through him. Most importantly, we meet Christ and find our identity in the word and sacrament of the liturgy. The liturgy is first and foremost where we encounter the Lord, where we encounter the one who is the truth.

Liturgy, truth, and the life of the world

> The living bread is broken for the life of the world.
> (Scottish Liturgy 1982)

In Alexander Schmemann's perception of the church, however, people are often not interested in understanding liturgy, much less theology; instead they are in search of some kind of 'spiritual experience, spiritual food' that is provided to those in a 'cultic society', a 'Jesus club'.[42] In a similar way, Bryan Spinks has observed the impact of consumerist culture on worship, resulting in a metaphorical worship mall where the worshipper is a fickle consumer and liturgy is the commodity.[43] The central problem which Schmemann, Spinks, and others seem to have perceived, in prosperous 'Western' societies at least, is the inward-looking focus on subjective experience, a defining symptom of the post-truth phenomenon. In the postmodern and post-truth age we must beware, as we have already seen, of the phenomenon of coming to church in order to find oneself, rather than to find Jesus Christ.[44] Christians are called to worship not simply in order to fulfil their own spiritual needs, but for the sake of the life of the world – the *kosmos*, the created order – in which that worship takes place.

The Gospels tell a story of how the life-giving power of God is breaking into the world, working in and through the ordinary events of life. And so it is that the supernatural and transcendent, in and through the church's worship, becomes visible in the natural and immanent world. We do not need liturgy in our life in order to have a place where we can go to escape the world, but we need liturgy in our life in order to receive the world again as it was given. For, as Schmemann and Fagerberg would have it, it is the liturgy that consecrates the world.

Against those who have said religion is abnormal, an escape from the world, it can be said that the liturgy is the very way to be 'normal'.

> Grace is perfecting nature everywhere we look. Now nothing in the world looks the same. To the naked, secular eye nothing looks different, but to the sanctified, consecrated eye every object and moment has a new potentiality. Once we have seen God invite himself into the house of Zacchaeus for supper, or stop for dinner in Emmaus after a long day's walk, there is no meal which is purely secular. Once we have seen Christ on the green hills of Galilee and the crowded streets of Jerusalem, we privilege neither the pastoral nor the political. Once we have seen God on the cross there is no corner of suffering or darkness where our spiritual eyes do not see him moving. Once we have

seen God in Hades, we know there is no length to which he will not go to find us.[45]

Like Christ, the Christian must stand at the centre of the world and bless God, both receiving the world from God and offering it to God. For the purpose in life of all Christians is to become the true 'liturgists of Jesus Christ', in the cosmic liturgy in which the human world itself must become worship of God, an oblation in the Holy Spirit.[46]

Christians are called to enter into the midst of the world and let it touch them. The church is a new way of living together as a community; it is a community of love, reborn through baptism; a community of faith, full of hope in a world marked by suffering; and a community of new life living according to the truth that is revealed in and through Jesus Christ, focused on sacrificial love and thanksgiving; the kind of sacrificial love and thanksgiving that is demonstrated at the heart of its liturgical life.

Questions for discussion

1 To what extent can truth be discovered outside the liturgical worship of the church?
2 How does the truth of the individual Christian's identity find expression in liturgy?
3 How far can truth be compromised in the non-verbal elements of worship and liturgy?

Further reading

D. W. Fagerberg, *Liturgy Outside Liturgy: The Liturgical Theology of Fr. Alexander Schmemann* (Hong Kong: Chorabooks, 2018).
L. P. Hemming, *Worship as a Revelation: the Past, Present and Future of Catholic Liturgy* (Tunbridge Wells: Burns & Oates, 2008).
L. Larson-Miller, *Sacramentality Renewed: Contemporary Conversations in Sacramental Theology* (Collegeville MN: Liturgical Press, 2016).
B. D. Spinks, *The Worship Mall: Contemporary Responses to Contemporary Culture*, Alcuin Club Collections 85 (London: SPCK, 2010).

Notes

1 'The elements of liturgy in the Orthodox Catholic Church', *One Church*, 13 (1959), 24.

2 Compare Chapter 2 (Jasper), p. 22.

3 *The Scottish Liturgy 1982: with Alternative Eucharistic Prayers* (Edinburgh: General Synod Office of the Scottish Episcopal Church, 1996); used with permission.

4 'The heavens are telling the glory of God; and the firmament proclaims his handiwork' (Psalm 19:1).

5 *De veritate*, Q. 1, resp.: Prima ergo comparatio entis ad intellectum est ut ens intellectui concordet: quae quidem concordia adaequatio intellectus et rei dicitur; et in hoc formaliter ratio veri perficitur. Hoc est ergo quod addit verum super ens, scilicet conformitatem, sive adaequationem rei et intellectus ('The first comparison of being to the intellect, therefore, is as it agrees with the intellect; this agreement is called the adapting of intellect and thing; and in this is formally fulfilled the matter of what is true. This is therefore what the true adds to being, that is to say, the conformity or equation of thing and intellect'). For this idea, see L. P. Hemming, 'Introduction', in László Dobszay, *The Restoration and Organic Development of the Roman Rite*, ed. L. P. Hemming (London: T & T Clark, 2010), pp. xiv–xvi.

6 W. P. Stephens, *The Theology of Huldrych Zwingli* (Oxford: Clarendon Press, 1986), pp. 248–50.

7 See N. H. Taylor, 'Stephen, the Temple, and early Christian eschatology', *Revue Biblique*, 110 (2003), 62–85.

8 Hemming, 'Introduction', p. xvii.

9 Ibid.

10 J.-Y. Lacoste, 'Perception, transcendence and the experience of God', in *Transcendence and Phenomenology*, ed. by Conor Cunningham and Peter M. Candler (London: SCM Press, 2007), pp. 1–20 (p. 20).

11 See A. Bartlett, *A Passionate Balance: The Anglican Tradition* (London: Darton, Longman and Todd, 2007); R. Williams, 'The Bible today: reading and hearing', Larkin Stuart Lecture, Toronto, 2007, available online at <http://aoc2013.brix.fatbeehive.com/articles.php/2112/the-bible-today-reading-hearing-the-larkin-stuart-lecture>; N. Taylor, 'Liturgy and theological method in the Scottish Episcopal Church', *Records of the Scottish Church History Society*, 47 (2018), 143–54 (especially pp. 143–4).

12 *Constitution on the Sacred Liturgy: Sacrosanctum Concilium* §14; official English translation on line at <http://www.vatican.va/archive/hist_councils/ii_vatican_council/documents/vat-ii_const_19631204_sacrosanctum-concilium_en.html> [accessed 13 December 2018].

13 The point was well made by Percy Dearmer at the end of the nineteenth century, when he commented, 'A modern preacher often stands in a sweated pulpit, wearing a sweated surplice over a cassock that was not produced under fair conditions, and, holding a sweated book in one hand, with the other he points to the machine-made cross at the jerry-built altar, and appeals to the sacred principles of mutual sacrifice and love' (*The Parson's Handbook* (London: Grant Richards, 1899), p. 5).

14 Benedict XVI, *Apostolic Exhortation: Verbum Domini* (2010), §52; official English translation online at < http://w2.vatican.va/content/benedict-xvi/

en/apost_exhortations/documents/hf_ben-xvi_exh_20100930_verbum-domini. html> [accessed 14 December 2018]

15 'Audiamus euangelium quasi praesentem Dominum ... Corpus enim Domini in quo resurrexit, uno loco esse potest: ueritas eius ubique diffusa est' (*In Ioannis euangelium tractatus CXXIV* ['124 Tractates on the Gospel of John'], 30, i; trans. John W. Rettig, *The Fathers of the Church: A New Translation*, vol. 88 (Washington DC: Catholic University of America Press, 1993), p. 22).

16 Isa. 43:15–21; 48:20–21; 51:9–11; Jer. 23:7.

17 Joachim Jeremias brings this out quite clearly in *The Eucharistic Words of Jesus*, trans. Norman Perrin (London: SCM Press, 1966), especially pp. 206–7.

18 L. Larson-Miller, *Sacramentality Renewed: Contemporary Conversations in Sacramental Theology* (Collegeville MN: Liturgical Press, 2016), p. 71.

19 See, for example, A. Bartlett, *A Passionate Balance: The Anglican Tradition* (London: Darton, Longman and Todd, 2007), pp. 90–117; R. Williams, 'The Word of God in Anglican tradition' (a presentation to the Ecumenical Gathering of Bishops associated with the Focolare Movement, Lambeth Palace, 8 September 2011), available online at <http://aoc2013.brix.fatbeehive.com/articles.php/2282/the-word-of-god-in-anglican-tradition-archbishop-addresses-focolare-bishops> [accessed 14 December 2018].

20 J. Taylor, 'The Author's Preface to The Apology for Authorized and Set Forms of Liturgy', in *The Whole Works of the Right Rev. Jeremy Taylor. Volume VII*, ed. Reginald Heber (London: Longman, 1834), p. 292.

21 The 1960s and 70s saw much controversy over the 'lectionary' basis of the composition of the New Testament documents; two key works were A. Guilding, *The Fourth Gospel and Jewish Worship: A Study of the Relation of St John's Gospel to the Ancient Jewish Lectionary System* (Oxford: Clarendon Press, 1960), and M. D. Goulder, *The Evangelists' Calendar. A Lectionary Explanation of the Development of Scripture*, The Speaker's Lectures in Biblical Studies, 1972 (London: SPCK, 1978); more recent reflection on the issues can be found in B. D. Chilton, 'Festivals and lectionaries: correspondence and distinctions', in *The Gospels according to Michael Goulder: A North American Response*, ed. Christopher A. Rollston (Harrisburg PA: Trinity Press, 2002), pp. 12–28, and John Tudno Williams, 'The Fourth Gospel and Jewish worship: Guilding's theory revisited', in *The Reception of the Hebrew Bible in the Septuagint and the New Testament: Essays in Memory of Aileen Guilding*, ed. David J. A. Clines and J. Cheryl Exum (Sheffield: Phoenix, 2013), pp. 126–45.

22 Lucetta Mowry, 'Revelation 4–5 and early Christian liturgical usage', *Journal of Biblical Literature*, 71 (1952), 75–84 (especially p. 84).

23 U. Vanni, 'Liturgical dialogue as a literary form in the Book of Revelation', *New Testament Studies* 37 (1991), 348–72.

24 Ibid., p. 356.

25 Ibid., pp. 356–64, 365–70.

26 See J. N. D. Kelly, *Early Christian Creeds*, 3rd edn (London: Taylor & Francis, 1972), pp. 1–29.

27 Geoffrey Wainwright, *Doxology. The Praise of God in Worship, Doctrine, and Life: A Systematic Theology* (London: Epworth, 1980), pp. 175–7.

28 See *The Practice of the Bible in the Middle Ages: Production, Reception, and Performance in Western Christianity*, ed. Susan Boynton and Diane J. Reilly (New York: Columbia University Press, 2011), especially Diane J. Reilly, 'Lectern Bibles and liturgical reform in the central middle ages', ibid., pp. 105–25.

29 *Doxology*, p. 176.

30 Ibid.

31 Ibid.

32 See the report of the Doctrine Committee of the Scottish Episcopal Church, *The Theology of Marriage* (2015), available online at <http://www.scotland.anglican.org/wp-content/uploads/2015/04/Doctrine-Committee-Theology-of-Marriage.pdf>, pp. 4–6 [accessed 13 December 2018]; for context see Taylor, 'Liturgy and theological method'.

33 See N. H. Taylor, *Lay Presidency at the Eucharist: An Anglican Approach* (London: Mowbray, 2009), chapter 1, especially pp. 25–9.

34 Wainwright, *Doxology*, p. 176.

35 Ibid., quoting J. Barr, *The Bible in the Modern World* (London: SCM Press, 1973), pp. 58–9.

36 Wainwright, *Doxology*, p. 176, quoting C. F. Evans, 'Hermeneutics', *Epworth Review* 2 (1975), 81–93 (p. 87).

37 See, for example, the provocatively headlined newspaper report on the promulgation of permitted alternatives to gendered pronouns referring to God in Scottish Liturgy 1982: 'God no longer male, Scottish Episcopal Church rules', *Daily Telegraph*, 6 September 2010, available online at <https://www.telegraph.co.uk/news/religion/7982904/God-no-longer-male-Scottish-Episcopal-Church-rules.html> [accessed 13 December 2018]. More recently, in relation to the Church of Sweden, see for example, N. Goodkind, 'Is God human? Spirit is both father and mother, says Church of Sweden', *Newsweek*, 24 November 2017, on line at < https://www.newsweek.com/god-gender-church-sweden-721647> [accessed 13 December 2018].

38 'Inclusive language and politeness', <https://thurible.net/2017/11/28/inclusive-language-politeness/> [accessed 13 December 2018]; see also his earlier post, 'We worship a non-binary God. Don't we?', <https://thurible.net/2016/05/20/worship-non-binary-god-dont/> [accessed 13 December 2018].

39 C. Hammond, *The Sound of the Liturgy: How Words Work in Worship* (London: SPCK, 2015), pp. 4.

40 Ibid., pp. 40–1.

41 N. T. Wright, 'Freedom and framework, spirit and truth: recovering biblical worship', *Studia Liturgica*, 32 (2002), 176–95.

42 See D. W. Fagerberg, *Liturgy Outside Liturgy: The Liturgical Theology of Fr. Alexander Schmemann* (Hong Kong: Chorabooks, 2018), pp. 191–205.

43 B. D. Spinks, *The Worship Mall: Contemporary Responses to Contemporary Culture*, Alcuin Club Collections 85 (London: SPCK, 2010).

44 Wright, 'Freedom and framework'; see above, p. 96.

45 Fagerberg, *Liturgy Outside Liturgy*, p. 204.

46 Cf. Rom. 15:16, *leitourgon Christou Iēsou*.

7

Truth and Experience: Prayer and Ascetic Practice

JOHN McLUCKIE

The mystery within one person's heart is the mystery within every person's heart.[1]

These words are from a significant twentieth-century book on prayer by the French monk, Henri le Saux, who took the name Abhishiktananda when he settled in India at the start of the 1950s. Abhishiktananda committed himself to the life of a Christian monk but in a context where he sought a deeper awareness of the presence of God in the same way as his Hindu fellow ascetics. This meant not only adopting Indian styles of dress, diet, and monastic life, but also exploring the deepest religious intuitions of Hinduism, guided by Hindu teachers. Although he found real tensions in his chosen path of complete immersion in two religious worlds, he remained convinced that the experience of the greatest mystery – that of the Absolute, the Real, the Divine – was shared by devotees of different faiths. For Abhishiktananda, God 'encompasses all things and pervades all things with his holiness; and yet he remains apart. No one indeed can know his immanence, if he has not first realized his transcendence.'[2] And the way that one follows this path towards such a realization, a path that leads from what is known to what is unknown, is by losing oneself in what transcends everything: 'The mind cannot grasp it and has no choice but to allow itself to be engulfed.'[3]

Abhishiktananda is stating some central aspects of Christian understandings of prayer. First, it is a path towards fuller realization of the nature of God. Second, the God whom we seek in prayer is both knowable and unknowable. Third, the path is one that entails a committed exercise of self-forgetfulness. Finally, there are common features to be found between different religious traditions at this level of the practice of silent prayer or meditation and, more than that, a shared experience of the Absolute. The Absolute, for Abhishiktananda, is not an idea or an abstraction, but the presence to be found in (and beyond) all that is – in every thing and every event we encounter. God is *real*.

When religious people talk about experiencing God as real when they pray or meditate, they are making a claim to some kind of knowledge about the deepest truth of how things are. But are they saying something that others can recognize as 'true'? And when they say that this God is 'ultimate truth', can this claim make any sense for those who do not share their religious commitment? In this chapter, I will ask whether it is possible to engage in a way of talking about the human experience of God in prayer that uses methods of inquiry into the nature of human experience which are acceptable to religious and non-religious people alike. Of course, it will not be possible to argue for a universally accepted measure of the truthfulness of human claims of an encounter with the Absolute. As we have seen with Abhishiktananda, many religious practitioners underline the ultimate unknowability of the Absolute to finite mortals. However, might it be at least possible to suggest that what is experienced as 'true' in prayer and meditation might shows signs that are not merely 'true for me'?

If interest in religious experience was strong in the highly religious culture of India for Abhishiktananda in the 1950s and 60s, we might ask whether it is still a relevant area for investigation in the seemingly post-religious context of Western Europe and North America in the new millennium. However, in her detailed 2014 study of Americans who describe themselves as 'spiritual but not religious', the American theologian Linda Mercadante encountered a wide range of accounts of religious experience and intuition. She draws out some common themes from those who have rejected exclusive religious truth claims and do not identify with a religious community. Among these themes is a nuanced exploration of the place that 'spiritual experiences' play in the search for meaning among this group. Many of those interviewed by Mercadante reported such an experience, often in relation to the natural world. One reported that 'being out in nature is one of the places where I would experience dropping into something bigger'.[4] Such experiences were rarely seen in isolation but might stand as an affirmation of one's spiritual quest or, where a spiritual experience was lacking, a confirmation of the inadequacy of a religious expression. Certainly, the truth of personal experience was placed above the credibility of dogmatic statements. This phenomenon is not entirely new, as can be seen in the distinction made by Simone Weil in her *Spiritual Autobiography* between experience and dogma where the former precedes and exists independently of the latter.[5] However, it seems clear that the priority of subjective experience over 'externally' formulated dogmatic claims has become a defining characteristic of the contemporary spiritual quest in the Western world.

To add another word to this language of spiritual experience, the phenomenon of a new spirituality which exists apart from a specific religious affiliation is, above all, one which emphasizes the *personal*. Ursula King broadens the scope of personal experiences which can be said to be spiritual by including those which are 'painful and disturbing' as well as those which are 'powerful and energising'.[6] The experiences cited by Simone Weil would certainly encompass this broader range. King charts a development in Western spirituality in which the traditional understanding of spirituality as a subset of religion is reversed. The prioritization of spirituality over religion entails taking responsibility for one's own relationship to the sacred and testing the claims of religious tradition against one's personal insights: 'What is crucial in the development of all personal spirituality is the deepening of reflection and an honest attitude towards oneself – an authenticity that recognizes truth and acknowledges a reality greater than oneself.'[7] This latter point is significant: personal spiritual experience is not necessarily introspective or solely self-regarding. Indeed, a common feature of experiences described in this way is that they are directed beyond the self and entail a degree of self-forgetting. Experiences of this sort include feelings of connection or unity, awe or wonder, ecstasy or clarity, gratitude or purposefulness. They may also, of course, include a sense of divine presence, splendour, forgiveness, care, or mercy and may be accompanied by specific thoughts or insights.

Religious or spiritual experiences are by no means absent from traditional Christian discourse. In the New Testament, St Paul describes an experience which is probably autobiographical in which he is 'caught up into paradise' in a manner that was not easily describable in familiar categories (2 Cor. 12:2–4). In the thirteenth century, St Francis received the stigmata following contemplation of the crucified Christ on Mount Alverna, an experience whose intensity is recounted by his biographers.[8] In the following century, Julian of Norwich recorded and reflected on her sixteen revelations on the passion of Christ and on his Mother. In a similar way, St John of the Cross in the sixteenth century reflected on intense experiences of divine love and absence through poetry to which he then added commentary. Into the modern era, we could look to the strangely warmed heart of John Wesley who encountered God's grace in a particular way at a meeting of Moravians in London in 1738. Nearer our own time, the Benedictine monk Bede Griffiths related a 'sense of presence' which he experienced in his teenage years while in the grounds of his boarding school.[9] These represent a very small sample from a vast range of mystical experience which is available to us in the form of autobiographical reflection and detailed theological investigation and we shall return to the question of how this tradition may be used in contemporary dialogue. However, two preliminary questions must be addressed. First, how reliable is personal experience as a primary locus for truthful discourse about the spiritual life? Second, is such discourse possible outside the frame of reference of a religious worldview? The first is a phenomenological question, the second theological.

To sound a note of caution before exploring what might be a fruitful phenomenological approach to spiritual experience, we turn to the writings of Maggie Ross, a scholar of spirituality and, as a vowed solitary, a practitioner of contemplative prayer. In her two-volume work on silence, Ross carefully and, at times, mercilessly deconstructs the notion of 'experience' as a reliable and definitive source of truth about God and our relation to God. Her critique is based on an understanding of the human mind which draws, to some extent, on the recent work of Iain McGilchrist[10] but which is more deeply based in her direct reading of early Christian texts on mystical theology, not least early Syrian writers such as Ephrem the Syrian and Evagrius Ponticus from the fourth century and Isaac of Nineveh from the seventh. She explores the concept of 'self-conscious mind' and 'deep mind' which corresponds to the left and right hemispheres of the brain in McGilchrist's model. The former is the finite, interpretive mind which creates a two-dimensional virtual world, sees things in linear terms and functions in a defining, discriminating fashion. Deep mind is not self-conscious and engages in a direct beholding of the world; it 'processes complex language but does not speak'[11] and is deeply engaged in the work of silence. Ross suggests that, for the mind to function optimally, it must be recentred in the deep mind but there is a circulation or internal dialogue between this side and the self-conscious mind. This circulation is achieved through paradoxical and apophatic language and through the repeated practice of 'attentive receptivity' such as is demonstrated in one-pointed meditation, a contemplative practice which is not focused on concepts or images, but which develops the mind's capacity for simple concentration on the present moment, free from distraction, introspection or active thought. In this way, the material generated by self-conscious analysis is constantly subjected to and transfigured (i.e. we change the way we 'figure things out') by the work of silence and the non-verbal working of the deep mind. A trivial example of this process might be seen in the recovery of a word that is 'on the tip of the tongue' by forgetting about it for a time.

For Ross, the notion of 'experience' is firmly rooted in the self-conscious mind because it is an entirely interpreted concept. Self-authenticating claims to a definitive experience, especially in the realm of spirituality, are fundamentally unreliable because of the self-conscious mind's tendency to construct simplistic or self-serving accounts.[12] She does not reject the usefulness of experiential analysis per se:

> While it might be appropriate to apply the term 'religious experience' to the reception, acknowledgement, and interpretation in religious terms of insights from the deep mind, it is nonsensical to speak of 'contemplative experience', for contemplation excludes the analytic faculty.[13]

However, she insists that the realm of 'experience' may only be safely explored when we remember that it is a construct which is virtual, provisional and sometimes deceitful. With this warning in mind, we shall now consider the possible fruitfulness of the interpretive process we bring to bear on the experiences that suggest to us a world of meaning and encounter that we call spiritual.

Such an interpretive project was the principal focus of the work of William James and it seems fitting to begin our exploration with his classic, if contested, work *The Varieties of Religious Experience*. We shall do so through the lens of a recent rehabilitation of his categories by the American theologian David Tracy. Tracy's concern with James's work is principally because of a shared interest in the question of religious pluralism but James's criteria have to do with the nature of religious experience and so Tracy's reframing of his work is relevant to our concerns. The first category Tracy explores comes out of a commitment to the investigation of plurality in religious expression. It concerns the search for analogies, 'similarities-in-difference' amid religious plurality.[14] Tracy calls this approach the 'analogical imagination'. James sought analogies between the experiences of 'saints and mystics' of various religious traditions:

> If you want to understand what human beings can be when they break out of self-centredness in Reality-centredness, then reflect, with James, not just on yourself but on the two extreme types: the cognitive extremity of the mystic and the action-transforming extremity of the saint.[15]

In other words, Tracy follows James in expressing a certain confidence in the human capacity to learn from the analogous experiences of paradigmatic exemplars of embodied religious commitment. At first glance, the intense experiences of the great mystics may seem remote from our 'everyday' exercise of religious faith, but they continue to communicate something essential to us because there is a familiarity in what they say about their encounters with the divine.

Second, Tracy notes James's concentration on the 'feeling' element of religious experience. While he may have neglected other essential characteristics of religions, such as their institutional life or their cognitive claims, James was notable for his insistence on what he called the 'full fact' of religious experience, that is 'a conscious field *plus* its object as felt or thought of *plus* an attitude towards the object *plus* the sense of a self to whom the attitude belongs'.[16] For James, it is not only possible to speak in analytical terms about religious experiences, but it is also desirable since this realm, that of the *personal*, is the one in which many religious people primarily locate their sense of the value of their religious belonging. Indeed, it seems to me that even the communal dimension of religion is often described experientially and personally. The analysis of a religion only in terms of its artefacts, doctrines and history will be a hollow thing if it does not also recognize the possibility of analysing data from the experiential, 'felt' accounts of its adherents. For religious people, their sense of what is true about their faith does not only exist in the realm of the more straightforwardly measurable dimensions of religion but also, and perhaps supremely, in the claim to a direct apprehension of the ultimate truth which is God. For James, this 'apprehension' is examinable.

Finally, Tracy outlines what he terms a 'rough coherence' in James between the evaluation of religious belief from 'within' and an assessment of religious experience from 'outside'.[17] Such analyses may draw on psychological, philosophical and ethical criteria and may focus on such questions as the experience of 'immediate luminousness' or the actual consequences of religious experience in individual or social terms. The former is an exploration of the character of experiences of the divine or transcendent and the latter a recognition that religious experience may rightly be judged on its consequences for the behaviour or outlook of the religious practitioner. In this, as in all of his assessments of religious experience, James does not allow any 'special case' treatment for religious experience as a realm inaccessible to normal categories of human inquiry based on the assessment of observable evidence.

Tracy is not alone in valuing James's approach to religious experience. The Irish Jesuit and popular mystical theologian, William Johnston, also found much to commend in his work. Like Tracy, Johnston was concerned with the dialogue between religions, particularly in the area of mystical experience and in the practice of meditation. His principal dialogue partner was Zen Buddhism as practised in his Japanese context (Johnston taught at Sophia University in Tokyo, where he lived most of his adult life). Johnston's engagement with James came in his early work, *The Still Point*, in an essay which sought to define mysticism in Buddhist and Christian traditions.[18] He saw James's phenomenology as a useful approach to place alongside theological and philosophical perspectives on the nature of mystical experience and he recognized James's proposed characteristics of mystical experience as being present in both Zen and Christian practice. These characteristics were that the experiences of practitioners have an *ineffable* quality and a *noetic* quality, that they are *transient* and that the practitioner describes the feeling of being a *passive* participant in the experience.[19] Johnston challenges the universality of some of these categories, such as passivity, which he does not consider to be characteristic of all forms of Buddhist understanding. However, Johnston recognizes the value of categories with which to evaluate and describe experiences which do appear in a variety of religious and non-religious contexts. In his next work, he also drew on neuro-scientific analyses of meditative states to suggest common shifts in states of consciousness among meditators of different religious traditions.[20] Science appears to confirm the proposition that the practice of meditation produces measurable changes in our neurophysiology such as an increased detachment and a decrease in self-interest.[21] Johnston relates this phenomenon to the 'state of pure beholding' that he encounters in the medieval English mystical work *The Cloud of Unknowing*, where the anonymous author describes how there is no distinguishing between friend and enemy in the work of contemplation, such is the state of non-attachment attained by the practitioner.

For all his enthusiasm for the possibilities opened up by various systematic analyses of religious experience, Johnston always insisted that these analyses have very limited value if they are not seen alongside the traditions of discourse about such experiences that arise from within the religious traditions. Systematic analysis of personal experience without theology can only give a partial account of the lived experience of spiritual seekers and adepts.

I will mention one final writer who values an analytical approach to felt spiritual experience as a source of truth alongside other forms of discourse. Kees Waaijman, in his wide-ranging systematic account of spirituality from a primarily Christian perspective, draws on Edith Stein's work on the nature of empathy as a way of understanding how one person might reasonably recognize the spiritual experiences of another. He summarizes Stein's approach to empathy as follows: 'In my experience I enter into the experience of an alter ego who is present as a psychosomatic unity that is involved with a reality that is also mine.'[22] There is a kind of projection we undertake as we seek to enter the experience of another. This projection is not based on the observation of outward phenomena and is not associational or analogical. Rather, it is an immediate and unmediated apprehension of the 'innerness' of another person's experience. Empathy is a true form of cognition which depends on a shared approach to attentive reflection on matters concerning the 'soul' or 'existential centre of a person's own being'[23] but is not concerned with agreement or disagreement with the way this unfolds in the other person's life, for that belongs in the realm of sympathy or antipathy rather than empathy. Waaijman's primary interest in this mode of cognition is mystagogical, that is, related to the shared work of development in faith such as we see in spiritual accompaniment. It may not, therefore, be as useful in more objective approaches to understanding experiential truth as it requires a level of shared commitment to the work of spiritual growth. However, his exploration of the place of empathy in allowing for a shared conversation about spiritual experience offers a further tool in the use of such experiences as rich material for the study of the human quest for spiritual meaning. One who observes the work of spiritual growth and the practice of prayer with a degree of empathy may, at the least, discover a realm of human experience that is not unrecognizable, even if the observer does not share the faith of the one observed.

We have briefly noted three theological writers' willingness to engage with experiential accounts of the spiritual life as a source for their theological reflections, that is, as a range of observable, truthful phenomena. When religious practitioners describe, in however limited terms, the effects of their prayerful encounters with the divine, they may be offering material for reflection by theologians – who is the God who is encountered? – and for those approaching religious practice with the methodologies of the human sciences – what are the common features of meditative and prayerful practice? None of these writers would regard such accounts as having a primary place in their inquiries and would be unwilling to allow 'experience' to trump other sources of knowledge. They all expressed the need to hold such sources in tension with theological, philosophical, ethical and empirical categories of knowing. Additionally, Maggie Ross reminds us of the need to regard all talk of spiritual 'experience' as a thoroughly interpreted concept. With these caveats in mind, is it possible to construct an approach to spiritual experience that treats it seriously as a rich source of material for a fuller understanding of the phenomena of religion and spirituality as a common occurrence in human societies? And could such an approach exist independently of specific religious traditions when used to analyse the reported experiences of those who do not espouse or who have rejected a religious identity?

To address both questions together, it seems to me that there are sufficient grounds to treat reported experiences of the transcendent seriously as usable material in the study of religion and spirituality. I suggest that they offer ways of describing and evaluating the character of spiritual experiences and their impact on the lives of practitioners. The work outlined above offers some provisional conclusions on the usefulness of such information. First, reports of spiritual experience are *recognizable* to the interpreter. Second, although occurring in different contexts, they are *comparable*. Finally, they are *consonant* with other modes of inquiry.

The *recognizability* of the spiritual or religious experiences of another person suggests an empathic mode of cognition which is reliable, if often difficult to articulate. If Stein was correct in her account of the nature of empathy, the empathic response is unmediated and, therefore, may lose something when translated into descriptive language, and this takes full account of Maggie Ross's concerns. However, the recognizability of such experiences is what allows for, and, to some extent, compels communal expressions of religious identity and practice – people seek affirmation and support from others with similar experiences. It is also the mechanism that makes growth in the spiritual life possible by the exercise of guidance or training. Outside the religious context, the recognizability of spiritual experiences as a common human phenomenon should also allow for a greater level of understanding across religious–secular divides.

If these experiences are recognizable, they are also, therefore, *comparable*. The comparability of spiritual and religious experiences suggests a certain common structure to the non-sensory human faculties of apprehension. It would be a step too far to say that a Christian in contemplative prayer and a Buddhist in a state of *samadhi* are 'experiencing the same thing' but it might be possible to say that they are 'experiencing something in a similar way' and in a comparable realm of a quest for ultimate reality. The experience of those engaged in inter-religious dialogue is that such comparisons allow for a fuller appreciation of the traditions of the other and, indeed, of one's own traditions and ways of articulating religious truth. In principle, comparability would also allow for a degree of assessment or judgement of the relative impact of spiritual experiences on the lives of the practitioner. It is possible and, indeed, desirable to examine the ethical or social outworking of stated beliefs or experiences and there exist traditions of such self-examination within religious traditions such as the daily prayer of the examination of consciousness in Ignatian practice.[24]

Finally, we repeat James's conviction that spiritual experiences do not form a separate category in the examination of human experience but are *consonant* with other comparable experiences. It is important here to indicate the kind of consonance I have in mind and I will tentatively suggest the following: the feeling of wonder and awe;[25] grateful responses to the perceived goodness of life, even when there is no divine being to thank; feelings of transcendence or vastness; complete absorption in the contemplation of beauty; a sudden experience of extreme clarity; profound feelings of stillness, peace or 'being at home in the world'; deep feelings of pity or compassion; a sense of connection to others or to the wider phenomenal world; a sense of being valued unconnected to specific human relationships. Connected to such positive feelings are their negative corollaries such as feelings of loss, abandonment, purposelessness or desolation, and it is important to include these, as noted above by Ursula King, not least because they feature strongly in the literature of spiritual autobiography.[26]

I began with a short quotation from Abhishiktananda which expressed a conviction that the mystery within one person's heart is the mystery within every person's heart. His own experience of the truth of God whom he encountered in the depths of contemplative prayer led him to conclude that this truth was universal. I have suggested some ways in which this claim to universality may be assessed by observing carefully the reported experiences of those who encounter the Absolute through the practice of prayer or meditation.

I have also suggested that these accounts of experiences of the transcendent provide a richly textured source of insight for theologians who reflect on the nature of the divine and who ask what sort of God is encountered in prayer and what is the nature of the change effected in us by such encounters. Experiential accounts can be sources of theological truth to be read alongside Scripture and its interpreters. These may be works of enduring spiritual insight, such as the great autobiographical works of Augustine, Teresa of Avila or Thomas Merton, or contemporary studies such as Linda Mercadante's.

For the believer who asks 'How can I know if my experiences of God are true?', these tools of analysis can offer a way of seeing one's own experiences alongside those of others in order to discern commonalities and examine the fruits of our experiences with a measure of objectivity. They are also tested against theological and ethical resources from the long practice of reflection on the life of faith.

However, we return also to the cautionary note sounded by Maggie Ross, whose observation from the point of view of an understanding of the human mind also resonates with a theological conviction about the ineffability of God. Any talk of our experience of God in prayer or meditation is a reduction of that experience to comprehensible categories. The truth of God – the One whom Abhishiktananda called 'the Real' – may be known at a deep level of our cognitive faculties, but that truth may only be communicated in approximations which deal with the *effects* of our encounter. Our spiritual experiences are a source of truth, but can never exhaust the ultimate Truth which we know now 'only in part'.

Questions for discussion

1. What realms of human experience would you describe as 'spiritual'?
2. If you can identify such experiences in your own life, what language would you use to communicate them to others?
3. How do these experiences relate to your understanding of ultimate truths, such as your sense of the meaning and purpose of life?

Further reading

W. James, *The Varieties of Religious Experience* (London: Longmans, Green and Co., 1902).

L. Mercadante, *Belief Without Borders: Inside the minds of the spiritual but not religious* (Oxford: OUP, 2014).

M. Ross, *Silence: A User's Guide, Volume 1: Process* (London: DLT, 2014).

K. Waaijman, *Spirituality: Forms, Foundations, Methods* (Louvain: Peeters, 2002).

Notes

1 Abhishiktananda, *Prayer* (Delhi: ISPCK, 1967), p. 29.
2 Abhishiktananda, *Saccidananda* (Delhi: ISPCK, 1974), p. 131.
3 Ibid.
4 L. Mercadente, *Belief Without Borders: Inside the minds of the spiritual but not religious* (Oxford: OUP, 2014), p. 89.
5 S. Weil, *Waiting on God* (London: Collins, 1951), p. 32. Weil is, however, a subtle thinker who recognizes the formative effect of a religious culture and spiritual milieu on any experience that might arise. She described herself as having always shared a Christian conception of life.
6 U. King, *The Search for Spirituality* (New York: BlueBridge, 2008) p. 12.
7 Ibid.
8 See, for example, chapter 13 of Bonaventure's *Legenda Maior – Bonaventure* in the Classics of Western Spirituality series (New York: Paulist Press, 1978).
9 B. Griffiths, *The Golden String* (Glasgow: Collins, 1979), p. 28.
10 I. McGilchrist, *The Master and his Emissary* (New Haven CT: Yale University Press, 2009).

11 M. Ross, *Silence: A User's Guide, Volume 1: Process* (London: DLT, 2014), p. 37.
12 Ibid., p. 78.
13 Ibid., p. 79.
14 D. Tracy, *Dialogue with the Other: the Inter-Religious Dialogue* (Louvain: Peeters, 1990), p. 30.
15 Ibid.
16 Ibid., p. 32.
17 Ibid., p. 36.
18 W. Johnston, *The Still Point* (New York: Fordham University Press, 1989), pp. 129–50.
19 Ibid., p. 144
20 W. Johnston, *Silent Music* (London: Collins, 1974).
21 Ibid., p. 39.
22 K. Waaijman, *Spirituality: Forms, Foundations, Methods* (Louvain: Peeters, 2002), p. 236.
23 Ibid., p. 939.
24 See entry at p. 292, P. Sheldrake (ed.), *The New SCM Dictionary of Christian Spirituality* (London: SCM Press, 2005).
25 See further Chapter 8 (Ballard) on Otto and awe.
26 See, for example, William Johnston's *Mystical Journey* (Maryknoll: Orbis Books, 2006), pp. 187–89 and his description of a 'dark night of the soul' related, in part, to his experiences of the Irish troubles.

8

Rudolf Otto: Truth and the Holy

STEVEN BALLARD

I have heard the *Sanctus Sanctus Sanctus* of the cardinals in St Peter's, the *Swiat Swiat Swiat* in the Cathedral of the Kremlin and the Holy Holy Holy of the Patriarch in Jerusalem. In whatever language they resound, these most exalted words that have ever come from human lips always grip one in the depths of the soul, with a mighty shudder exciting and calling into play the mystery of the other world latent therein. And this more than anywhere else in this modest place, where they resound in the same tongue in which Isaiah first received them and from the lips of the people whose first inheritance they were.[1]

Rudolf Otto, the German theologian and philosopher of religion, wrote these words during his visit to North Africa in 1911–12. In a synagogue at Mogador, now Essaouira in Morocco, the experience of worship made a profound impression upon him. Entry to the synagogue by way of a dark passage, suggestive of the mystery which religious places often express, heightened the dynamic effect of worship. Otto, who was so sensitive to these things, found himself fascinated by his participation in the Jewish liturgy.

The work for which Otto is best known is *Das Heilige* (1917). In its English translation this appeared as *The Idea of the Holy*.[2] A hundred years after its publication I returned last year to the German University town of Marburg, where Rudolf Otto lived and taught, to celebrate the book's centenary. The conference in Marburg in September 2017, *Medien Materialität Methoden*, addressed itself to modern interpretations of religion from sociological and anthropological perspectives, but appropriately, in *Das Heilige*'s centenary year, it included a panel to discuss the significance of Otto's work. During the conference, I visited the cemetery at Marburg where Otto lies buried. The simplicity of the words on the headstone are striking. It gives only the dates of Rudolf Otto's life, 1869–1937, over which are cited the words, 'Heilig, Heilig, Heilig ist Gott, der Herr von Sabbaoth.' (Holy, Holy, Holy, is the Lord God of Hosts). There is nothing said about the man himself. It is as if the wording is designed to suggest that it is enough to give the briefest details of the human being, of whom in relation to the Holy One there is no more to be said. Otto's grave symbolizes his deepest insight into where the truth about the human condition lies. Human beings come and go, but God, the Holy One, abides forever.

It is important to state the context in which *The Idea of the Holy* achieved such an enthusiastic and widespread response. Together with Karl Bath's *Der Römerbrief* [3] it offered something important to those who had so recently experienced the events of the First World War. A generation which had witnessed the flower of Europe's youth mown down by the machine gun looked to something which had far more to offer than liberal hopes in human progress. Readers of Otto found, in the context of a wrecked Europe, a new theology which declared that human life is meaningful only in relation to the transcendent. Just as Karl Barth envisaged the Word of God breaking into man's existential crisis and calling for a decision in favour of Christ, Otto too introduces us to a realm in which encounters with the sacred open us up to the Truth that lies at the heart of all things.

There is, however, a crucial difference between Rudolf Otto and Karl Barth in their beliefs about how Truth can be apprehended. While both men were deeply Christian, Otto believed that some elements and understandings of God's truth were present also in the other great world religions. This was anathema to Barth, who saw religions apart from Christianity largely as idolatrous human constructs.

One of the key challenges, especially in the earlier part of Otto's academic career, was that in popular thinking science had seemingly dethroned religion and demonstrated that the latter was rationally inferior in explaining how the world works. Facing the challenge of science, Otto insists through his philosophy of religion that religious experience offers a means of apprehending the Truth which is in no way inferior.

Otto was well aware that scientific reductionism, when it looked to explain all things in terms of natural processes alone, posed considerable threats to Christian theology and he set himself the task, therefore, to maintain the autonomy of religion in relation to its scientific counterpart. He makes this clear in the opening words of his book, *Naturalism and Religion*: 'The title of this book, contrasting as it does the naturalistic and the religious interpretation of the world, indicates that the intention of the following pages is, in the first place, to define the relation, or rather the antithesis between the two, and second to endeavour to reconcile the contradictions, and to vindicate against the counter claims of naturalism, the validity and freedom of the religious outlook.'[4]

It is the conviction that religion is *sui generis* that underlies Otto's interpretation of it and his analysis of religious experience. How then does he proceed with the daunting task of providing a phenomenological account of religious experience? The starting point for him is that historically Christianity and its theology in the West has placed too much emphasis on the rational aspects of deity. The Nicene Creed, for example, does this expressly, as the Divine is described in terms such as Person, Being, Substance, and True God. A correction was needed leading him to analyse what it is that lies at the heart of the 'feeling which remains where concepts fail'. Otto located this in what he calls the 'numinous'. He also uses the term 'the sacred', which results in an experience that has a duality about it. There is awe in the presence of the Wholly Other which also possesses a power of fascination. To emphasize that he is working with an experience that cannot be precisely conceptualized or expressed in terms of conventional language, Otto made use of Latin terminology. These become what Otto calls 'ideograms'. Thus, he writes of the *mysterium* which lies at the heart of things, and refers to the sacred's quality of *tremendum* – its tendency to induce the feeling of awe. Further, he ascribes to the nature of the numinous the element of *fascinans* – the capacity the sacred has to draw the devotee nearer.[5]

There are, indeed, criticisms of Otto that can be made. First, by making the non- or supra-rational the primary element in religion and only then bringing in the rational-ethical within the category of the Holy, is his structure designed to interpret religion both artificial and unconvincing? Second, does his analysis of religious experience draw too heavily from the predominant Judaeo-Christian forms of religion with which he was most familiar himself as a Christian theologian? Does his emphasis on the overpowering, urgent, and energetic qualities of the numinous as *tremendum*, for example, accord with a religion like Theravada Buddhism, with Nirvana as its goal, and how does his description of the numinous play out in the case of mysticism?

Clearly, Otto has provided us with a phenomenology of religion which tends to characterize religious experience by its strongest types, though he does point out that encounters with the sacred do not always involve such dynamic and powerful types of feelings. He writes that 'the awe or "dread" *may* indeed be so overwhelmingly great that it seems to penetrate to the very marrow, making the man's hair bristle and his limbs quake. But it may steal upon him almost unobserved as the gentlest of agitations, a mere fleeting shadow passing across his mood.'[6]

It is notoriously difficult, Otto suggests, to put certain kinds of experience into words. How can a person describe the frisson that occurs, for example, when listening to a Beethoven symphony, or convey the feelings that are experienced in admiring a beautiful scene of nature which is suggestive of the sublime? Otto was surely right when he suggested that in religious experience it is inevitable that its subject matter will overflow the normal conceptual categories. Despite this, however, there is an important aspect of Otto's work where he is open to attack, namely that his interpretation of religion is unnecessarily irrationalistic. In the foreword to the English version of *The Idea of the Holy*, it is clear that Otto was eager to defend himself against this view. He states, 'Before I ventured upon this field of inquiry I spent many years of study upon the *rational* aspect of that supreme Reality we call God ... And I feel that no one ought to concern himself with the '*Numen ineffibale*' who has not already devoted assiduous and serious study to the '*Ratio aeterna*'.[7] Otto sets out his case even more strongly in the author's notes on the Translation of *The Philosophy of Religion based on Kant and Fries*,

> in an exposition and criticism of W. Wundt's *Theory of Religion*, I had begun to give expression to my ideas on the non-rational factor in Religion; these were afterwards developed in my book, *The Idea of the Holy*. In *The Philosophy of Religion* I wished to present the 'rational' factor in Religion, which, for me, is no less important and essential than the non-rational.
> ... *On no account* do I wish to be considered as a "non-rationalist". In all religion, and in my own religion, I indeed recognize the profundity of the non-rational factor; but that deepens my conviction that it is the duty of serious theology to win as much ground as it can for Ratio in this realm, and even at the point where our rational concepts desert us, to satisfy the demands of judicious theological teaching by framing "ideograms" as accurately as possible, where dogmatic concepts are impossible.[8]

It may well be that Otto regretted later that the terminology he had chosen made him susceptible to the charge that his work is irrationalistic in flavour. If instead of using the word 'irrational' he had made it clear that he did not mean the 'irrational' but rather was referring to that which is 'supra-rational', that would probably have been far better. It is ironic, in fact, that Otto's work was challenged on the basis that it tended towards irrationalism because as a philosopher of religion who was influenced strongly by Kant and Fries, the framework of Idealism which Otto uses to construct his analysis of religious experience is firmly grounded in Kantian categories of 'pure reason'. The philosopher J. M. Moore recognized this in his book, *Theories of Religious Experience with Special Reference to James, Otto and Bergson*, where he comments on Otto that 'in spite of his emphasis upon feeling and the non-rational, his interpretation of religious experience depends at every crucial point upon the historic presumptions of rationalism.'[9]

It becomes apparent, on further investigation of Otto's work, that his description of the experience of the numinous is embedded in a wider comprehensive scheme, designed to validate the Truth that is the Holy at a number of different epistemological levels. To demonstrate this we must mention briefly the key influences on his thinking. Thus we can achieve a better understanding of the schematic nature of his work and understand Otto's claim that the sense of the Holy, mediated through the experience of the numinous, constitutes the most significant means through which Truth is made known. Apart from Martin Luther (Otto remained a devout Lutheran Christian throughout his life), there are at least five other influential thinkers who helped to shape his understanding of religion, all of them German.

The first, the philosopher and theologian Friedrich Schleiermacher (1768–1834), is most notable for Otto for attempting to define, as Otto did himself, what is at the heart of religion. Schleiermacher located this in the sense of dependence upon the Creator. It is only when a person knows him or herself to be in this state of dependence, for Schleiermacher, that the spirit of true religion can proceed. This gives rise to reverence, both in relation to the Creator and the Creation, and the practice of humility. While Schleiermacher's search for what is central to religion has some merit for Otto, where he parts company with Schleiermacher is that he believed Schleiermacher's understanding does not do justice to the phenomenology of religious experience. The idea of creatureliness occurs, for Otto, not so much as the result of reasoned thinking which looks to understand selfhood in relation to the natural order, but as a result of the numinous object, experienced generally in powerful emotions and sensed as breaking in from the outside. Thus, Otto asserts, 'Creature feeling in itself indubitably has immediate and primary reference to an object outside the self.' He adds, 'this "feeling of reality" – the feeling of a numinous object objectively given, must be posited as a primary immediate datum of consciousness.'[10]

The second thinker who influenced Rudolf Otto greatly was Immanuel Kant (1724–1804). In *The Critique of Pure Reason* Kant proposed that fundamental conceptual categories must be posited to constitute the mechanism through which the mind operates. They must be located at reason's first base, as *a priori*. The categories Kant proposed were logic, ethics and aesthetics. Otto found common ground with Kant in working with such concepts as the *a priori* and pure reason, but he believed that Kant was mistaken in treating religion as derivative of ethics. True, the springs which Otto's philosophy of religion draws from are Kantian, but it needed to be shown that religion occupies its own autonomous ground. It is this compulsion which led to Otto's modification of the Kantian model and to postulate a fourth *a priori* category, the idea of the Holy.

The third key person to influence Otto was a former student of Kant himself, the philosopher Jakob Fries (1773–1843). While Fries's philosophical framework was Kantian, Otto found in him a sympathetic ally who was prepared to grant religion a greater degree of autonomy than Kant had allowed it. The problem with Kant, for Otto, was that he placed religion in the realm of faith, and not knowledge. While Kant would never have denied that there are transcendental realities, because they lie beyond the limits of possible knowledge they must be the object of faith. Fries, in a development that moved away from Kant, proposed that human understanding comprises three areas: '*Wissen*', which was logical or scientific knowledge, '*Glaube*', which denoted rational belief, and '*Ahndung*', which equated to a religious and aesthetic intuition.

Ahndung, as it is conceived by Fries, provided the cognitive basis that Otto was seeking in his theory of religion. It signifies a presentiment or foreboding, an intuitive reaching out towards the Eternal. Fries called *Ahndung* 'a necessary conviction of pure feeling'. Otto is never closer to Fries than when in *The Idea of the Holy* he writes of 'the glimpse of an Eternal in and beyond the temporal and penetrating it, the apprehension of a ground and meaning of things in and beyond the empirical and transcending it. They are *surmises* or *inklings* of a Reality fraught with mystery and momentousness.'[11] The work of Jakob Fries interested Otto because it appeared to offer a solid epistemological base for a theory of religious knowledge, though later Otto admitted that the Friesian model did not maintain the autonomy of religion as much as he might have wished. *Ahndung* conflates feelings of a religious kind with those of the sublime under the same category, and so Otto looked for yet another principle for his developed theory of religion. He found this in two other religious thinkers.

The work of the liberal theologian Albrecht Ritschl (1822–89) was significant for Otto in his proposition that religious experience is not merely to be understood in terms of its own feeling states, but also because it consists in autonomous value judgements which are uniquely religious. That the influence of Ritschl upon Otto was decisive becomes clear when he writes, 'I shall speak, then, of a unique "numinous" category of value and of a definitely "numinous" state of mind, which is always found wherever the category is applied.'[12] Otto develops his thinking around religious experience comprising a category of meaning and value in relating this to the concept of the sacred.

The importance of employing this Ritschlian category of value was that in siting religion in its own autonomous ground, it is set free from its subjugation to Kantian ethics. Furthermore, it brought to religion a higher cognitive status than what for Schleiermacher was essentially the product of piety and feeling. Thus it is not surprising that the influence of Ritschl's thinking upon Otto has long been recognized. R. F. Davidson, for example, comments of Otto, 'his own idea of *the Holy* as an autonomous religious category of value is based directly and unmistakably upon Ritschl's concept of the independent religious value judgement.'[13]

The final notable figure to influence Otto in his understanding of religion was the theologian and philosopher of history Ernst Troeltsch (1865–1923). Troeltsch's thinking influenced Otto in two main ways. First, Troeltsch, like Otto, was concerned to understand the place that Christianity had in relation to the other major world religions, and he sought a way to regard them within a global perspective which recognized their values and commonalities. Otto, as we shall see, found a practical outlet for these concerns in the years following the First World War through his initiation of the *Religiöser Menschheitsbund*, the Religious League of Mankind. A more fundamental connection between Troeltsch and Otto lies, however, in Troeltsch's location of religion within its own *a priori* order of reality. The advantage of this religious *a priori* was that it guaranteed the freedom of religion's subject matter from the dominance of science. It also released religion from its subordination to Kantian ethics. Consequently, in *Das Heilige*, Otto proposed that the sacred, the numinous object of religion, constitutes its own *a priori* category distinct from logical reasoning, ethics and aesthetics.

In their own way each of these five scholars offered to define where the essence of religion and its Truth has its roots. Rudolf Otto located this in religion's experiential dimension and incorporated it within a composite religious-ethical category which he termed *Das Heilige*, 'The Idea of the Holy'. This source of religion was for Otto just as valid, and perhaps a more valid method of apprehending the Truth than the other *a priori* categories that Kant identified. So it is the experiential dimension that is at the heart of Otto's most significant work, *Das Heilige*, and his importance for religious studies was secured because in his analysis of religious experience Otto illuminates in a way which no one had quite done before some key aspects of religious worship and behaviour.

Rudolf Otto's *Idea of the Holy* and the challenge of a 'post-truth' society

The chapters in this book seek to contribute to the question of where Truth can be found in relation to developments in a society which, it might be said, has moved towards 'post-truth'. How might these 'post-truth' developments be described?

There has been, as many commentators have noted, a tendency in contemporary society, especially noticeable since the advent of the Internet and social media, for appeals to populist emotion to replace the evidence of both fact and reason. Internationally, alarm bells have been ringing on account of a number of the world's leaders who have been cynical manipulators, even corrupters of Truth, for their own political ends. While this phenomenon has been evident at both extremes of the political spectrum, the current tendency is for the Truth to be hijacked by the Far Right.

No author has portrayed how far Truth can decay when people and nation states embrace totalitarian ideals better than George Orwell. What could better describe some of the tendencies in a society that has moved down the road of post-truth than Orwell's novel *Nineteen Eighty-Four*[14] which pictures four ministries in the super state of Oceania? Realities become inverted as the Ministry of Love concerns itself with torture, the Ministry of Peace with war, the Ministry of Plenty with starvation and the Ministry of Truth with lies. Orwell provides us with a dire warning about how appalling and inhumane society can become when it produces grotesque distortions of fact and cuts itself adrift from anything which is reasonable and true.

What parallels do we find when we go back to the time in which Rudolf Otto lived and our own age? When I read papers from the Otto archives, from the years following the First World War, one note was evident –'*Nie Wieder*!' 'Never Again!' should there be war on that scale which had so devastated humanity on the continent of Europe. 'Nie Wieder!', in fact, became a popular movement in Germany and its ideals were echoed across Europe . One of the key initiatives of that era was the League of Nations, which it was hoped would lead to countries discussing their disputes and coming to the peace table before any declaration of war. It is one of the tragedies of the early 1920s that the setting up of the League of Nations was so unsuccessful. Reparations demanded of Germany had the effect of sinking the German economy and led to hyper-inflation, thereby sowing the seeds which allowed the ruthless ambition of Hitler and the Nazis to come to power. But what of Otto in all of this?

Otto was an unusual theologian, perhaps, in that although he remained a devout Christian and in no way wished to promote a religious syncretism which would satisfy no one, he valued much more than most of his theological colleagues either before or since the riches that other religious traditions could offer. At a museum in Marburg, *Die Religionskundliche Sammlung*, 'The Religious Collection', contains many of the cult objects Otto had brought back from his extensive travels. He secured the purchase of these through lobbying of the regional government for the necessary finances. The *Religionskundliche Sammlung* remains an important part of Otto's legacy and offers an important resource for scholars working in the field of religious studies today. It is very clear that Otto favoured what brought men and nations together rather than what set them apart. Two of Otto's works which demonstrate his openness to other religious traditions and indicate that he was trying to understand coherences between religions in a systematic way are his *India's Religion of Grace and Christianity Compared and Contrasted*[15] and *Mysticism East and West*.[16] His position on world religions is more briefly expressed in *Religious Essays*.[17] Here Otto includes an essay entitled in its English translation 'Parallels and Convergences in the History of Religion'.[18] After considering manifestations of religion across different eras and cultures and noting how commonalities are evident, ranging from religion's earliest forms in Greece, the Near and Far East, in India, China and in Western Christianity, Otto concludes:

> These parallels lend overwhelming conviction to one great fact, namely the fundamental kinship of the nature and experience of mankind in general, East and West, North and South; by reason of their basic similarity, it works itself out in these parallels, manifesting similar phenomena, and in diverse territories producing similar results.[19]

In the belief that the great world religions possess many riches and that people of different faiths could learn from one another, Otto played a pivotal role in the formation of the *Religiöser Menschheitsbund*, 'The Religious League of Mankind'. In his essay 'An Inter-Religious League', also in *Religious Essays*, Otto sketches out some of the principles and ideals that would be enshrined in this new inter-religious movement. That it was highly idealistic can be seen as Otto writes:

> The meaning and purpose of this league put in a nutshell, is (1) to work for an authoritative world conscience, and to unite men of principle everywhere that the law of justice and the feeling of mutual responsibility may hold sway in the relationship between nations, religions

and classes, and that the great collective moral tasks facing cultured humanity may be achieved through a closely knit co-operation.[20]

Otto also affirms, idealistically, under principle 3:

we cherish the belief that it is possible through the awakening of conscience and the co-operation of men of faith to remove the course of world events from the dark tyranny of a blind 'social law' and the demoniac forces of group egoism, and to rationalise and subject it to the idea of justice and common interests.[21]

Highly idealistic and optimistic the *Religiöser Menschheitsbund* may have been, but its setting up was no mean logistical feat on the part of Otto and those who supported him. From 1920 onwards, the Otto archives show how much time and energy he was investing as he rallied people at home in Germany, in other European countries, and in the English-speaking world to his cause.

The first meeting of the *Religiöser Menschheitsbund* (RMB) took place on 1 August 1922 at Wilhelmslagen, near Berlin. Representatives from eight different religious groups participated.[22] In the early 1920s the RMB met with considerable support and its international outreach stretched as far afield as Japan. The records of the RMB indicate that in 1923 its membership was 471, many representing non-Christian religions.[23] In an age when communication technology was very different from our own, the work of Otto and his co-founders was truly impressive. It is very much to Otto's credit that in the early years of the twentieth century he played a key role in facilitating interreligious dialogue, and that the agenda of the RMB sought to bring people of the different world faiths together to work in ethical ways to promote the universal good. However, the heady enthusiasm of Otto proved to be short-lived. The growing economic crisis in Germany, burdened by its war debts, resulted in a period of rapid inflation and gradually this impacted upon the finances the RMB had at its disposal. The upshot of all this was that despite efforts to revive the organization from 1927 onwards through opportunities for travel and the promotion of a Religious Peace Conference, the RMB lost its way. The rise to power of Fascism in Germany resulted, eventually, in the formal disbanding of the League by the Nazi Party.

Thus, for all the efforts of Otto and those who helped him in setting up an organization dedicated to universal peace and goodwill, its deepest flaw was that it never managed to anchor the high ideals it set out in a practical programme for action. Gregory D. Alles, in an article entitled 'Rudolf Otto and the Politics of Utopia',[24] indicates how every issue of social concern found its way into the literature produced by the organization. That was one thing. It was quite another to address the causes it spent much time talking about. Its vision remained a Utopian dream.

> Out flowed almost every moral and social dream of the early 1920s: the solution to the question of the 'guilt' for the last war; the elimination of 'poison' from the press; intervention in world crises before they came to a head; the creation of social justice, for example, between classes; the elimination of filth (*Shmutz*) from literature and public life; the elimination of alcoholism, 'the mother of many and the nurse of most social and ethical evils'; solutions to women's workers' and racial problems; advocacy of the oppressed, of national and social minorities, and of the conquered against the conquerors; and the sharing of cultural riches, from East to West as well as from West to East. No wonder Otto claimed in the same letter that he cherished the Utopia.[25]

In spite of Alles' comments which expose all that was weakest in the RMB, was there anything positive in the attempt on the part of Otto and his co-workers to stand for what they believed to be *true*? Certainly, for all the RMB's flawed ideals it was a noble vision which inspired its organizers to engage in the work of breaking down the barriers which separate humans from their fellows and sow the seeds of religious intolerance and racial conflict. In the current climate of the twenty-first century where racial hatreds, religious intolerance, and cynical attempts to twist the truth by political extremists are still much in evidence, we may judge that for all their naivety and weaknesses, those who were active in the RMB were honest people, committed to the idea of truth which had universal obligations.

For Otto himself, the efforts he poured into creating the RMB were made because he believed that the Truth that was to be found in the Holy was present to some degree in all the major world religions. The Truth of the Holy committed Rudolf Otto and his co-workers to take a stand for the ethical good which was an absolute obligation and was never to be sacrificed to the interests of political expediency. Certainly, in the light of the brutalities that were to follow under the Nazis, we might even say that Otto and those who supported this work were clearly on the side of the angels.

There is another important area to consider, however, when we raise the question of where, ultimately, Otto believed the Truth was to be found in the Holy. As a Christian theologian he sought throughout his life to come to terms with how the Truth, that is, the Holy, can be related to the person of Jesus Christ. This, for Otto, was not merely academic but it represented a quest for the Truth that would nurture the wellsprings of his faith. There is evidence from both the Otto archives and from material that Philip Almond has made public in his book *Rudolf Otto: An Introduction to his Philosophical Theology* (1984) that there were times, especially in his early university career, then later after he had retired from teaching, when Otto struggled with his faith. Otto, whose health was often not good, suffered from periods of depression and it was then that what he believed in was sorely tested.

It would seem from archival papers and letters, which include a large amount of personal correspondence, that there was never a Damascus Road experience in Otto's life. Yet while there were times when he struggled to hold onto faith, he remained a devout Lutheran to the end, and never departed from his belief that the highest revelation of God's truth is to be found in the person of Jesus Christ. Otto's writing on the subject of Christology is, in fact, an area of his work which is generally overlooked, and indeed now seems somewhat dated.

Two publications which come respectively from the beginning and the end of his career show how much his thoughts developed on this subject. The first work on Jesus and his ministry was *Leben und Wirken Jesu*, which appeared in English as *The Life and Ministry of Jesus*.[26] Although it was not considered a radical work, it met with opposition from conservative theologians who took issue with it because they believed it undermined the historicity of the Gospels. The picture which emerges in *Leben und Wirken Jesu* is of Jesus as a religious-ethical teacher whose life is the supreme example of piety and righteousness, and the stress that Otto places on the importance of ethics for Jesus and his ministry clearly indicates Kantian influence. The criterion for Otto, when he wrote this early work on Christology, was that only that which can be judged rationally and historically acceptable by the processes of religio-historical enquiry can stand the test of authenticity in the Gospel narratives. Sixteen years after *Leben und Wirken Jesu* was published it is apparent that in the two chapters of *Das Heilige* which are Christologically based, Otto was noticeably more open to the element of mystery in Jesus's life and ministry.[27]

The second work which shows that Otto's ideas on the subject of Christology had undergone a substantial revision, *Reich Gottes und Menschensohn*,[28] is nowhere starker than in the placement of Jesus's work firmly in the framework of eschatology. Few scholars today would agree with Otto tracing New Testament thinking back to ancient Aryan and Iranian influences, but these are what he held to be significant in the evolution of Jesus's teaching on the Son of Man and his identification of it with himself. Throughout this later Christological book emphasis is placed upon the role of Jesus as a prophetic, charismatic figure. Contrasting the ministries of John the Baptist and Jesus, for example, Otto maintains that 'our primary assertion [is] that Jesus was a charismatic evangelist who was also an exorcist.'[29] Otto was well aware that in the works of power attributed to Jesus in the Gospels many people who encountered him regarded him as the Son of God. The position of whether Jesus was the Christ of God, in the fuller Christological sense, was, for Otto however, beyond the scope of religio-historical enquiry. The answer depended, as a Ritschlian principle, on a unique value judgement which is specifically religious.

On what, then, does Otto's Christian faith ultimately depend? For him, the person of Jesus Christ marked the highest revelation of God's presence in the world. It is notable, though, that Otto does not, in his Christology, lay much weight on the doctrine of the Incarnation. As a scholar who was familiar with Eastern religions and had translated a number of religious Indian texts into German for the first time, he was well aware that the idea of incarnation was a frequent one, especially in the mythology of Hinduism. The uniqueness of Jesus lies instead for the Lutheran Otto in the atonement. Thus, in *The Idea of the Holy*, he proposes that the highest forms of religious intuition have to do with the death of Christ on the cross. It is the atonement, which finds its historical context in Jesus's death alone, that becomes the mark distinguishing Christianity from other great world religions:

> No religion has brought the mystery of the need for atonement or expiation to so complete, so profound, or so powerful expression as Christianity. And in this too, it shows its superiority over others. It is a more perfect religion and more perfectly religion than they, in so far as what is potential in religion in general becomes in Christianity a pure actuality.[30]

In this quotation we can detect a problem with Otto's work. Here it becomes apparent that he has abandoned a phenomenological, scientific study of religion and nails his colours to the mast as a Christian theologian. There are three different strands to his interpretation of religion; theology, philosophy and phenomenology – and he wears these various hats at different times. This is the main reason why Otto's work is not regarded as highly in Germany as we might expect, because while scholars recognize that his work attempts commonalities of understanding between theology and *Religionswissenschaft*, they see it as insufficiently academically rigorous to be one or the other. In the English-speaking world, however, this has tended to play out more favourably. The fact that Otto's thinking is more open-ended and that issues in theology, philosophy and phenomenology intersect in his work maintain his position as an important thinker.

So finally, where does the work of Otto stand today in relation to contemporary developments in a society which seems to be abandoning Truth for post-truth? Two things might be said. First, it is impossible to understand the history and present context of mankind without taking into account the importance of the religious dimension in our collective existence. Rudolf Otto sought, as a Christian theologian, to describe what is universally at the heart of religious experience in the most accurate way he could. Second, his commitment to the belief that we can learn from the truths that are to be found in other world religions led him to promote inter-religious dialogue. In this respect, Otto was one of its earliest pioneers. Suppressing the religious beliefs and the racial identities of others at the expense of Truth would lead, as Otto would come to see, to the evils of totalitarianism in his own nation, and all this resulted ultimately in Germany's ruin.

For Rudolf Otto, the Holy was the Truth, the Truth was the Holy. While Truth might be decayed and distorted, as a facet of the Holy it remains an absolute reality. As Otto must have seen as the 1920s in Germany gave way to the next decade, there are huge dangers in departing from the Truth. The corruption of the Truth fails each one of us in the end.

Questions for discussion

1 Central to Rudolf Otto's understanding of religion is the sense of the numinous and the awareness of the sacred. How relevant is his work in the context of contemporary society in which the notion of the sacred is accorded either no meaning, or little value?
2 Rudolf Otto's phenomenology of religion locates the essence of religion in its experiential dimension. Has Otto emphasized this at the expense of other dimensions of religion which may be equally important?
3 In the light of the dangers that a post-truth culture poses, mirrored historically in extreme forms of politics where religious and ethnic minorities have been targeted and attacked, does Rudolf Otto's work in establishing his Religious League of Mankind offer any encouragement in promoting tolerance on the part of global religious communities today? Was the Truth that Otto stood for meaningful only in its own historical, social context, or is it still important and relevant today?

Further reading

R. Otto, *The Idea of the Holy: An Inquiry into the non-rational factor in the idea of the divine and its relation to the rational* (Oxford: Oxford University Press, 1923).

R. Otto, *Religious Essays: A Supplement to The Idea of the Holy* (Oxford: Oxford University Press, 1931).

These two books are core to the understanding of Rudolf Otto's work.

P. C. Almond, *Rudolf Otto: An Introduction to his Philosophical Theology* (Chapel Hill NC: University of North Carolina Press, 1984). A clear, readable introduction to Rudolf Otto's work, which includes some fascinating biographical material.

S. Ballard, *Rudolf Otto and the Synthesis of the Rational and the Non-Rational in the Idea of the Holy* (published in the series THEION, Annual for Religious Culture vol. XII, Peter Lang, 2000). This book, which was the published version of my own Dr Theol thesis submitted to the University of Marburg, seeks to make connections between some key theoretical ideas of Otto and the practical initiatives in which he was engaged.

R. F. Davidson, *Rudolf Otto's Interpretation of Religion* (Princeton NJ: Princeton University Press, 1947). Now rather dated, but it offers a helpful analytical presentation of Rudolf Otto and the idea of the Holy.

Notes

1 Quoted by Peter R. McKenzie in his 'Introduction to the Man', in Harold W. Turner's *The Idea of the Holy – Commentary on a Shortened Version* (Aberdeen: Aberdeen People's Press, 1974), p. 4.

2 R. Otto, *Das Heilige*: Über das Irrationale in der Idee des Göttlichen und sein *Verhältnis zum Rationalen* (Breslau: Trewendt and Granier 1917). ET – *The Idea of the Holy: An Inquiry into the non-rational factor in the idea of the divine and its relation to the rational* (Oxford: Oxford University Press, 1923).

3 K. Barth, *Der Römerbrief* 1, 1919. Translated into English by E. C. Hoskyns as *The Epistle to the Romans* (London: Oxford University Press, 1933).

4 R. Otto, *Naturalism and Religion* (London: Williams and Norgate, 1931), p. 1. German original: *Naturalistische und religiöse Weltansicht* (Tübingen: J.C.B. Mohr, 1904).

5 See especially Otto's analysis of the experience of the 'numinous' in chapters III to VI in *The Idea of the Holy*.

6 Ibid., p. 16.

7 Ibid., in 'Foreword by the Author to the First English Edition'.

8 Author's Notes on the Translation, *The Philosophy of Religion Based on Kant and Fries* (London: Williams and Norgate, 1931). German original: *Kantisch-Fries'sche Religionsphilosophie und ihre Anwendung auf die Theologie* (Tübingen: J.C.B.Mohr, 1909).

9 J. M. Moore, *Theories of Religious Experience with Special Reference to James, Otto and Bergson* (New York: Round Table Press, 1938), p. 106.

10 *The Idea of the Holy*, footnote to p. 11.
11 Ibid., p. 147.
12 Ibid., p. 7.
13 R. F. Davidson, *Rudolf Otto's Interpretation of Religion* (Princeton NJ: Princeton University Press, 1947), pp. 4f.
14 G. Orwell, *Nineteen Eighty-Four* (London: Secker and Warburg, 1949).
15 R. Otto, *India's Religion of Grace and Christianity Compared and Contrasted* (London: SCM Press, 1930). German original: *Die Gnadenreligion Indiens und das Christentum. Vergleich und Unterscheidung* (Gotha: L. Klotz, 1930).
16 R. Otto, *Mysticism East and West* (New York: Macmillan, 1932). German original: *West-Östliche Mystik – Vergeich und Unterscheidung zur Wesensdeutung* (Gotha: L. Klotz, 1926).
17 R. Otto, *Religious Essays: A Supplement to The Idea of the Holy* (Oxford: Oxford University Press, 1931).
18 Ibid., chapter X, pp. 95–109.
19 Ibid., p.107.
20 Ibid., p. 151.
21 Ibid., p. 151.
22 R. Otto, 'Menschheitsbund Religiöser', in *Die Religion in Geschichte und Gegenwart*, 2nd edn (Tübingen: J.C.B. Mohr, 1927–1931.) III, 2122–3.
23 Otto Archive (OA) no. 1833.
24 G. D. Alles, 'Rudolf Otto and the Politics of Utopia', *Religion* 21 (1991), pp. 235–56.
25 Ibid., p. 239.
26 Rudolf Otto, *The Life and Ministry of Jesus* (Chicago: The Open Court, 1908). German original: *Die historisch-kritische Auffassung vom Leben und Wirken Jesu* (Göttingen: Vandenhoeck and Ruprecht, 1901).
27 See chapters XIX and XX of *The Idea of the Holy*, entitled respectively 'Divination in Primitive Christianity' and 'Divination in Christianity Today'.
28 R. Otto, *Reich Gottes und Menschensohn : Ein religionsgeschichtlicher Versuch* (München: C.H. Beck, 1934). Translated into English as *The Kingdom of God and the Son of Man* (London: Lutterworth Press, 1938).
29 *The Kingdom of God and The Son of Man*, p. 67.
30 *The Idea of the Holy*, p. 56.

9

Truth, Non-Truth and Reality in the Pastoral Context

ROBERT A. GILLIES

Institutional denial and deceit

In his novel *Professor Schmoot Has Lost His Keys Again*, Christopher Morse caricatures a liberal-minded theological seminary. In one 'Episode' we read:

> Tucker had settled upon a new book proposal outlining the hermeneutical issues at the core of the 'fake news' charges and counter charges that had first drawn headlines in the 2016 presidential campaign and election and, with the intriguing title *Fake News and The Good News* questioning the relevance of factuality as the test of truth in either case, had quickly secured a publishing contract.

In the same 'Episode' Morse refers to a 'postmodern destabilization of meaning'.[1] The context for this comment refers to a dilemma for the President of the seminary where Tucker was employed, who, when faced by evidence, used this latter turn of phrase to justify how he was employing truth in a particular way and doing so in a manner that was, to his mind, objectifiably secure. Clearly, as the narrative develops, it was not.

Morse's narrative of events in this seminary revolves around a sequence of such truth-denying scenes. In each the President (particularly) seeks to secure ongoing funding from a rich and ageing benefactress by deceit. Having departed from the conservative orthodoxy of its founder (the benefactress' grandfather) the now ultra-liberal seminary is hard-strapped for cash. The benefactress must be led to think that the seminary is as it was in the days of her grandfather. The contortions of reality and truth-telling that the President deploys seeking to maintain this duplicity form the majority of the thirty-seven Episodes of Morse's book.

In the end this duplicity can carry its own weight no longer. It bears too heavy a load and the book closes with due serious dialogue towards truth. The falsehood of the deceptions created by the President is exposed through a combination of empirical verification and fiscal examination. The truth becomes self-evident; as indeed does the deception.

One can imagine the situation of Star-Cross Seminary presented as a real-life scenario in any one or number of business, economic, social, or political contexts where institutional denial and deceit has eventually been exposed by the light of truth shone from without; be that investigative journalism, 'whistle blowers', or the straightforward intolerable burden and weight of self-imposed deceit and denial.

In the chapter that follows I will identify precursors of 'not-truth telling' as a backcloth against which we then consider a sequence of pastoral situations. We shall see how failure to tell the truth, or lying, or living a lie, have variously brought the church and Christian faith into disrepute. Historical antecedents where truth-telling is given relative status, graded significance, and absolute status are then noted. Finally, there follows a more substantive reflection on Dietrich Bonhoeffer's note on truth-telling with related expository thoughts, and particularly upon Phil. 2:5.

Not a new problem

In recent times the problem of deep-seated institutional deceit has come prominently into focus. With this have arisen questions about the nature of truth and the value we place upon it. Should the centrality of truth within our thinking and practice be given the emphasis that most would, or ought to, think it should? Should lying, or failing to tell the truth when required to do so, or dissembling the truth by avoidance or careful concealment beneath language, become more admissible?

Some simple definitions are important. 'Lying', for example, is an act of commission. 'Failing to tell the truth' may be either one of commission or omission. Withholding truth is a complex moral act – and one of the most pressing in pastoral situations. Many clergy will testify to the restraint necessarily exercised in holding back the truth that a particular parishioner is a pain in the neck!

Through all this an age-old problem has fused with the relatively new, often facilitated by social media, desire (or is it 'pleasure') to create 'fake news' or false truths in contexts where truth-telling has less traction than it should. Friedrich Nietzsche wrote in the nineteenth century:

> A great man – what is he? ... He rather lies than tells the truth; it requires more spirit and *will*. There is a solitude within him that is inaccessible to praise or blame, his own justice that is beyond appeal.[2]

The reality of deceit is also noted by Bok in her citation of Machiavelli:

> Men are so simple and so ready to obey present necessities, that one who deceives will always find those who allow themselves to be deceived.[3]

The home of such guile has ancient provenance. Athena, addressing Odysseus in the *Odyssey*, says that:

> even a god might bow to you in ways of dissimulation. You! You chameleon ... Two of a kind, we are, contrivers both.[4]

In recent times such dissimulation has found its home in recent presidents of the United States. On 17 August 1998 President Clinton admitted that which he had explicitly denied in a speech on 26 January earlier that year.

Duplicity is by no means restricted to those in political office. The church is also culpable. Dr Martin Warner, currently the Bishop of Chichester, has, in his submission to the Independent Inquiry into Child Sex Abuse (IICSA), said:

> it is clear to me there had been a historic bias in the Diocese in favour of adults in positions of power and authority [which has] led to an unwillingness to take allegations of sexual abuse made by children or by adults sufficiently seriously.

He continued:

> It reflects a wider social attitude of deference, a culture of deferring unduly to those in power and a culture of ... defensiveness.[5]

The church's failure to hear and act upon truth claims made by survivors of (mainly) clerical abuse has led to a serious diminution of trust in the church as an institution and in its clergy as individuals. Also reflected here are hierarchical relations and their associated power dynamics, all of which might, and probably will, have influenced what people feel they were, or are, able to say to authority figures.[6] The Archbishop of Canterbury, Justin Welby, was explicit in what he said to the same inquiry. The 'insanity of clericalism' in the Church of England by which senior clergy shift blame on to others to save their reputation and that of the Church is 'absurd' and a 'failure of human duty'.[7] He added that he 'was ashamed of the church'.

Telling lies, withholding and denying truth, damages those who perpetuate such as well as those who are denied justice by it. All too belatedly has the church discovered this in its pastoral practice and institutional leadership structures.

A situation that has further led to loss of trust in the church was highlighted in the sudden and, to many, shock resignation of Cardinal Keith Patrick O'Brien, formerly head of the Roman Catholic Church in Scotland.

Cardinal O'Brien had taken a strong campaigning stance on a range of issues affecting current society. However, in 2013 *The Observer* newspaper published allegations of sexual misconduct, dating from the 1980s, against the Cardinal. Initially O'Brien denied the allegations but within two days had resigned. An obituary of O'Brien in *The Daily Telegraph* of 20 March 2018 spoke of the crisis:

> O'Brien's accusers continued to demand justice and an acknowledgement of the truth of their claims that O'Brien had used his position as a seminary rector and a bishop to pressure young men into sex.

A report was commissioned but was never published. As a consequence the four accusers never 'had their day in court', so to speak, to have their accusations tested. Whether the report had laid open facts justifying their claims remains hidden from wider scrutiny. Such dissembling of the truth is surely to be regarded as a further injustice.

As one might expect this affair led to a serious crisis for the Roman Catholic Church in Scotland. Whatever the truth of accusations against Cardinal O'Brien might be, the fact of openly untested allegations of abuse of power by church leaders over their juniors, as well as now-admitted accusations of child abuse elsewhere, has brought discredit and shame upon the church across many countries.[8] Where there is official denial of what is true and/or a failure to hear truth told, discredit comes to some and sheer offence to others. Those who have perpetuated the injustice of lying and the failure to hear and respond to truth, or who have concealed investigations, have brought discredit and mistrust upon the very institution they sought, ill-advisedly, to protect.[9]

In the more open society we now have dissembling is perhaps increasingly unlikely, even if not evenly so, and is certainly more open to challenge. Many who previously told lies and denied truth in defence either of themselves or the institutions they served have in our day become the victims of their own deceit.

Lest however we consider the 'big headline' cases too exclusively, let us bring our attention to what are the more likely day-to-day issues that might face clergy and lay people in our church congregations and institutions.

The nativity play and the funeral

The presence of children in a Christmas nativity play is well-known and much loved. Let us suppose that one year it does not go well. The minister dutifully and in fulsome terms praises the children and their leaders for what they have done and speaks of how moving it has been for everyone present when in reality the whole performance has been cringingly embarrassing. Is this a lie? Or is it a pastorally justified action? Let us examine this hypothetical but nonetheless all-too-real situation.[10]

The minister's justification for her words of praise was that the effort the children and their leaders had put in needed positive acknowledgement. What she said, however, patently did not reflect what happened at the performance. That much was clear. We recognize that the minister's words were a denial of the truth in relation to what had happened. What she said was sublimated to the personal and pastoral needs of people who, as volunteers, were seeking to give of their best even if it had all failed.

Let us suppose that the minister in question is prone to telling 'white lies'. These are seemingly superficial untruths. One or two white lies 'now and then' may occasion little or no harm. If this is the case then those with whom this minister interacts will soon question her probity. Initially this might be in individuals' minds. But the risk for the minister is that her 'white lies' might become 'the talk of the town'. Telling 'white lies' risks becomes habit forming. One such lie might have no discernible effect. But more might be added on further occasions. In the relatively tight-knit communities where clergy serve, word soon risks passing from one person to another that 'the minister cannot be trusted to mean what she says.'

If this is the minister who then stands up in front of the audience to give the valedictory vote of thanks at our hypothetical nativity play then in all likelihood her intended praise before the woebegone performers and audience will come across as lacking integrity and worth. Knowing her to be a liar in the normal ebb and flow of life, those gathered at the nativity play witness further disingenuousness in a minister whose word cannot be trusted to be true, let alone honourable. In the normal run of things lies are tested against the bar of truth as known and shared by those concerned. Those who find themselves lied to will not easily trust the word of the liar, and certainly not the habitual teller of 'white lies'. If the liar is the parish minister then that cleric's whole ministry will risk discredit as a consequence.

Another situation concerns the funeral eulogy. In the Anglican Book of Common Prayer there is no provision for a eulogy, or address, or other form of homily in respect of the departed person (or 'corpse' as the Prayer Book puts it).

The eulogy at a funeral is a relatively modern invention. As a priest of forty years' service I have always offered an address at funeral services but have noted that in recent times families have started presenting me with full texts on the person's life. Sometimes these are of great length. If a request, or a demand, is given that this text is read in full and it contains no reference to Jesus' victory over death, the resurrection life, or for that matter, repentance for sins committed or good not accomplished, then the Christian pastor and priest has his or her hands firmly tied by way of pastoral practice.

In one situation, where fortunately I had a good relationship with a particular family, I was able to say to the family (after they had sent me a very long eulogizing text for the departed person) that 'it is easy to eulogize someone beyond recognition'. The point was taken and a good pastoral outcome resulted.

Less fortunate was the funeral of my uncle who, at a humanist 'celebration of his life',[11] had all his many merits praised so that he seemed to have lived a faultless and blameless life. Such is never the case and if failings are not admitted or alluded to then we deceive ourselves and the truth is not in us. In cases like these we are faced, not with Christopher Morse's 'institutional deceit', but rather with the realities of personal life and interpersonal relationships being denied.

On another occasion, I was asked to advise on a situation where a family explicitly required a cleric to remove ten lines from a eulogy he had prepared, and which he had shared with the family in advance. In that paragraph reference was made to the deceased's seriously troubling, troublesome, and aggressive personality. I advised that it be removed; the family's grieving would be compounded by felt hurt and potential insult were it to remain and angry correspondence and formal complaints might have followed. Many years later, I still continue to reflect on the question of whether honesty, and with it truth, was best served by my action. On balance I feel I acted appropriately, but nonetheless my action was at the expense of truth. The unease remains[12] and the question remains through these pastoral circumstances: when are we in denial of truth, and victims of its evasion and its avoidance? Worse still perhaps is the question, do we feel telling the truth matters? And its rider, is truth always to be sublimated on the one hand to institutional need and reputation and, on the other, more locally perhaps, to pastoral need and request?

Furthermore, how do we guard ourselves against becoming the habitual teller of 'white lies' whom I referred to above? To this last question I fear there may be no answer. It is a sad fact of life that the one who is guilty in this regard lives a life of greater or lesser self-deceit in such a way as to render them unlikely to heed or even hear the word of advice that might be given in respect of their failing. Moreover we live in an age in which social media access allows previously voiceless victims of injustice an opening to air their grievance and voice their need for truth. Deliberate dissemblance is therefore very likely to be uncovered.[13]

Conversely, and negatively, social media allows every advantage to those who seek to create confusion. Their delight is to cause potentially serious damage by misrepresenting, often under the protection of anonymity, what is true or false, right or wrong, just or unjust through dissemination of that which has been given the title 'fake news'. For such as these the propagation of that which is false, or which may be mischievous by false imputation, can be mendacious and a pernicious attraction. Furthermore, the deliberate goal of those purveying 'fake news' over longer time-spans is to generate doubt on *all* sources of news. Such has to be a denial of the will of God as instanced in Jesus Christ. To this we shall return at the end of this chapter.

Before closing this section we must also make mention of those situations where mendacious accusations are made against clergy and church lay workers. Such do appalling damage and cause sometimes irreparable hurt as local gossip exacerbates the worry to those who, in such cases, are being falsely and vexatiously accused. Inadequacies in the church's own investigations and information gathering processes, where they exist, can make the situation worse.

In one case that has come to my attention the accused cleric was not interviewed by those gathering information on behalf of the church nor given any reason why opportunity would *not* be given for [him or her] to present their own response to the accusations. This cannot be the best way to assemble the facts of a case from every vantage so as to form a perspective on where truth resides and thus to gain direction on the best way to proceed next. In a situation such as this truth is ill-served even if 'due process' and legal advice is being followed.

TRUTH, NON-TRUTH AND REALITY IN THE PASTORAL CONTEXT

Reprise

Our reflections have admitted that denial of truth is no recent phenomenon. We have suggested how and why truth-telling is important in the pastoral context. Through narrative, we have contended that where truth is denied, not admitted, or not disclosed, then pastoral trust and personal integrity risk being compromised. The risk might be small, medium or large; but risk there is, nonetheless. However, we do not yet have a secure ground to argue what *should* or *ought* to be operative in the pastoral context. This comes as no surprise, for no narrative of what *is* the case can determine or posit an obligation towards what ought to be. Narratives, however, even if not determinative, can be indicative.

Against this background we now consider how truth and lying have been viewed historically. St Augustine of Hippo (354–430 CE) and Immanuel Kant (1724–1804), with others, figure largely in this next section. More recent theological reflection then follows whereby we track the German theologian Dietrich Bonhoeffer along a suggestive line of thought and ally this with the importance of prayer and pastoral practice for the Christian disciple 'in Christ'.

How Augustine and others might have responded

Augustine had no doubts upon the matter of lying. In *The Enchiridion* he writes:

> every liar says the opposite of what he thinks in his heart, with purpose to deceive. Now it is evident that speech was given to man, not that men might therewith deceive one another, but that one man might make known his thoughts to another. To use speech, then, for the purpose of deception, and not for its appointed end, is a sin.[14]

Thus we see that lying is presented as simultaneously having one thing in the heart but saying something else with the clear intention to deceive. Doing this is a denial and frustration of God's purpose for speech. However, Augustine recognized the problems of an absolutist position in respect of lying. If all lies are a sin then how does one address the human complexities that are involved when lies need to be told in order, for example, to protect someone from assault. The same could be said in what amounts to spying. Here is an example.

The Chief Constable of one of Scotland's former police forces spoke of the absolute nature of truth needed in his profession at a church event with an essentially lay audience. It was not long before a member of the audience asked about the need to lie in undercover policing, and in the infiltration of suspected criminal networks. For the wider public to be protected lying needs to be the order of the day in such contexts. The Chief Constable acknowledged the validitiy of the question. But here is Augustine again:

> Nor are we to suppose that there is any lie that is not a sin, because it is sometimes possible, by telling a lie, to do service to another.

Thus we see that even Augustine was prepared to acknowledge that there can be gradations of lying. In fact Augustine set up an eightfold schema; lies told in catechetical formation being the most serious, and lies which harmed no one, the least. In the end, for Augustine all lies remain sins and for this reason cannot be advocated. If there is to be any mitigation for telling lies then it resides in the intention of the one who does the lying. If the intention (even where there are mixed motives) is to prevent or minimize harm and/or where benefit or protection arises, then praise of the intention can carry with it divine pardon – even if not commendation – of the lie.

St Thomas Aquinas (1225–74) developed this thinking into a more formularized system in his *Summa Theologica*. The outcome was not without difficulty. The problem with the positions of Augustine and Aquinas is that, increasingly, people would adapt the schema and hierarchy of lies not to suit the needs of the occasion but also to satisfy their own preferences. Thus the smart thinker and quick speaker could find ways to justify anything he or she wanted to.

Blaise Pascal (1623–62) railed against the classical thinking of both doctors of the church:

> A man may swear ... that he never did such a thing (though he actually did it), meaning within himself that he did not do so on a certain day, or before he was born, or understanding any other such circumstance, while the words which he employs have no such sense as would discover his meaning. And this is very convenient in many cases, when necessary or conducive to one's health, honour, or advantage.[15]

He concludes that this is both a lie and, additionally, perjury.

Hugo Grotius (1583–1645), Dutch legal theorist and philosopher, challenged Augustine's approach by arguing that among his schema were things that should not be considered to be lies. Determining what constitutes 'lying' or 'a lie' is fundamental. Where something does not conflict with the rights of the person to whom the 'lie' is told then that should not be considered to be a lie. Upon such a basis it is perfectly correct to lie to a person in order to thwart his or her evil intent if such is their desire. Grotius' legal persuasion, formed from his commitment to natural law arguments, led his thinking. Grotius' perspective has some force. We might even think of it as 'common sense'.

Immanuel Kant (1724–1804) brings us more closely to modernity. A philosophical heir of the European Enlightenment, Kant's ethical thinking impacts as powerfully now as it has since the day his words were first published. It is perhaps surprising that Kant espoused a 'truth at all costs' position, if it may be so described. He writes:

> Truthfulness in statements which cannot be avoided is the formal duty of an individual to everyone, however great may be the disadvantage accruing to himself or to another.[16]

Kant is explicitly suggesting that all lying is wrong and those who lie, or fail to tell the truth, harm themselves by doing so. It follows also that the one who is lied to is also harmed by the lies told him or her. But, we must ask, how might Kant have considered cases where there is a conflict of duties – for example where telling the truth to one person leads to others' harm. The point is well made, against Kant's absolutist position, that if it is legitimate to use actual physical force to defend someone against harm then it should be equally legitimate to lie, similarly to protect.

Bonhoeffer's *Ethics*

A short section towards the end of Dietrich Bonhoeffer's *Ethics*[17] is remarkable for its insights into the nature of truth, not least because it was composed while Bonhoeffer was in prison in 1943 and out of which it was smuggled. He asks the questions, 'What does it mean to tell the truth?' and 'What does it demand of us?' Bonhoeffer sets his argument by saying that '"telling the truth" means something different according to the particular situation in which one stands'.[18] This contextual nature of truth is crucial, for 'account must be taken of one's relationships at each particular time'.

For Bonhoeffer, it is fundamental that one owes full truthfulness to the living God who entered our life and our manifold of relationships. The truthfulness we owe to God must be given concrete expression in the world we inhabit. He goes on to say that truth telling 'is not solely a matter of moral character; it is also a matter of correct appreciation of real situations'.[19]

Bonhoeffer offers the example of a classroom teacher who asks a small child in the class a question whether the child's father comes home drunk at night. The child replies that he does not even though this is not true. Bonhoeffer's point behind this example is that the teacher has put the child in a difficult situation in a public environment for which the child is not yet prepared. Bonhoeffer comments, 'As a simple "no" to the teacher's question the child's answer is certainly untrue; yet at the same time it gives expression to the truth that the family is an institution *sui generis* and that the teacher had no right to interfere in it.'[20] The child therefore gave a 'real answer' that honoured the integrity of the family even though factually untrue. Bonhoeffer says, 'Telling the truth is, therefore, something which must be learnt ... the ethical cannot be detached from reality, and consequently continual progress in learning to appreciate reality is a necessary ingredient in ethical action.'[21] None of this happens in a vacuum. To speak truthfully one must orientate oneself towards the way by which the 'real exists in God and through God and for God'.

In this vein, I remember a conversation with the former Archbishop of Canterbury, Rowan Williams. I recall him saying, and I paraphrase, that one's prayer should lead one into the mind of Christ so that his mind becomes our mind thus to guide our will and our actions to his desire. Bonhoeffer again:

> If my utterance is to be truthful it must in each case be different according to whom I am addressing, who is questioning me, and what I am speaking about ... If it is detached from life and from its reference to the concrete other man, if 'the truth is told' without taking [this] into account then this truth has only the appearance of truth, but it lacks its essential character.[22]

It is service of 'Satan' which requires truth devoid of reference to the reality of human concrete, i.e. 'real', situations, Bonhoeffer tells us. And yet the obvious question raises itself: 'How does his position guard itself against the all-too-human tendency to decide truth according to personal preference?' This leads Bonhoeffer to the observation that 'The usual definition of the lie as a conscious discrepancy between thought and speech is completely inadequate ... the essential character of the lie is to be found at a far deeper level than in the discrepancy between thought and speech'.[23] He continues:

> the lie is the denial, the negation and the conscious and deliberate destruction of the reality which is created by God and which consists in God, no matter whether this purpose is achieved by speech or by

silence. The assigned purpose of our words, in unity with the word of God, is to express the real, as it exists in God; and the assigned purpose of our silence is to signify the limit which is imposed upon our words by the real as it exists in God.[24]

This is encountered not as a 'consistent whole' but rather in a 'condition of disruption and inner contradiction which has need of reconciliation and healing ... [for there are] ... different orders of the real'. In search of this reconciliation and healing our words are 'repeatedly drawn in into ... prevalent disunion and conflict'.[25]

In a final paragraph to this piece, added from a letter by his editor, Eberhard Bethge, Bonhoeffer notes that not everything that 'is' should be disclosed. God (and referring now to Genesis 3:21) has given us clothes to conceal our nakedness. Concealment, by analogy therefore, is God-given; 'concealment and secrecy' contest 'fanatical' devotion to truth-exposure that denies the reality of God's creation and human fall.[26]

Philippians 2:5 'Let the same mind be in you that was in Christ Jesus'

Though not referred to in 'What is meant by telling the truth' this single verse from Philippians takes us to the heart of that Christian discipleship discipline that Bonhoeffer invokes. Lest it be thought that we are taking one verse out of context and imposing upon it too heavy an interpretive burden we must make clear that it stands for many others in the New Testament and that it is at the heart of the Christological and soteriological theology of Christ's redemptive work and the pneumatological force of the Holy Spirit in accord with the will and plan of God for his creation (see note 24).

It is in the Christian's life in response to Christ's call, through prayer, service and outreach that he or she is called to model in person-to-person relationships the relationship that each has with Christ. How this comes to be is crucial if we are to understand both this passage and Bonhoeffer properly.

It is Christ who is the archetype of all human behaviour. Those in every generation who have heard the call from Christ that leads to discipleship see in him the foundation of how all things should be. Philippians 2:5 reads, 'Let the same mind be in you that was in Christ Jesus'.[27] Care must be taken when reading and interpreting this verse to avoid seeing Christian discipleship as *imitating* what Christ did. Bauder in *The New International Dictionary of New Testament*

Theology reminds us that, '[Christ] is the archetype, not an *exemplum*, but the *exemplar*'.[28]

Thus, if one lives the life of the disciple one is not following a particular way of life that was modelled by a particular holy man (Jesus Christ) but rather one sets one's life to be the way of life that arises from having been called, forgiven and redeemed through faith in the one who alone can make that possible. Bauder, again, where he considers 'imitation of Christ' as 'being in Christ' rather than following Christ's example through good and holy living, states:

> [Imitation of Christ] is not the way to salvation through pious achievement, but an attitude of thanks in response to the salvation that has been given ... The summons to discipleship can only be fulfilled, when a [person] is grasped by Christ and undergoes the transformation which existence under the Lordship of Christ involves.

It follows that actions where explicit truth cannot be told openly (for example in such a way as would benefit a malefactor) have to be measured with the total reality of the situation as given in Christ when he assumed unique, unambiguously human life. In this form he was explicitly delivered to death but then broke the power of that death. Living in Christ means that those who align their minds to his will see everything from the vantage of salvation won through Christ-like obedience to God rather than through improved moral living.[29] The more one is aligned to the mind of Christ, by being transformed into his being, the more one will see reality from Christ's perspective and so model the articulation of truth in ways that equate to the mind of Christ. This is an aspect of Christian discipleship and requires spiritual discipline on the part of each Christian believer so to orientate their lives to Christ that what Christ's will and being is, theirs should also be. Such life comes to Christian believers as a gift of the Spirit and is the stress of 1 Corinthians 2:14–16. Like all gifts of the Spirit it must be tested, put into effect and refined so that the gift of truth-telling is apposite to the mind of Christ in all things.

Lying to protect an institution, whether that institution be the church or another, is a sin and, in Bonhoeffer's terms, would give victory to Satan. Lying can be distinguished from failing to tell the truth, or even from telling an un-truth, most especially where it honours and protects the well-being of another and gives no advantage to one with mendacious intent.

People most often tell lies and deceive to defend themselves in some way or to promote a personal cause. We are self-protective and self-deceived, but the cost of honesty can be searing shame and exposure (as can the cost of deception, ultimately). None of us want to be seen naked before our neighbours or before God. So to follow Bonhoeffer we need to believe, and this is not always easy, in the absolute loving gaze of a gracious and loving God. In the confessional, as in supervision, there is space for talking about those times when one has lied, or withheld truth, with beneficent intent and purpose. This self-examination, with a rigorous guide as companion, can, when used honestly and properly, be an essential mechanism to avoid falling into an easy expediency that leads to self-preferencing. Consulting the community of Christ and receiving correction offers an essential check and balance mechanism within the living body of Christian community and is a means of accessing what it might be to live the mind of Christ. Correction like this would do much to mitigate the worst aspects of lying and self-deception and, through mutual criticism and critique, seek to ameliorate such aspects as might be deliberately against the will of Christ.[30]

Conclusion

Clearly this is not the end of the story. Our case studies have exposed a wide spectrum of questions and approaches to the matter of truth and lying. Nonetheless it is in the approach which Bonhoeffer offered, and which in turn led to our exposition of Philippians 2:5, that we find best direction given.

The life of Christian discipleship is not one characterized by following a good example, whether that of Jesus Christ or another. Rather the life of Christian discipleship is characterized by the life that the person lives in Christ. The disciple of Christ lives the mind of Christ in all things. For our present purposes this comes with living Christ's truth in the reality of all situations, thus giving no advantage to deception and to powers that seek to undermine it and which thereby seek to undermine the mind of Christ in the world he redeemed.

Questions for discussion

1 Identify a time recently when you deliberately told a white lie with the intent of making yourself seem important.
2 Identify a time in your life when you deliberately either said something false, or withheld something that was true, in order to protect yourself.

3 Can you think of a time when you were the victim of someone else's false statements and as a result of which you were hurt or seriously offended?
4 If possible these questions should be discussed in a group with others in which you will feel safe sharing such personal questions.

Further reading

C. Morse, *Professor Schmoot Has Lost His Keys Again* (Resource Publications for Wipf and Stock, 2017). This novel explores through a series of 'episodes' institutional deceit and lying. It is also an allegory of the 'Emmaus Road' story in the Gospel of Luke, 24:13–35.

S. Bok, *Lying, Moral Choice in Public and Private Life,* 2nd edn (New York: Vintage Books, 1999). This is an important and systematic examination of lying and of the failure of truth-telling at all levels.

D. Bonhoeffer, 'What Is Meant by Telling the Truth' in *Ethics,* ed. Eberhard Bethge, trans. Neville Horton Smith (New York: Touchstone edition, 1995), pp. 358–67. This brief section in *Ethics* is signally important for truth-telling for it introduces the category of the 'real' to the discussion and relates this to Christian discipleship now.

Notes

1 C. Morse, *Professor Schmoot Has Lost His Keys Again* (Resource Publications for Wipf and Stock, 2017), p. 128 and p. 131.

2 Quoted by S. Bok, *Lying, Moral Choice in Public and Private Life,* 2nd edn (New York: Vintage Books, 1999), p. 17, from Nietzsche's *The Will to Power.*

3 Bok, p. 28.

4 Cited from Bok, pp. 29–30.

5 *Church of England Newspaper,* 23 March 2018, p. 4.

6 On truth, power and authority see also Chapter 1 (Taylor) and Chapter 2 (Jasper).

7 *Church Times,* 23 March 2018.

8 Dr Eric Stoddart has written to me in relation to this chapter and on this point in particular, 'I wonder if shame might actually be a significant issue in all our talk about lying – because some lies are deemed worse than others. Pastoral dynamics of shame (and shaming) may well be important in how/if/what sort of truth is told'.

9 I must make a footnote comment on allegations, levelled many years after his death, against Bishop Bell of Chichester. I share the view of many that those who investigated these allegations rushed to hasty and peremptory justice on this issue, serving ill the memory of a revered wartime bishop, nor yet did they serve adequately the woman who made the allegations.

10 The minister could have deployed other measures such as picking out what had gone well and drawing a veil of silence over the embarrassing bits

(even if that was most of it). However, for the purposes of our examination the situation as described, even if seemingly contrived, is what we will remain with.

11 The word 'funeral' is not normally used at humanist burials and cremations.

12 That said, I console myself that in doing what I did I consciously sought to be faithful to God's witness to me in Christ.

13 So too is inconsistency when, for example, comparing tweets on either side of, say, a five-year gap.

14 St Augustine, *On Faith, Hope and Love (The Enchiridion)*, ed. Philip Schaff, trans. J. F. Shaw, chapter 22 (Kindle edition). Compare, in a different context, Plato on rhetoric in the *Phaedrus*.

15 B. Pascal, *The Provincial Letters* trans. Thomas M'Crie (1857), ed. A. Boer, Sr, (Veritas Splendor Publications; Letter 9; republication 2012) (Kindle edition).

16 Cited from Bok, p. 268.

17 D. Bonhoeffer, 'What Is Meant by Telling the Truth', in *Ethics*, ed. Eberhard Bethge, trans. Neville Horton Smith, (New York: Touchstone edition, 1995), pp. 358–67.

18 *Ethics*, p. 358.

19 *Ethics*, p. 359.

20 *Ethics*, p. 362.

21 *Ethics*, pp. 359, 360.

22 *Ethics*, p. 360.

23 *Ethics*, pp. 363, 364.

24 *Ethics*, p. 364.

25 We note that some Christian groups (as in other religions) have justified deception and seduction precisely on the contextual relativism/relationalism that could be thought to derive from Bonhoeffer. For example, 'it is ok to sleep with someone if that brings them into the group' or to be untruthful to them 'because you are going to save their soul'. Such take one to the need for a strong doctrine of sin and costly grace-led forgiveness as a counteract. I am reminded (*pace* St Augustine) that acknowledgment of forgiveness brings with it the awareness of sin and thus of the wrongs that associate with it.

26 *Ethics*, pp. 366–7 (note).

27 The verse may also read, 'Let the same mind be in you that you have in Christ Jesus'.

28 W. Bauder in *The New International Dictionary of New Testament Theology*, Vol. 1 (Carlisle: Paternoster Press, 1986), p. 492. Bauder also cites other passages in similar vein.

29 This obedience includes not just Gethsemane and Golgotha, as might be first thought, but also table fellowship, the Wedding at Cana of Galilee, asserting himself as a teenager vis-à-vis not telling his parents where he was, upturning the money-changers tables in the Temple and so on. I am indebted to Dr Stoddart for this reminder.

30 I express my gratitude to Dr Eric Stoddart, the Revd Prof Stephen Pattison and the Revd Prof Christopher Morse for valuable advice and direction on the course and content of this chapter.

10

Sciences and Truth: A Scientist's View

ERIC PRIEST

We shall not cease from exploration
And the end of all our exploring
Will be to arrive where we started
And know the place for the first time.
(T. S. Eliot, *Four Quartets*)[1]

For now we see through a glass, darkly; but then face to face: now I know in part; but then shall I know even as also I am known.
(1 Corinthians 13:12, AV)

Science demands also the believing spirit. Anyone who has been seriously engaged in scientific work of any kind realizes that over the gate of the temple of science are written the words 'Ye must have faith'. (Max Planck, 1932)[2]

Introduction

The author of this chapter is an applied mathematician and solar physicist, whose aim is to give a personal perspective on what it is like to be a practising scientist and a person of faith, a perspective that is accepted by many scientists who are also Christians on how the sciences claim to know reliable things about the universe.

The first two quotations above, from the visionary T. S. Eliot and St Paul, express something of the nature of the scientific search for Truth. Absolute or universal truth is something that is true at all times and in all places, that is unalterable and permanent. We shall denote it by Truth, with a capital T. For example, it includes truths that may be proved by logic, such as propositions of Euclid, or the statement that there are no round squares. In contrast truths that change in time or depend on culture, such as moral truths, are relative.

In science, by its nature, our understanding evolves over time and there is a difference between mainstream science, where the understanding is unlikely to change, and frontier science which is evolving rapidly. Science involves a combination of empirical truths, which are based on evidence that may be wrong or incomplete, and theoretical arguments that also may be improved in future. The aim though is to progress towards an absolute understanding, which becomes part of mainstream science and which may often be regarded as part of Truth. Of course, as time proceeds, some accepted results may be shown to be false after all, while others may be shown to be limited in their nature so that they remain true provided certain conditions hold.

The third quotation, from an early twentieth-century pioneer of quantum physics, stresses that part of the very essence of science is the fact that scientists have faith in the intelligibility of the physical universe and they hold beliefs, such as the idea that the universe always follows the same rules.

For practising scientists, such as the present author, the usual belief is that Truth in some form lies behind the phenomena they are investigating, and that it may be partially accessed by scientific investigation.

However, we live in an age of post-truth, fake news, a loss of truth in public life, a misunderstanding of the role of science and a loss of respect for authority, including science. So, it is important to stress that:

- sciences are about searching for Truth;
- scientific results are always provisional and so humility is crucial as scientists remain open to new possibilities;
- sciences that have been tested and confirmed by experts should be respected, like other specialisms such as electronics or dentistry;
- but that respect needs to be earned by scientists communicating the nature of their science and their results to a general audience and remaining open to alternative interpretations of observations or experiments.

There is also a difference between:

- mature science, where a large body of observations has been gathered over a long period of time and the core interpretations are well accepted; and
- frontier science, where new observations are being made and their interpretation is rapidly evolving.

One example of mature science would be evolution, since the existence of evolution and the role of genetics is well established by most biologists and is consistent with a vast range of evidence. However, the frontier aspects of evolution, such as the mechanisms of epigenetics and of the extended evolutionary synthesis, are matters of current research and are open to debate.

We shall find deep connections between science and aesthetics, since science is far from being the cold logical activity that follows a rigid method. Rather, at its core the scientist is behaving in ways that parallel those of an artist, and, as Michael Polanyi has stressed, there is a role for personal judgement.

In this chapter, I make the assumption that Truth is a fixed and eternal concept that does indeed exist, and will ask 'How can the sciences help us approach it or illuminate it?'

As we shall see, this requires a more nuanced and complex view than is presented by either a pure realist or a non-realist understanding of the nature of reality

Then I describe the nature of science and the scientific method for a scientist, pointing out that there is a wide range of sciences and of scientific methods. Genuine science adopts a subtle and balanced view between the two extreme views of scientism and postmodernism. In addition, an integrated view of science and faith is proposed, stressing the role of reason and revelation in the work of a scientist.

Finally, I give an account of what it is like to do science, including Thomas Kuhn's ideas of paradigms and Michael Polanyi's stress on personal judgement and touch briefly on a comparison of the books of nature and Scripture, and the importance of beauty, reason, and revelation for a scientist.

The nature of reality

I shall take Truth in the first instance to be a metaphysical concept concerned with bedrock questions of reality (such as the ultimate laws of nature), a definition that could be acceptable regardless of one's belief. *Scientific* truth is the part of Truth that is concerned with the nature, properties and behaviour of the universe, with seeking to understand what is, namely, the environment within which we live. Physical science, in particular, restricts itself to natural causes and deals with matter, energy, and their interactions in space and time. It assumes that the universe always follows the same rules.

Different *metaphysical assumptions* may be adopted about the nature of the world that sciences investigate, namely, non-realist, realist or critical realist:

1. A *non-realist* or *anti-realist* view would suggest that ideas are invented or constructed by scientists to make sense of their observations, but they say nothing definitive about what's out there and have no correspondence with an independent reality;

2 A *realist* view would attempt to discover truths about the universe, a world out there which we can access and whose properties we can attempt to predict.

Most scientists, including the present author, feel that they are indeed in the process of discovering reality. Their motives for doing research are 'intellectual curiosity and a desire to know the truth' (Hardy, 1940).[3] However, they follow many scholars in science and religion (such as Michael Polanyi (1962), Tom Torrance (1969),[4] John Polkinghorne (1994),[5] Ian Barbour (1997), and Arthur Peacock (1996)[6]), in preferring a modification of the realist view, namely:

3 *Critical realism,* which recognizes the existence of reality, while acknowledging that any view of the world we gain through scientific activity is provisional and liable to improvement in the light of future experiments, observations or theories. Therefore, we hope to become closer and closer to Truth, while not yet perfectly achieving it, as T. S. Eliot and St Paul realized in the first two quotes at the beginning of this chapter.

Mathematics

It is worth mentioning here the special case of mathematics, which may be thought of as the 'language' of science. Many scientists are struck by what Eugene Wigner[7] referred to as 'the unreasonable effectiveness of mathematics' in describing the physical world, leading them towards an understanding which sees mathematics as encapsulating aspects of deep truth about the physical world.

The fact that the physical world is *underpinned by mathematics* is quite amazing and is consistent with being construed in the mind of the Creator. The orderly nature of the universe, as well as the mathematical symmetry and elegance, are uncanny, since they mirror patterns in nature and are not just a human invention but suggest a rational heart to the universe and a reality behind the world with its uniformity, regularity, and intelligibility. The mathematics represents a deeper level of reality than mere description, a reality that can be discovered and that describes the links, relations and behaviour of physical phenomena. Indeed, Hardy (1940) distinguishes between 'physical reality', which can often be described by mathematics, and 'mathematical reality' itself, such that our function is to discover it.

Mathematical knowledge is acquired by *pure reason,* using logical mathematical arguments: an example would be Fermat's last theorem (which states that there are no three positive integers a, b, c, such that $a^n + b^n = c^n$ for any integer n greater than 2). This was posed by Fermat in 1637 but proved by Andrew Wiles only in 1994; in other words a mathematical argument was presented that demonstrates that the theorem is true. In many cases true statements in mathematics are those that are provable within a formal axiomatic system. However, as Gödel and Turing have shown, there are some statements that are true but which cannot be proved within the system, while Russell has highlighted the existence of paradoxical statements.

In addition, aesthetics can have a part to play in mathematics, as in reflections on the characteristics of God (goodness, beauty, and so on). Many mathematicians and scientists find amazing beauty in the structure of mathematical equations. For example, Euler's formula $e^{i\pi} + 1 = 0$ relates the base ($e = 2.71828...$) of the natural logarithm (e), the imaginary number (i) and the ratio ($\pi = 3.14159...$) of the circumference to the diameter of a circle, and it also contains examples of the three mathematical functions of addition, multiplication, and raising to a power.

Again, as a scientist, I find the equations of magnetohydrodynamics (a unification of the equations of fluid dynamics with electromagnetism, describing much of the behaviour of our Sun) to be as beautiful as a sunset, a Bach fugue or a Monet painting.

Deep questions seeking answers here include: Why are there mathematical laws at all? Why is nature mathematical in form? Why are the laws universal? Theological perspectives might offer ways of responding to these questions by noting the grounding of our universe in the outworkings of the will of a God who has affirmed its goodness from its very point of origin. Humans may apprehend aspects of that goodness through their perceptions of beauty, harmony, and orderliness in the universe.

What is science or the sciences?

There are many unsatisfactory dictionary definitions of science, but it is better to refer to 'sciences' rather than 'science', since there is now a huge range of different kinds of science, ranging from pure mathematics to social science, which employ a diverse range of methods.

Consequently, I shall adopt the following definition:

Science is the systematic study of the structure and behaviour of the physical and natural world through observation, experiment, or theoretical modelling.

This is much broader than an understanding of the natural world through physical processes alone, since it also includes other fields such as the human sciences. Moreover, it excludes 'spiritual' or faith aspects, even though such realities do exist for scientists with a faith perspective.

For the physical sciences a *'naturalist'* or *'physicalist'* approach assumes that the object under investigation can be treated as a purely material entity with repeatable behaviour obeying physical laws, without reference to supernatural causes.

Whereas *metaphysical naturalism* holds that there is nothing but natural elements, principles, and relations of the kind studied by the natural sciences, many of us scientists are *methodological naturalists*: when undertaking scientific investigations we use only the methods of science, but we do not necessarily deny the existence of a religious realm. Indeed, our religious beliefs may affect the way we think about the implications (often moral) of our work and the ways we try to interact with our colleagues.

Scientism, postmodernism or an integrated attitude

Science needs to be distinguished from two extreme views which I do not accept. The first is *'scientism'*, common to new atheists or to logical positivism, which holds that science is the main or the only way to find Truth and to interpret what we experience. Scientism imposes its own understanding on all aspects of human life and distorts human experience by insisting that it be understood through one particular lens. A follower of scientism may, for example, suppose that God does not exist, but the existence of God is not a scientific question: rather, it is a philosophical or theological one.

There are many aspects of my life which I cannot demonstrate absolutely but that are nevertheless important and which I may accept provisionally. Thus, whereas pure mathematicians can indeed prove that some results are absolutely true, there are many ideas, models, and theories that, as an applied mathematician or physicist, I cannot prove are correct, and this affects my attitude to the fact that I can also never prove the existence of God. But what I can do is ask whether my theory for solar flares, say, is consistent with the observations, and similarly whether the existence or non-existence of God is more consistent with my experience. For the moment at least, the existence of God is much more consistent, and so I am prepared to live my life under the assumption that God does indeed exist.

For me, being open-minded is a key aspect of being a scientist. However, many followers of scientism such as Richard Dawkins are in my view actually militant fundamentalist propagandists rather than being genuine open-minded scientists. He has famously defined 'faith' as 'belief in something in the absence of any evidence', which implicitly defines 'evidence' as only scientific evidence and is not the definition of faith or trust that I recognize. Indeed, as we shall see, and, as Max Planck recognized in the quotation at the head of this chapter, faith is an important ingredient of being a scientist.

The second extreme is a *postmodern* view, which has attractive features of tolerating a variety of cultures and beliefs, but it rejects absolute truth and therefore the critical realist position that I have advocated in the previous section. Not surprisingly, few scientists would accept the relativist aspects of postmodernism.

Instead, I adopt a more measured approach between these extremes in which science is an important source of knowledge which should be recognized as the authority when addressing scientific questions. Moreover, of course I recognize its limitations, since there are many non-scientific questions which the sciences cannot address, so that they have a limited amount to say about many important aspects of human life such as morality, purpose, love, and beauty.

Rather than there being a battle between the sciences and faith, the sciences and humanities (including theology) may be regarded, in my view, as an integrated whole in which reason and wonder play key roles.[8] What united them in classical times and before the nineteenth century was Aristotle's idea that *scientia* and *religio* are different kinds of virtue. For Aquinas (1225–1274), *religio* refers to inner piety, interior acts of devotion and prayer, whereas *scientia* is a habit of mind, an intellectual virtue, a personal quality. What unites them today, according to Priest (2016), is a common search for understanding, which involves both reason and imagination.

The methods of sciences

Scientific methods

Just as it is misleading to talk about one 'science', since there are many sciences, so also it is a mistake to talk about one 'scientific method'. The many sciences differ from one another not just in their object of study but also in the methods they use in approaching and analysing that object: from mathematicians who use reason to deduce theorems, to physicists and chemists who emphasize evidence-based techniques and repeatability, to palaeontologists who use fossil finds to understand extinct species and establish plausible evolutionary links, to plant taxonomists who categorize different plants, to social psychologists who use questionnaires to understand human behaviour.

What, then, might be said about the methods which underpin the sciences? The so-called scientific method involves the following five steps:

- asking a question;
- stating a hypothesis;
- conducting an experiment;
- analysing the results; and
- drawing a conclusion.

However, the methods of science are far more complex than this would have us believe. Sometimes one may stumble on a result by accident without asking a question; in other cases, one may start with an experiment or may gather data and seek a pattern; again, an experiment may not be possible (e.g., in astronomy) or it may not be ethical (in medicine) or it may not be appropriate (e.g., in geology or anthropology, where one gathers data instead).

Sometimes, science proceeds instead by the 'inductive method', whereby lots of observations are made or data collected, and patterns are sought that lead to an explanation for them all. David Hume realized that, although induction is not made by reason (i.e., by deduction), it does use custom and habit to draw connections. Moreover, once a scientific result has been obtained by induction, it does not stop there, since theoretical modelling may be able to add understanding. Also, future observations either agree with the explanation and add confidence to it or they disagree, in which case the explanation is either modified to take account of the new result or it is thrown over and a new explanation is sought.

Falsifiability

It is clear that, with the exception of pure mathematical theorems, a *scientific theory can never be proved true*, since there is always the possibility of future arguments, experiments, or observations that disprove it. This led the philosopher Karl Popper[9] to suggest instead that a theory should be 'falsifiable', i.e., that it should be inherently disprovable before it can become accepted as scientific. No number of positive experiments can prove a scientific theory, but a single negative one can disprove it.

The implication is that, if a theory is falsifiable and supported with evidence, then it can temporarily be accepted as true. For example, Newton's theory of gravitation was accepted as true for several hundred years since it fitted the evidence. Then Einstein's theory of relativity made new falsifiable predictions concerning gravitational lensing of light and the precession of Mercury, which were later shown to agree with observations. As a result, Newton's theory was replaced by Einstein's theory under conditions of extreme gravity or relativistic speeds, although it remains acceptable outside these conditions since it is simpler.

Many physical scientists accept falsifiability as a tenet. For example, some have suggested that the idea of a 'multiverse' is not testable and so it has a lower status than falsifiable theories. However, the criterion of falsifiability has its limitations. It is not applicable to many aspects of social science, nor to observational or descriptive results. Furthermore, often scientists do not in practice try to work out how a theory could be falsifiable in order to add credence to it. It is certainly true that scientists are only too aware that their work is transitory and could be supplanted in future. But credence is added in practice not by showing the falsifiability of a theory but by finding new evidence and new reason that lends support to it. Another point is that in practice, science often advances not by falsifying theories, but by showing that a theory needs to be developed or generalized in order fully to account for new observations. In such cases, the theory is modified or expanded rather than discarded.

Just as Christianity cannot be scientifically proved to be true, so also it cannot be proved to be false.[10] In spite of not being falsifiable, it does have one aspect in common with scientific theories, namely, that faith implies that it can be temporarily accepted. There is the possibility that it might be shown to be inconsistent with experience in future, but for the time being it may be accepted until that happens.

'Doing science': Consistency, paradigms, laws, faith, and community

Scientific truth is often described in terms of theoretical models and scientific laws, but these are nearly always provisional and approximate and so never equate to 'absolute truth' but often give approximations to or windows on the Truth. The hope is that, as science evolves, the models will become closer to the Truth. We have noted above that scientists can never say their theory (for solar flares or black holes, say) is *true*; all they can say is that the theory is *consistent* with the observations of the time. New observations either support a theory or lead to a minor revision of it or disprove it, but they never prove it, since it is always open to possible disproof in future.

SCIENCES AND TRUTH: A SCIENTIST'S VIEW

As more observations appear, the theoretical models are usually improved and modified by adding in extra effects and making the model more sophisticated. Very occasionally, the new observations or understanding show the previous approach to be completely wrong, so that, as Thomas Kuhn[11] realized, a *paradigm shift* is needed and a radically new theory is developed. Sometimes, the paradigm shift means the previous understanding has very little value, as for instance when Newton's theory of gravitation replaced Aristotle's idea that balls fall because they have a natural tendency and desire to seek the earth's centre. Often, however, the paradigm shift implies that the former model is still applicable, but only under a restricted range of parameters: thus Newton's laws continue to be relevant for many circumstances, but need to be replaced by general relativity when travelling at relativistic speeds and by a quantum theory at very small scales. In other words, scientific truth has the subtle quality that any scientific statement holds only when appropriate conditions, assumptions and limitations hold.

Although (as we have seen) scientific results are always provisional, since they may be modified or even overturned by new insights, there is a big difference between results that are part of the *scientific mainstream*, which are very unlikely to be overturned, and those that are at the *frontiers* of knowledge and are far from being well established. The ways that ideas become well established are by being repeated and examined closely, and by finding consistency with new observations or experiments and experience. Of course, mainstream ideas are still open to being changed, but they are less likely to change than frontier hypotheses.

It is worth noting that the unfortunate habit of calling scientific principles '*laws*' originated in the sixteenth and seventeenth centuries and continued throughout the nineteenth, but the word 'law' is too rigid, since it tends to suggest a result that is set in stone. Rather, scientific ideas are always provisional and open to change. For example, Newton's laws are now located in a broader theory that reveals the limits of their application, and the same is true of Faraday's and Ampère's laws of electromagnetism. Preferable to 'laws' are the words '*principles*', '*theories*' or '*theoretical models*', or, when the ideas are highly tentative, '*scientific hypotheses*'.

From the above, it will be clear that a sense of *community*, as well as faith in the methods of science and the workings of that community, are crucial in the search for scientific truth. Whereas some scientific endeavours are undertaken by individuals, most are now the product of teams or groups of scientists, sometimes in twos or threes but occasionally in teams of hundreds or thousands. Often it is the diversity of talents and experiences that enables a group to make much more progress than a single scientist. The creative spark at the core of scientific discoveries can appear out of nothing to an individual or it can occur during discussions when 'two or three are gathered together' who respect each other and have an extensive shared understanding as well as their own unique insights.

A further aspect of the dynamic of a scientific community is the way discoveries are communicated via publications, talks and discussions. This is a prerequisite for the checking and validation of novel ideas by the community, a 'community of verifiers', as Michael Polanyi (1962) puts it. In this way, a new result or idea can start out at the fringes of knowledge (where all is uncertain and unvalidated) and become accepted as part of mainstream science (where it may remain for a long time). Indeed, the Truth to which the practice of science guides us is crucially shaped by the insights of other scientists, namely, by what Polanyi called the 'community of explorers'.

It is clear that researchers are not simply automata or detached observers, recording observations like machines. Rather, they exercise skill in the pursuit of their craft: skill which has been gained through instruction, training and practice, so that scientific discovery is an art. Polanyi felt that pure scientific objectivity, completely detached from the person who is making a discovery, is not what happens in practice. For him, the idea of such objectivity had evolved from the rationalism of the Enlightenment and has undermined the commitment of the enlightened scientist to transcendent values of seeking Truth, liberty and justice. He stressed the role of personal judgement and commitment in the practice of science. Examples of the personal dimension to knowing include choosing the questions to tackle, assessing the reliability of measurements, developing skills and theories, as well as being driven by hunches, commitment and a longing for discovery.

For Polanyi, personal does not just mean subjective, which could tend towards relativism. Rather, scientists are committed to the belief that there is indeed a hidden reality waiting to be discovered. They are on a quest for Truth, but their current understanding is not yet complete and is open to correction in future. Such openness to new insights is a hallmark of scientists as they move forward in faith, personal responsibility and hope.

This brings us to the topic of the reproducibility of scientific experiments. Such experiments are often regarded as 'objective': if I conduct an experiment and obtain a particular result, then it is assumed that if you conduct the same experiment under the same conditions, you will obtain the same result. However, insofar as our skills may not be identical and you may interpret the results in a different way, there is a personal component to science, as mentioned above. In the field of quantum physics, too, the dominant Copenhagen interpretation of quantum phenomena is one of many interpretations of the data and emphasizes the role of an observer in bringing about events at the quantum level.

Of course, there are many other aspects of the conduct of research, such as its funding and the question of career progression, assessment and peer review, as well as political and governmental choices in what areas of research are to be funded. Such broader social constraints influence the ways in which scientists operate, but they have no direct bearing on the methodology of science, or on the orientation of science towards the pursuit of Truth.

Communicating the philosophy and results of sciences to non-scientists is an important responsibility, but it can only be done in general terms, since the techniques and tools of science are highly specialized. For example, it may take more than ten years of study of mathematics to reach the deep level of understanding of the mathematical underpinning for the theory of black holes or for the origin of sunspots. Nevertheless, the best scientists will be able to communicate the essential significance of their subjects to a wider audience.

Links with theology: Books of nature and Scripture, beauty, reason, and revelation

In the past (such as, for example, in the seventeenth century when the Royal Society was founded), many scientists regarded their role as a sacred responsibility, being inspired and motivated to try and understand the nature of God's universe using the minds and talents God has given them, motivated by the belief that the universe is orderly, good and worthy of study. Indeed, the sciences can be regarded as a means that God has given us to grow in understanding of Truth and reality. This view stems from the idea that God's revelation is contained in two books: the book of Scripture and the book of nature. Indeed, it was partly the Western church reformers' replacement of an allegorical approach to the Bible with a literal one that encouraged a scientific approach to the book of nature in the sixteenth and seventeenth centuries.[12]

In this search for Truth, scientists today often experience beauty, wonder, mystery, humility, and a sense of being carried along on a voyage of discovery[13] guided by the promptings of the Holy Spirit. Some scientists have a sense of spirituality without being attracted to traditional religion. Others do not share such beliefs, but it is possible they are indeed being guided by the Holy Spirit without realizing it.

Since (on this understanding) scientific truth is part of Truth, when religious and scientific truth are understood properly they must either be responses to different questions or be consistent with one another. When they appear to contradict one another, there is a responsibility to ask whether the religious or scientific understanding is at fault; to determine, for example, whether a given question (such as the existence of climate change or the evolution of life or of the universe) is a scientific rather than a religious question, and vice versa. It is not acceptable just blindly to reject one or the other. In such apparent contradictions, it is therefore important to be aware of the domains of scientific and religious thought and the types of questions they address.

A further helpful link with theology is the interplay of reason and revelation. Many scientific discoveries result from a combination of reason (in the form of theoretical modelling using mathematics) and revelation (in the form of observation or experiment). The metaphor of 'revelation' is used here to describe the result of an observation or experiment in the sense that it is a truth from the book of nature waiting to be revealed. Even when a discovery appears to be purely by revelation (such as the discovery of a black hole or a planet around a star), there is often a background of theoretical modelling that has played a role, so that data can be theory-laden.[14] Indeed, both the interpretation of a new observation or experiment and the motivation for making it are often deeply embedded in the theoretical understanding of the time.[15] Since science is a human activity, the biases of the scientist may affect the conduct of an experiment, but the aim is always to be as objective as possible, so that others may be able to verify the results.

In other cases, it is reason that leads to revelation: for example, one of the most brilliant advances was the proposal of a new equation by Paul Dirac in 1928 that generalizes Schrödinger's famous equation of quantum mechanics to incorporate special relativity. This 'Dirac equation' implied the existence of a new particle called a *positron*, which is the anti-particle of an electron and possesses a positive charge. The predicted positron was later discovered experimentally in 1932 and led to the realization that there must be a host of other anti-particles for every normal particle.

Conclusion: Sciences, belief, and truth

From the above, we have seen:

- 'Sciences' is a preferable term to 'science', since they cover a very wide range of fields which adopt a wide range of different methods of study.

- Neither of the overly objective or subjective approaches of 'scientism' or 'postmodernism', respectively, have appeal to most scientists as a means of explaining many phenomena.
- Rather, most scientists are 'critical realists', who are searching for absolute truth (i.e., Truth), but who nevertheless recognize that their current understanding is provisional and open to change.
- Mainstream science is unlikely to change but may occasionally suffer a major paradigm shift; the frontiers of knowledge are by their nature rapidly evolving with openness to change being part of their very nature.
- Scientists also tend to be 'methodological naturalists', who adopt the methods of science when pursuing their science, but who may be open to theological insights for non-scientific aspects of their life.
- When addressing purely scientific questions such as 'Is the global temperature of the earth increasing?' or 'Have humans evolved over millions of years?' the preferable approach is to ask the specialists in those sciences for answers and to respect their answers, but the scientists themselves need to earn that respect and to communicate widely the significance and philosophy of their results.
- Faith, trust, and belief are important attributes of scientists: faith that the universe is orderly, good, and worthy of study; trust in the integrity of other scientists; and belief in the intelligibility of the universe as it follows the same rules as in the past.
- In addition, openness, beauty, wonder, and a sense of community are key aspects that lie at the core of much science.
- The conflict model for the relation between science and religion is now regarded as outmoded, and so a more appealing model for many is a unified one, in which the sciences and humanities (including theology) form a rainbow tapestry of rich diversity that is united in its search for understanding using a combination of reason and imagination.

Thus, most scientists, as critical realists, are searching for scientific truth as part of absolute Truth, sitting in between the extremes of scientism and postmodernism. They acknowledge the provisional nature of their scientific results, and also follow T. S. Eliot and St Paul in hoping their results are related to reality but will become closer (or asymptote) to the Truth as time proceeds.

Furthermore, they accept the complementary roles of reason, revelation, and imagination, which weave their ways through this chapter, and an understanding that the practice of science demands faith and a believing spirit. Finally, the current limited understanding of the mysterious nature of space, time, and matter, as well as the origin of the universe, the origin of life and the nature of consciousness, will, to be sure, continue to inspire us in a search for understanding God's wonderful universe.

The aim of this chapter has been to give a personal view, shared by many scientists who are also Christians, of what it is to be a scientist and how to seek Truth. The next chapter explores other philosophical, literary and theological aspects of the subject.

Questions for discussion

1 Would you describe the relations between science and religion as being in conflict, complementary, or unified? Why?
2 Describe and compare the activities of doing scientific research and painting a work of art.
3 Describe the origin and evolution of the universe and of life from both a scientific viewpoint and a theological viewpoint.
4 What are the roles of science and of religion in your life?

Further reading

I. Barbour, *Religion and Science: Historical and Contemporary Issues* (New York: Harper One, 1997). A classic in the study of science and religion by one of its pioneers.

T. McLeish, *Faith and Wisdom in Science* (Oxford: Oxford University Press, 2014). Starting with the book of Job and ancient wisdom literature, this leads to a unified account of faith and science that suggests science is a deeply religious activity.

M. Polanyi, *Personal Knowledge: Towards a Post-Critical Philosophy* (London: Routledge, 1962). An account by an eminent scientist about the art of knowing and the role of personal beliefs in scientific activity.

E. Priest, *Reason and Wonder: Why Science and Faith Need Each Other* (London: SPCK, 2016). A proposal that the sciences and humanities be regarded as part of an integrated whole, together with chapters by an eminent collection of scientists, philosophers and theologians on the relation between science and faith.

Notes

1 T. S. Eliot, *Four Quartets* (Boston: Harcourt, 1943).
2 M. Planck, *Where is Science Going?* (New York: Norton, 1932).
3 G. H. Hardy, *A Mathematician's Apology* (Cambridge: Cambridge University Press, 1940).

4 T. Torrance, *Theological Science* (Oxford: Oxford University Press, 1969).

5 J. Polkinghorne, *Science and Christian Belief* (London: SPCK, 1994).

6 A. Peacock, *God and Science: A Quest for Christian Credibility* (London: SCM Press, 1996).

7 E. Wigner, 'The Unreasonable Effectiveness of Mathematics in the Natural Sciences', in *Communications in Pure and Applied Mathematics*, vol. 13 (New York: John Wiley & Sons, 1960), pp. 1–14.

8 E. Priest, *Reason and Wonder: Why Science and Faith Need Each Other* (London: SPCK, 2016).

9 K. Popper, *The Logic of Scientific Discovery* (New York: Basic Books, 1959).

10 But compare with Chapter 5 (Hart), and the discussion concerning J. H. Newman's *The Grammar of Assent*.

11 T. Kuhn, *The Structure of Scientific Revolutions* (Chicago: University of Chicago Press, 1962).

12 P. Harrison, *The Fall of Man and the Foundations of Science* (Cambridge: Cambridge University Press, 2007).

13 See, for example, T. McLeish, *Faith and Wisdom in Science*, Oxford: Oxford University Press, and E. Priest, *Reason and Wonder: Why Science and Faith Need Each Other* (London: SPCK, 2016).

14 T. Kuhn, *The Structure of Scientific Revolutions*.

15 M. Polanyi, *Personal Knowledge: Towards a Post-Critical Philosophy* (London: Routledge, 1962).

11

Sciences and Truths: A Theologian's View

MICHAEL FULLER

> The good thing about science is that it's true whether or not you believe in it. (Neil deGrasse Tyson)

The principal assumption of the last chapter – that scientists see themselves as pursuing truth – has been strikingly borne out by research carried out in the USA. (Interestingly, this research has also noted that scientists there express a wide range of responses to religions, and to the notion of the spiritual, and that a wide range of responses towards the sciences is similarly expressed by people who identify as religious.)[1] This chapter explores two further – and radically different – ways of thinking about science and truth which are regularly encountered in the twenty-first century West. The first is that science is the *only* way in which truth can be ascertained – and, moreover, that the sciences are of necessity opposed to all other outlooks on life, such as religious outlooks. The second is that science embodies particular (Western, Enlightenment) values, and cannot claim any especially privileged position when commenting on issues like truth. This chapter then goes on to ask: How can dialogue between those holding different views come about? If there are different understandings of truth, must those espousing them necessarily be at loggerheads with one another?

The first of the views above is nicely caught in the celebrated aphorism of the contemporary American astrophysicist Neil deGrasse Tyson which stands at the head of this chapter. The popularity of this comment is such that it has appeared as a slogan on T-shirts. It expresses clearly the idea that science straightforwardly generates 'truth', and that it is to be contrasted with 'belief'. Let us begin by unpacking this slogan, and the assumptions that lie behind it.

Tyson's statement clearly assumes that there is a single thing called 'science', and that this is an uncontested term with a clear and unambiguous meaning. Another is that science is a means of establishing 'truth' (although no indication is given of what the content of such truth might look like, or what the criteria for judging truth might be, or what – if any – constraints there might be around truth obtained through scientific means). Then there is the assumption that science is something which is entirely independent of 'belief', and which (presumably) can be contrasted with things that do require belief (implicit here is the understanding that 'science' is to be contrasted with 'religion', the former being concerned with 'facts' and the latter with 'beliefs'). But are any of these assumptions actually 'true'? What do we mean when we talk about 'science'? Is science capable of establishing truth? If it is, what kinds of truth is it capable of revealing? And is science entirely independent of belief? Are there, in fact, unstated (and possibly unconscious) beliefs which underpin the assumptions and practices of science?

Science or sciences?

Consider the question of what is meant by the word 'science'. Some responses to this question might be as follows. (i) Science is some all-encompassing and all-sufficient metaphysical system, which can answer any question which it is sensible to ask. (This is a position which is known as 'scientism'.) Alternatively, (ii) science might be considered as a methodology, a way of studying the world; or, perhaps, (iii) as a means of establishing truth over falsehood, and fact over opinion; or simply (iv) as an understanding of the material world as operating solely under the physical and other laws of nature.

I will deal with scientism later. What of the idea (ii), that 'science' consists of a variety of studies united by a common method? In fact, as Eric Priest has pointed out in the previous chapter, there are many 'sciences', which differ from one another not just in their object of study but also in the method(s) which they use in approaching and analysing that object. From particle physicists who conduct experiments in hi-tech accelerators, to palaeontologists who attempt to fit fossil finds into an evolutionary narrative, to social scientists who try to elucidate aspects of human thought and behaviour using tools such as questionnaires and focus group, to data scientists who sift huge quantities of data in attempts to derive useful information from them, the range of activities conducted under the umbrella term 'science', and the range of methodologies used in prosecuting them, are extremely broad, and varying degrees of certainty may be attached to their findings – and hence to any truths which they might be said to convey.

It has been maintained that the contemporary use of the term 'science' brings together activities which have in the past been considered under two separate headings: natural philosophy and natural history.[2]

Broadly, natural philosophy, as pursued from ancient times until the eighteenth century, was an attempt to understand how things function, with a view to predicting how they will behave in the future: it was about the elucidation of laws governing the behaviour of material objects. Newton's *Principia* of 1687 – 'The Mathematical Principles of Natural Philosophy', to give it its full title – might been seen as a climax of this pursuit; and the natural sciences – physics and chemistry – continue it today. Natural history was concerned with seeking an understanding of how things have come to be the way they are: it was about the interrelatedness of things. Evolutionary science, geology, and archaeology continue this pursuit. (In contrast to natural philosophy and natural history, the term *scientia* in the past simply referred to an ordered or systematized body of knowledge, which might relate to any subject: it included disciplines we would now place in the domain of the humanities, such as music, philosophy, or theology.) So, from the outset of the modern (post-Enlightenment) use of the word 'science' it has combined different approaches and sought to understand different things about the objects of its study. The idea that there can be a single 'scientific method' is therefore inevitably problematic.

What about (iii), understanding science as a means of establishing truth? As we shall see in the next section, this also requires qualification. Least problematic of the understandings above is to treat 'science' in sense (iv), as an understanding of the natural world which sees it as operating solely through physical processes. However, we may immediately note two things relating to this understanding: first, that it may be considered to be a *belief* about the natural world (it is an assumption, not something which has been demonstrated in any way); and second, that this assumption excludes from the outset any consideration of engagement with 'spiritual' or other realities from a scientific perspective (although from the assumption that we may study the natural world in this way it does not, of course, follow that such realities do not exist).

Does the scientific method establish truth?

The physical sciences are often considered to be the paradigm of a scientific approach to the world. How do they work, in practice? It is often assumed that such scientists construct theories, from which they derive hypotheses which can be tested experimentally. They then conduct repeatable experiments, from which objective data about the phenomenon being studied ('scientific facts') may be obtained through a process of observation; and these data enable them to refine and develop their hypotheses, so that a greater understanding of that phenomenon is produced. A number of critiques of this method may be raised, some theoretical and some practical.

The sort of approach described here – undertaking many observations, and establishing reliable laws on the basis of them – is known as the inductive method. David Hume's criticisms of this method in the eighteenth century, and the response by Karl Popper to those criticisms in the twentieth, have been rehearsed in the previous chapter. Popper's novel way of thinking about science – that instead of a 'scientific fact' being considered as something that *has* been proved *true*, it should be considered to be something that *may* be proved *false* – has found widespread acceptance (although it has not been without its critics[3]). In other words, scientific ideas are distinguished from non-scientific ones by virtue of their being testable and, through testing, being falsifiable. So, for example, a theory about (say) the behaviour of particles in a magnetic field may be tested (given the right kind of equipment and an adequate budget): it is therefore a scientific theory (which may or may not continue to be verified by such testing). On the other hand, a theory about, say, the existence of an afterlife may not be tested, and is therefore not a scientific theory (not that it is necessarily any the worse for that).

Given that any truth generated by scientific processes is, by this understanding, only provisional, and liable to be overturned by future experiments, Popper coined the term 'verisimilitude' to describe the goal of scientific endeavour. We may not attain to absolute *truth* through the method associated with scientific investigation, but we may come to greater and greater degrees of verisimilitude in the ways in which our understanding maps onto physical reality.

It is also worth noting that the individual scientific practitioners are not simply automata, recording observations in the way machines would do so. Rather, they exercise practical *skill* in the pursuit of their craft: skill which has been gained through instruction, training and practice. This instruction and training effectively constitutes an apprenticeship, which itself will imbue the neophyte with particular values and beliefs. Eric Priest has drawn attention, in the previous chapter, to the important work of Michael Polanyi concerning the role played by individuals in the practice of science. Polanyi commented that 'making sense of experience is a skillful act which impresses the personal participation of the scientist on the resultant knowledge'.[4] This suggests that insofar as the skills and training of scientists may not be identical, there is an irreducibly subjective component to the harvesting of scientific data. This component may be a negligibly small one in the case of the physical sciences; it may be considerably more significant in the case of the historical or social sciences, where the past experience of a scientist may play an important role in the harvesting of data, or in its careful interpretation. Any truth which that data reveals may be considered to be imbued with particular values and emphases which its interlocutor brings to the observations which they have made. (This may be seen particularly clearly in the work of today's data scientists, in their efforts to extract meaningful information from extremely large and heterogeneous datasets.[5])

Are there beliefs involved in the practice of science?

Most of the time, of course, experiments do not overturn the findings of the past. This is because most of the time scientists are doing what the philosopher Thomas Kuhn referred to as 'normal science': that is to say, science conducted according to the norms and expectations embedded in the thought-world, or paradigm, within which they are operating.[6] Periodically results obtained in experiments will violate the expectations generated by this paradigm: if such results accumulate, and are confirmed, this leads to what Kuhn called a 'crisis' period in which various possible new paradigms capable of explaining the new results jostle one another for acceptance. Eventually one of these finds general approval and there is a 'paradigm shift' towards it, following which 'normal science' continues within this new paradigm. (In so far as a paradigm generates what we might term 'lower-case-t truths', this means that we might consider such truths to shift too, as paradigms do.)

Kuhn's understanding of scientific progress has also been much criticized,[7] but he draws our attention to the fact that scientists operate within a set of guiding assumptions, or beliefs, about the object(s) of their investigation. These beliefs are shared by the 'scientific community', and may or may not be obvious to individual scientific practitioners, depending on the extent to which they question the presuppositions of that community. Kuhn's approach also draws attention to the way in which disputes over competing paradigms are resolved not simply through appeals to reason or logic (since different paradigms may themselves have different understandings of what reason and logic are), but may involve factors such as aesthetics (for example, the better of two competing understandings is often held to be the one which is the simpler of the two).

There is a further practical issue around the way in which science is conducted. Even if an experiment is in theory repeatable, in practice many are never repeated. This is for the simple and practical reason that research is expensive and time-consuming, and most scientific practitioners (naturally enough) are more concerned about pursuing new work than reproducing what someone else has already done. Given this, it is striking to note that the Royal Society, a major force in the driving forward of science in the UK since its foundation in 1660, has as its motto *Nullius in verba*, which may be translated as 'take nobody's word for it'. Although this is clearly an exhortation to accept as true only those things one has verified for oneself, few, if any, scientific practitioners are in a position to take that exhortation literally today; they must proceed on the basis of trusting that reports produced by their colleagues are true. (As one might expect, misconduct in this matter, such as the misreporting or even the fabrication of results, is treated with the greatest severity by the scientific community.) This might be reckoned as another crucial aspect of the belief which necessarily lies at the heart of scientific practice: belief in the trustworthiness of colleagues.

Reality

What of the nature of the reality which the sciences investigate, and of the theories by which we attempt to understand it? How is that reality 'captured' by a scientific theory? Do such theories give us direct access to some capital-T Truth about the way the universe is – access to some quasi-Platonic world of eternal verities? Or are they simply human constructs, allowing us to make sense of the observations that we make but having no direct relation to anything 'out there'? The distinction between these positions is sometimes referred to as 'realist' versus 'non-realist' understandings of science. It is nicely caught by the question: do we *discover* reality, or do we *construct* or *invent* it?

The qualifications on scientific knowledge indicated by Popper have led many to assume that a straightforwardly realist view is untenable: any understanding of the world we gain through scientific activity is provisional, and liable to correction in the light of future experiments. On the other hand, there are aspects of scientific experience which militate against a fully non-realist perspective. It is sometimes observed that models devised to account for one aspect of what we observe can also account for other, apparently unrelated, phenomena, suggesting that our models are not purely arbitrary. For reasons such as these, many have inclined to a form of 'critical realism' in science: recognizing the provisionality of our models, but believing them also to be in some way related to a reality 'out there' to which it is possible for us to have access. Critical realism underscores the conclusion that the sciences are able to access aspects of truth about the natural world, even if our understandings of them are always liable to revision. Some commentators have further urged that critical realist thinking of this kind resonates powerfully with religious thinking about the existence and nature of God, who is presumed to be a real entity 'out there', but regarding whom our knowledge can only be partial, and revisable. This position, championed influentially by Ian Barbour,[8] has been adopted by many other commentators in the field of science and religion, although it has also been subject to serious criticism.[9]

An alternative approach has been developed by Nancy Cartwright, who argues against the realist insistence 'that the laws of our best sciences are true or are approaching the truth ... [and] that they are "few in number", "simple" and "all-embracing"', suggesting rather that 'the laws that are the best candidates for being literally true ... are numerous and diverse, complicated and limited in scope'.[10] Cartwright therefore argues for an understanding of reality that is 'dappled', in which knowledge gleaned through a variety of disciplines using a variety of approaches is combined in efforts to solve 'real-world' problems, without straitjacketing it into a single framework.

Truth or truths? The role of narrative

In simple terms, we have so far been looking at the idea of 'scientific truth' in more or less realist terms; that is to say, we have assumed there to be some reality 'out there', some capital-T Truth, to which the sciences might afford at least some partial access. (And as we have seen, this is the assumption of most scientists.) Another way of thinking about truth is that it is something which is constructed by human beings in particular contexts, leading to many understandings of truth which may or may not relate to an absolute Truth beyond ourselves.

Let us return to the ways in which sciences are pursued. We have seen that these will involve observation and the collection of data. (Depending on the science in question, those observations may consist of anything from a reading on a meter in a laboratory to the collection of a fossil on a field trip.) In short, observations generate data. But those data in and of themselves do not *mean* anything: their meaning only becomes apparent when they are understood within the paradigm within which the scientist interprets them. In other words, any truth which a piece of data (of whatever kind) may be said to contain is contingent on the narrative into which it is placed. When Einstein interpreted the photoelectric effect in terms of the quantization of light, he framed his interpretation in terms of a story about the corpuscular nature of light. Observations about the diffraction of light are framed in terms of a story about the wave-like nature of light. (Stories do not have to be mutually compatible for them to make sense in their own terms. In the Christian context, it can readily be seen that there are inconsistencies in biblical narratives: for example, on one occasion the risen Jesus appears to be incorporeal, in that he appears without warning in a locked room (John 20:26), yet on another his physicality is stressed through his eating with his disciples (Luke 24:42–43). Whatever a resurrected body is like, it is clearly different to the bodies we normally encounter.)

In thinking about how we develop an understanding of truth, we can therefore see that a crucial role is played by *narrative* – by the way in which we join together data in order to enable a comprehensible and meaningful story to be told. A reading made by experimenters at the Large Hadron Collider at CERN means nothing until it is fitted into a story which allows it to be interpreted as indicative of the presence of a particle which might produce such a reading. A fragment of bone uncovered on an archaeological dig in Africa means nothing until it is fitted into a story which allows it to be interpreted as part of the mandible of an early hominin. On a grander scale, narratives allow us to bring together, and make sense of, many diverse aspects of our lives.

Some scientific popularizers believe that 'science' should be understood as such a narrative: that 'science', understood as an overarching grand narrative, is a means of explaining everything that is worthy of explanation. Such a narrative is set out by sociologist Christian Smith (and contrasted by him with other narratives, such as religious ones) in the following terms:

> For most of human history, people have lived in the darkness of ignorance and tradition, driven by fear, believing in superstitions. Priests and lords preyed on such ignorance, and life was wearisome and short. Ever so gradually, however, and often at great cost, inventive men have endeavoured better to understand the natural world around them. Centuries of such inquiry eventually led to a marvellous Scientific Revolution that radically transformed our methods of understanding nature. What we know now as a result is based on objective observation, empirical fact, and rational analysis. With each passing decade, science reveals increasingly more about the earth, our bodies, our minds. We have come to possess the power to transform nature and ourselves. We can fortify health, relieve suffering, and prolong life. Science is close to understanding the secret of life and maybe eternal life itself. Of course, forces of ignorance, fear, irrationality and blind faith still threaten the progress of science. But

they must be resisted at all costs. For unfettered science is our only hope for true enlightenment and happiness.[11]

Smith calls this 'the scientific enlightenment narrative'. It is a narrative which informs the lives of many people in the West today. It accounts for a lot of things, facilitated by its Whiggish approach to history – an approach to history which sees it as progressive, with all past events leading inexorably upwards to the present day – and by the way in which it expresses a particular vision of what reason is (and of how that vision of reason has overcome other narratives). It can be very helpful in allowing people to construct a framework within which to order their lives. However, it can lead to the position known as scientism: the understanding that science is the *only* correct means by which to interpret *all* the phenomena we experience. Anything, such as a religion, which attempts any alternative explanations is then by definition wrong.

Against the scientistic view, it has been argued that science should not be seen as in any way privileged as a means of describing and engaging with the world. Paul Feyerabend was a particularly vocal writer in this respect, commenting that 'Knowledge is a local commodity designed to satisfy local needs and to solve local problems ... Orthodox "science", in this view, is one institution among many, not the one and only repository of sound information'.[12] How, then, can science relate to Truth? For Feyerabend it cannot: scientists 'insinuate that their standards are *essential* for arriving at the Truth, or for getting Results ... [but] science is only one of the many instruments people invented to cope with their surroundings. It is not the only one, it is not infallible, and it has become too powerful, too pushy and too dangerous to be left on its own'.[13] This view may be seen as an expression of the postmodern understanding that expresses a distrust of all 'master-narratives' which claim exclusive access to 'truth'.[14] Critics like Feyerabend maintain that science itself has come to be seen as such a master-narrative, imposing its own understanding on all aspects of human life whether or not it is sensible to do so, and distorting human experience by insisting that it be understood through one particular lens. (Of course, the view that there are many narratives, none of which can claim ultimate superiority over others, is itself a narrative, which allows other narratives to be understood in relation to each other and to it. Feyerabend might be criticized for failing to make clear that a relativizing narrative such as his cannot claim to have any 'master-narrative' status itself: it is just one more narrative alongside the rest.)

In short, it is possible to have coherent, reasonable and strongly-held views that might (on the one hand) place science on a unique pedestal when it comes to ascertaining matters of truth, and (on the other) dismiss it as simply one view among many. Where does one go from here? Who is 'right'?

Kuhn observed that scientists inhabiting different paradigms may not be able to communicate with one another, since they are effectively speaking different languages.[15] In a similar fashion, it is very difficult for someone deeply embedded in a narrative such as the scientistic narrative to communicate with someone outside it. That defines the terms of engagement by assuming (for example) that there is no God, and that there could never be evidence for the existence of God. Indeed, Richard Dawkins has defined 'faith' as 'a state of mind that leads people to believe something – it doesn't matter what – *in the total absence of supporting evidence*' (my italics).[16] Dawkins understands the concept of 'evidence' in a particular way, as it might be understood in the context of a scientific experiment. But the evidence a believer in something – it doesn't matter what – is likely to advance in support of their belief may well not be of this scientific kind. They might point to personal experience, or to 'gut feelings', or to the testimony of others whom they consider reliable; all of which can dismissed as evidence by a scientistic narrative, and attributed to (respectively) delusion, indigestion, and gullibility (*nullius in verba*!).

Smith makes the important point that 'what *is* evidence is *itself* largely made significant, if not constituted for us, by our narratives'[17]: in other words, the narrative you inhabit does not only shape the world you live in, it is self-reinforcing because it admits as relevant to your life only those bits of evidence which support the narrative. A scientific narrative cannot admit the evidential role of instinct, say – unless, of course, it can give a naturalistic account of what instinct is. (Incidentally, this is why we are bombarded with stories about how this, that or the other bit of human behaviour is 'evolutionarily advantageous', or 'determined by our genes': indeed, attempts have even been made to explain belief in God by such means.[18] This is because it is the only way in which a scientistic paradigm can admit the reality of such behaviour – by fitting it, however uncomfortably, into a narrative that allows it to be 'explained'. Narratives not only indicate the nature of truth for those who inhabit them: they dictate the way(s) in which it may be reached, too.)

All this suggests that there can be radical difficulties in communication where such issues as truth are concerned, because the truth of something may be seen differently from within different narratives. Those difficulties can become problems if the desire to communicate becomes swamped by the desire to have one narrative definitively prevail over another. Decrying those who inhabit a different narrative for believing in 'fake news', for example, or for being a 'climate change denier', will only deepen their suspicion that the news others believe to be fake is in fact trustworthy, or that climate change is not real. A deeply corrosive consequence of this is an erosion of mutual trust, and the possible arising of unscrupulous individuals who exploit such erosion for their own personal or political ends.

Can there be communication between narratives?

Where does this leave someone who (like the present writer) believes that, irrespective of the status accorded to truths supported by scientific means, there is in fact a Truth which can be accessed by humans – a Truth which is bound up in the revelation brought by the one who said, 'I am the way, and the truth, and the life' (John 14:6)? To be sure, that Truth can be known by any individual only partially and imperfectly: 'For now we see in a mirror, dimly', as St Paul put it (1 Cor. 13:12); but we may still claim to have some apprehension of it. Might it not be urged that we simply inhabit a narrative, like anyone else; a narrative that shapes not only how we order and give expression to our experiences in the world around us, but which also guides and informs our ongoing encounters with that world in such a way as to confirm and reinforce that narrative?

The answer to that question can only be: yes, of course we inhabit such a narrative. And, while our justification for inhabiting it will vary from person to person, most will doubtless offer a reason for it along the lines of: this is a narrative which fits with every aspect of my life; a narrative which not only allows me to appreciate the achievements of human reason, as expressed in the sciences, but also to understand a bigger picture into which these achievements fit. This bigger picture allows me to integrate aspects of my life and experience, my thoughts and feelings, which the sciences cannot always address, including those subjective phenomena that are only accessible to me, as a conscious individual. It also allows me to understand and appreciate those experiences of love, joy, awe, wonder, and peace (and, likewise, of sadness, pain, and loss), which you can never fully access or account for, because they are *my* experiences.

How might my (or any other) worldview be communicated to you? There can be no straightforward way of doing this. Your experiences will be different from mine: you may find other worldviews fit better with them. What I can do is listen with humility and respect to you, in the expectation that you will similarly listen to my account of the worldview that generates 'the hope that is within me' (cf. 1 Pet. 3:15). One of the tragedies of the 'post-truth' age we now inhabit is that a readiness to listen to others in this way appears to be in short supply, as people close down the possibilities for dialogue. There is an alarming extent to which advocates of scientism simply refuse to listen to (or wilfully ignore) the views of religious advocates (the God Delusion!), just as 'Brexiters' in the UK refuse to listen to 'Remainers' (Project Fear!), and supporters of the current US President refuse to listen to his opponents (Fake News!) – and of course the blame for a breakdown in communication can equally be attributed the other way, in all these cases. But divisions between individuals, and within societies, cannot be understood – let alone healed – in this way. The genuine exchange of ideas requires flexibility, openness, goodwill, and respect on both sides, and without such an exchange a genuinely pluralist society is impossible. Not only that: without such an exchange no one's view, no matter how harmful to social cohesion or planetary well-being it may be, will ever be changed. The remark attributed to Aneurin Bevan, 'This is my truth, tell me yours', might perhaps serve as a helpful maxim in enabling such conversations to take place. Perhaps a mutually-recognized truth can best be approached through such patient conversations.

But the genuine communication of understanding between people is likely to involve far more than the exchange of words or arguments: what we *do* can be as effective in this respect as what we *say*. 'Preach the gospel at all times: if necessary, use words', St Francis of Assisi is alleged to have said: as the New Testament Letter of James puts it, 'I by my works will show you my faith' (James 2:18).

Conclusion: science, belief, and truth

We saw in the last chapter that some people (including many, if not most, scientists) see science as a means to access an eternal capital-T Truth, which they may see in Platonic or even in theological terms (indeed, in the past some scientists have understood their vocation as 'thinking God's thoughts after him', as the astronomer Johannes Kepler (1571–1630) expressed it). The present chapter has identified and discussed a Scylla and Charybdis that may follow from either the over-enthusiastic acceptance or the outright rejection of this view. On the one hand, those espousing scientistic positions assert that truth is the preserve of science alone, and that anything to which the label 'truth' can be applied can and must be founded on a scientific approach. On the other hand, some people question science, seeing it as a 'master-narrative' which embodies a particular Western Enlightenment understanding of notions such as truth, fact, and evidence. Science (such thinkers might maintain) has become equated with a particular kind of materialist metaphysics, in a narrative which sets it on a collision course with other narratives (such as those of religions); in fact, none of these can claim privileged access to truth, since all rest on unprovable metaphysical assumptions.

I suggest that the most helpful way of thinking about the relationship between science and truth sits in between the extremes outlined above. One can question the claim made by some, that science is potentially capable of addressing every question which humans might sensibly wish to ask, quite reasonably feeling that Richard Dawkins' dismissal of 'why is there something rather than nothing?' as a 'vacuous existential question'[19] simply will not do. One can accept the critiques of Popper and others, noting the provisionality of the relationship between the knowledge and understanding generated by the sciences and any form of absolute truth. However, one can also have serious reservations about extreme forms of cultural relativism, which dismiss science as having nothing truly objective to say to us about the physical world around us – and hence about the nature of truth, in so far as this finds expression in that physical world.

Returning to the Tyson slogan with which I began, perhaps this might more accurately be rendered: 'The good thing about science is that it is a generally effective means of approaching the truth about some natural phenomena, which itself requires belief in unprovable assumptions.' (This would, of course, require small print or a very large T-shirt; but it is the unfortunate nature of a slogan to prioritize brevity over accuracy.) More helpful, though, in a 'post-truth' age, would be a slogan affirming the radical need for mutual respect and trust between those advocating competing truths. I leave it to the reader of this chapter to devise one.

Questions for discussion

1 How persuasive (or otherwise) do you find either scientific or postmodern approaches to truth? Why?
2 How would you give an account of the narrative you inhabit (a) to a fellow-traveller, and (b) to someone coming from a different perspective?

Further reading

J. H. Brooke, *Science and Religion: Some historical perspectives* (Cambridge: Cambridge University Press, 1991). A book which gave a huge boost to scholarly work on the history of the relationships between science and religion, advancing what was subsequently dubbed Brooke's 'complexity thesis' as a more accurate way of thinking about those relationships than the much-touted 'conflict thesis'.

N. Cartwright, *The Dappled World: A study in the boundaries of science* (Cambridge: Cambridge University Press, 1999). A philosopher advocates an approach to science that eschews uniform understandings of science in favour of a 'patchwork of laws' model.

P. Harrison, *The Territories of Science and Religion* (Chicago: University of Chicago Press, 2015). A careful, and occasionally provocative, work which helpfully probes the roots of the perceived antagonism of science and religion.

W. H. Newton-Smith, *The Rationality of Science* (London: Routledge, 1990). A helpful critique of some of the classic thinkers in the philosophy of science, including Popper, Kuhn, and Feyerabend.

C. Smith, *Moral, Believing Animals* (Oxford: Oxford University Press, 2003). A contemporary sociologist explores (inter alia) the ways in which narratives shape how we understand the world around us – including the beliefs of others.

Notes

1 See E. H. Ecklund, *Science vs. Religion: What Scientists Really Think* (Oxford: Oxford University Press, 2012) esp. Chapter 1; and E. H. Ecklund and C. P. Scheitle, *Religion vs. Science: What Religious People Really Think* (Oxford: Oxford University Press, 2018).

2 See P. Harrison, *The Territories of Science and Religion* (Chicago: University of Chicago Press, 2015), p. 3.

3 See, for example, W. H. Newton-Smith, *The Rationality of Science* (London: Routledge, 1990), esp. chapter III.

4 M. Polanyi, *Personal Knowledge* (London: Routledge, 1962), p. 62.

5 See M. Fuller, 'Big Data: New science, new challenges, new dialogical opportunities', *Zygon* vol. 50 no. 3 (2015), pp. 569–82.

6 See T. S. Kuhn, *The Structure of Scientific Revolutions*, 2nd edn (Chicago: University of Chicago Press, 1970).

7 See, for example, Newton-Smith, *The Rationality of Science*, esp. chapter V.

8 I. G. Barbour, *Religion and Science: Historical and Contemporary Issues* (London: SCM Press, 1998), pp. 115ff.

9 See, for example, N. H. Gregersen, 'Critical Realism and other Realisms', in R. J. Russell (ed.), *Fifty Years in Science and Religion: Ian G. Barbour and his Legacy* (Aldershot: Ashgate, 2004).

10 N. Cartwright, *The Dappled World: A study in the boundaries of science* (Cambridge: Cambridge University Press, 1999), p. 10.

11 C. Smith, *Moral, Believing Animals* (Oxford: Oxford University Press, 2003), p. 71.

12 P. Feyerabend, *Farewell to Reason* (London: Verso, 1987), p. 28.

13 P. Feyerabend, *Against Method*, rev. edn (London: Verso, 1988), p. 166.

14 Cf. Lyotard's definition of 'postmodernity' as 'incredulity toward meta-narratives' (J.-F. Lyotard, *The Postmodern Condition: A Report on Knowledge*,

trans. G. Bennington and B. Massumi (Manchester: Manchester University Press, 1984), p. xxiv.

15 Kuhn, *The Structure of Scientific Revolutions*, pp. 149 ff.

16 R. Dawkins, *The Selfish Gene*, new edn (Oxford: Oxford University Press, 1989), p. 330.

17 Smith, *Moral, Believing Animals*, p. 87.

18 See J. L. Barrett, *Cognitive Science, Religion and Theology* (West Conshohocken: Templeton Press, 2011) for an example of such an approach.

19 R. Dawkins, *River out of Eden* (London: Phoenix, 1996), p. 113.

12

Today's Church and the Politics of Post-Truth

ALISON JASPER

Lying, deceiving, and 'being economical with the truth' are not new ideas within the minority world communities of the so-called West[1] in spite of the sense in which a discourse of 'post-truth' that has, in part, inspired this collection, has emerged recently. In its ancient literature – including the Bible – there are many 'trickster figures' who mislead and lie in order to gain some advantage for themselves or their kin. Think of the figure of Abram, whose, arguably, somewhat disreputable trick is to procure the family's future by offering his wife Sarai to Pharaoh in the guise of his marriageable sister (Genesis 12). Or there is the story of Rebecca helping Jacob to disguise himself in order to cheat his brother Esau out of his birthright (Genesis 27). Nor is this just characteristic of the ways in which the human characters behave in the Bible. It is clear enough that YHWH is sometimes participating as trickster-figure-in-chief, within these ancient story cycles[2] as providential ends are being divinely shaped. Sometimes, certainly, in the Bible, there is also condemnation, for example, of deceit for personal gain: King David is called to account by the prophet Nathan when he schemes to kill a man through trickery so that he can take his wife, Bathsheba (2 Samuel 11). Ahab is similarly pulled up by the prophet Elijah because of his trickery in having Naboth killed so that he can take the man's vineyard (1 Kings 21). In the New Testament, Jesus speaks out against the deceptions and tricksome hypocrisies of the authorities of the day (Matt. 23:27):

> Woe to you, scribes and Pharisees, hypocrites! For you are like white-washed tombs, which on the outside look beautiful, but on the inside they are full of the bones of the dead and of all kinds of filth.

He warns his listeners against those liars who dress themselves as prophets in sheep's clothing 'but inwardly are ravenous wolves' (Matt. 7:15).

It would appear however that, as readers of the Bible, we are, millennia before the age of President Trump, nevertheless familiar with a world in which truth is lauded as a principle or value but often faked by the unscrupulous. 'You shall not bear false witness against your neighbour' might be one of the Ten Commandments (Exod. 20:16), but our culture is, and has been for centuries, laced with a full range of irony, fibbing, dissimulating, spinning, and manipulation. That this ambivalence seeps into the texts of the Bible is, therefore, perhaps only to be expected. Representations of a world in which there is only ever unadulterated truth on the one hand and unadulterated falsehood on the other, fail to measure up to the real and actual complexities of human living and dying on this planet.

One of these complexities emerges during the period of what might be called modernity, a period in broad terms stretching forward in the minority world from the Renaissance into the European Enlightenment and up to the present. During this time a kind of knowledge has gained currency in which truth doesn't need divine authorization. It is empirically verified – something apparently much clearer and more transparent than reference to forms of revelation. This we commonly refer to today as scientific truth[3]. The prestige of this scientific methodology – often invoked with little understanding of the far from clear and transparent translations involved in reaching its conclusions[4] – has been powerfully advanced by its relationship with industrial technologies. They have delivered significant benefits and riches to some humans. At the same time, by expanding human capacities to use up the world's resources they have also contributed to an accelerating rate of devastations and extinctions affecting many others[5] both human and non-human.

One consequence of these changes in our approach to truth is the extent to which a degree of feeling or subjectivity implicit in the process of assessing truth has become clearer. In those parts of the world of the eighteenth and nineteenth centuries that were inheritors – as colonial or unwilling subjects – of Christian thought and culture, this was exemplified in challenges or approaches to the sacred authority of the biblical text; making its fictional narratives, ironies, fantasies, fables, and symbols explicit, laying them bare in a more scientific manner on the dissecting tables of higher criticism.[6] The subjectivity implicit in our reading of the Bible, and the evidence that many of its claims could not stand up to standards of empirical proof, has been enough to discredit it for many. Thus the biblical text has become ever more detached from our shared language of cultural symbols and crowded out of our understandings of the sacred. In consequence we have lost sight of the ways in which our discourse as a whole depends upon subjective factors. Not everything is established in our hearts and minds through simple reference to scientific methodology, though people sometimes act as if subjective assumptions can be eradicated from our understanding of the truth just by shutting up the Bible and closing down church buildings. In fact, we still value and trust in a whole range of objects, people, ideas, institutions, and idealizations (liberty, capital, humanity, democracy, and human rights, to name a few) that are not substantiated for us by scientific methods. In many ways, our behaviours and assumptions, in respect of a so-called modern secular world, conform to the same model as those belonging, in the past, to the biblical view of the world. We stick with them because we have some evidence but principally because we believe they deliver order, continuity, justice, or profit. In other words we think we have moved from the age of faith to the age of reason but actually we have not done so, at least not entirely. More than this, we frequently fail to notice how scientific 'truth' is itself ruled and directed by human desire. We work obsessively to discover the truth about human cancers for example, but we learn much less of truths about the flourishing of insects or sea critters[7] that seem to us to be unconnected with human life or living.

Another characteristic of the more recent situation in which we find ourselves perplexed by questions of truth, has been the emergence of a feminist critique and this refers back to a focus in this book on the contexts within which truth is defined, As women have come out from the shadows cast by societies geared to the interests of men, the truth has to be seen in relation to these differently gendered contexts. One problem is that women's access to the truth is still routinely blocked by the circulation of authoritative (un/truthful?) stories that cast doubt on women as subjects worthy of equal respect. Activists for women's rights have demanded that they should have equal access to the goods that truth implies: justice, fairness, integrity, and honesty from those in public office. but stories are still being told about how women are untrustworthy witnesses.[8] In contexts formed and dominated by elite men in the minority world,

> women who allege sexual violence or harassment will almost certainly face one of two lines of argument: 'he said/she said' or 'nobody really knows what happened', both of which ... signal that the pursuit of truth will be abandoned as 'unknowable'.[9]

In a male dominated society, the judicial system – the system for establishing truth – often discounts women's voices as a matter of course. In one recent high-profile case in the United States (September 2018), alleging historical sexual assault against Judge Brett Kavanaugh, Dr Christine Blasey Ford drew on her own academic expertise as a professor of psychology to support her claim that because trauma results in highly selective memory,[10] she could remember the actions and voices of her assailants but not how she arrived at the place of her attack or how she returned home. This is not just the voice of one woman. There is a body of work available to support the idea that victims of sexual abuse and violent assault may suffer a whole range of effects that impair their capacity to revisit or assess their experiences.[11] None of this prevented President Donald Trump from publicly ridiculing Dr Ford, undermining her trustworthiness as a witness, because she could not remember all the events surrounding the alleged assault.[12]

It is not surprising, then, that the feminist philosopher of science Donna Haraway is so interested in stories, when we see that those that predominate within the culture as a whole can be so damaging to the truth. Haraway believes passionately – and believes as a scientist[13] – that ongoing critical interrogation of the kinds of stories within which we frame our notions of truth is absolutely vital. She would say that even science is not about replacing an unproblematic lie with new unassailable truth. Even they have to go on changing the stories because it is human scientists and not some kind of idealized and essentialized, 'cold hard facts' that frame actions and drive what we do to achieve actual flourishing or destruction. Our story-telling is the expression of our imaginary capacities to grasp or fail to grasp what is new, different and crucially, truer, juster, fairer, and more honestly a reflection of the totality of our changing experiences. For this reason, Haraway is strongly attracted by the genre of science or speculative fiction and by some of its authors. As one exponent, whom Haraway admires, says:

> fantasists are perhaps trying to assert and explore a larger reality than we now allow ourselves. They are trying to restore the sense – to regain the knowledge – that there is somewhere else, anywhere else, where other people may live another kind of life.
>
> The literature of imagination, even when tragic, is reassuring, not necessarily in the sense of offering nostalgic comfort, but because it offers a world large enough to contain alternatives and therefore offers hope.[14]

We live in a time of intensifying environmental fragility but the point made here by the writer Ursula Le Guin is not so much that we do not know what to do about it, but that the stories in which our most precious assumptions and values are embedded sometimes act to prevent us. Haraway, taking up the same line, reflects that a desire for gripping stories,[15] may be sustaining a reluctance to accept a different, less dramatic call to engage in the 'attentive practices of thought, love, rage and care'[16] that might really help us, in the words of the title of her book, to 'stay with the trouble'. Her message overall is that this is a far better way to deal with the current 'urgency' as she understands the term, resisting both naïve faith in technofixes (Christian or otherwise) or defeatism.[17] She[18] draws in this book on the work of Michael Klare:

> [who] details the large and growing global national and corporate investments in renewables; clearly, there are big profit and power advantages to be had in this sector. And at the same time, every imaginable, and many unimaginable, technologies and strategic measures are being pursued by all the big global players to extract every last calorie of fossil carbon, at whatever depth and in whatever formations of sand, mud, or rock, and with whatever horrors of travel to distribution and use points, to burn before someone else gets at that calorie and burns it first in the great prick story of the first and the last beautiful words and weapons.

In what Klare calls the Age of Unconventional Oil and Gas, hydrofracking is the tip of the (melting) iceberg: 'Melting of the polar seas, terrible for polar bears and for coastal peoples, is very good for big competitive military, exploration, drilling, and tanker shipping across the northern passages.'[19]

The gripping (and true/actual) story referenced here is not dissimilar to the fictional case described by Le Guin in relation to the skillful hunters of prehistoric times who – maybe – came 'staggering back with a load of meat, a lot of ivory, and a story' that was a lot more interesting than the story of how 'I wrested a wild-oat seed from its husk, and then another, and then another, and then another and then another …'[20] As she says, '[i]t wasn't the meat that made the difference. It was the story.'[21]

So, the point to take from these reflections is that what we think and the kind of stories we tell, truly matter.[22] Representing only certain perspectives or contextualized framings, one single thought or story will not do for the truth of all our futures or all our living and dying well. In the present time, called the Anthropocene,[23] though for Haraway the term is over-dramatic and much too anthropocentric, the truths of environmental fragility are frequently sidelined. They may be sidelined by the dramatic story of the deals we can or cannot make through the exploitation of our environment, or because we have convinced ourselves that they are not issues we need to or are able to address.

Over the centuries, some Christians, claiming that final salvation is not material or earthly anyway, have bought into this version. Isabelle Stengers, philosopher of science, cautions her readers[24] that

> [t]he sciences, as they are taught, that is, as they are presented once their results are unlinked from the practices of science 'as it is practiced,' do not have a meaning that is appreciably different from a religious engine of war, point out the path to salvation, condemning sin and idolatry.

In other words, what Stengers sees in science, as she has seen in some forms of institutional Christianity in the minority world, is a kind of striving for domination – closing down all the spaces for negotiation, conversation, or questioning and, instead, drawing attention to the speakers and their sources of seeming unchallengeability. It is another form of Haraway's 'prick story'. Yet Stengers had also observed a 'passion for truth'[25] in the scientific community that could not be gainsaid and that she did not dispute. And so, she looks instead for ways of upholding truths 'that are not hierarchical and polemical,'[26] bringing us back to another of the key themes of this book: that there are different kinds of truth.

This then, as a premise for exploring truth and the church, is to claim that the question of truth still matters profoundly to us, but also that some root and branch thinking is desperately needed to change the framework of domination within which it is commonly understood. The practice of Christian theology – like that of the practice of much science – is always getting caught up in a lethal kind of human hierarchical exceptionalism that has the effect of stopping humans from finding ways to be properly 'at home in the universe'.[27] Drawing on the philosophy of Whitehead which stresses an understanding of God as mutable and responsive in a changing world, theologian Catherine Keller and philosophers of science Stengers and Prigogine challenge the way in which theologians and scientists alike tend to understand 'nature' as 'stripped of any property that permits man to identify himself with the ancient harmony of natural "becoming".'[28] In other words, what we need to understand about truth and the church is, arguably, that neither of these concepts can be usefully understood in the present 'urgency' as standing still or standing apart; truth cannot be hitched up to something unchanging, unaltered, unaffected. And this is likely to be a hard point to digest in contexts where '[a] dominological Christianity had branded any deep sense of belonging within the flux as pagan, irrational – and chaotic. Science superseded and mirrored the ontotheology of timeless truth'.[29] In other words the central claim I am making here is that truth is always within relationships – and not fixed and eternal. This is a difficult idea for many, perhaps most Christians brought up with a traditional view of God's nature as rigidly fixed: non-temporal (eternal), unchanging (immutable), and unaffected by the world (impassible). Yet even in a world in which there is evil, pain, and suffering, why should such unchanging characteristics necessarily serve us better, given that our vulnerability is as much the root of our capacity to truly love and be affected by each other as to suffer violence?

To sum up at this point, in relation to the politics of post-truth, I have suggested, looking at the work of scientists as well as storytellers, that the church needs to take its stories in hand. This is not, as is sometimes implied in media features or casual conversation, because its stories do not any longer measure up to standards of 'scientific truth'. Rather it is to say that the truth to which the church is committed theologically can only be maintained by a commitment to constant critical challenge, imaginative thinking and rethinking, and considered practices, seeking out alternatives that offer warning and hope in a world that does not stand still. One of the ways in which liberation theologians in particular have claimed that the churches' stories might need to change – going back to Stengers' point – is in respect to those concepts of domination and hierarchy. A highly gendered form of domination is still inextricably entangled in its language, worship, imagery, and theology, not to speak of its institutional framing and praxis. Its stories also encompass exactly the sense of (male) human entitlement that Haraway contests so strongly. These are the stories of 'the hunter', 'on a quest to kill and bring back the terrible bounty'[30] or the 'prick stories' already referred to. There may still be scope for these exciting tales of the hunter or perhaps of the saviour hero, but, as Haraway says, what do they say meantime about all the others? Huge swathes of non-human animals, plants, organisms and materials are hereby simply cast as 'in the way, to be overcome, to be the road, the conduit, but not the traveller, not the begetter'.[31] And there is a great deal of evidence already to illustrate how this exceptionalism, with its roots in some ways in certain interpretations of Gen. 1:28–29 as a rationale for human exploitation of the non-human world, has already damaged our earthly home.

A different way to look at traditionally all-important biblical and theological storytelling is, perhaps, in terms of 'the carrier bag theory' of literature as suggested originally by Elizabeth Fisher.[32] Biblical stories can be these kinds of (non-plastic, recyclable) carrier bags too – intended to carry home all the potatoes you have dug up and cannot eat at once.[33] This could be roughly translated as all the possible meanings and interpretations that are not revealed at a first reading which might itself be quite a nice definition of biblical revelation more broadly. We have seen, for example, how feminist theologians and biblical critics have reread the story of Eve, disgraced for centuries if not millennia as 'the devil's gateway'[34] and the ultimate cause of all the trouble including the death of Christ, to generate stories of her wisdom, her desire for knowledge, her initiative, and her in-tuneness with the divine.[35] They have done the same with the uppity Syro-Phoenician woman who impels Jesus into taking a helpful new step into new and difficult territory.[36] They have put the stories of God as midwife [37] and as the tehomic/amniotic waters of creation[38] into this bag and scooped up narrative seeds for growing stories about outsiders, misfits, and sexual non-conformers.[39] Perhaps in the light of Haraway's work we could even throw in a sympoietics[40] of yeast and bacteria at work in all kinds of breaking down and recombining, including bread and wine. We also need new and other stories too; living conduits challenging toxic monopolies. Memories of the past need to be preserved, respected, and brought to mind because they establish belonging and preserve a wisdom. At the same time, memories also need to be made anew and projects of cross-species' co-operation and of living and dying well[41] provide hope. Perhaps to protect us from hurt, loss and death, we would be better off with fewer heroes, hunters and Lords – of whatever gender – and more storytelling to keep our notions and communities/communions of truth-telling alive and functioning.

So what does this mean for post-truth and the politics of the church? First a very little about me and about any claim I might have to contribute to this volume. I have a long association with the Scottish Episcopal Church and community. It fostered my academic career in theology and a certain poetics as well as ethical values and emotional resonances. Over the last thirty years I have worked to exclude from my theological reflection and writing the politics (and accompanying polemics) of domination to which I believe the title of this chapter implicitly refers. As a Christian feminist theologian, the task has been about challenging an overwhelming and now, arguably in the current urgency, an anachronistic obsession with demonstrating mastery and defeating – in contrast to engaging with – the opposition. In this scenario, neither party can represent the truth on its own. Even when this mastery is configured as opposition to suffering, pain, and environmental disaster, the terror of what is different and other that is reflected in much traditional apocalyptic imagery and theology emphasizes for me a misogynistic and human exceptionalism.[42] In these contexts, the claim to 'truth' seems just to become another stick with which to beat others/the Other into submission or just another story with which to demonize what we struggle to understand or account for in our experience. Christianity, I would argue, is founded on an incarnational insight and I identify with the legacy of Christian thought embedded in the statement that the Word became flesh. Yet I would say that this fertile mystery represents, for me, neither light unalloyed nor the 'darkness of religion'[43] but a call to address what reason, logic and the evidence of my senses is telling me in new stories and old stories retold, about a theology of becoming and of living and dying well alongside all my fellow human beings and companions.

An example taken from Haraway's book helps bring together some of the points I have been making about telling stories and thinking about truth in the context of the church. Key ideas in what I have said have focused on the relational context of different understandings of truth, commitment to critical thinking-through truth as a notion associated with power in a changing world and my own attempt to dismantle talk about God and truth within frameworks of domination – patriarchal and human exceptionalist in particular. The point of the example – Haraway's chapter on pigeons, called 'Playing String Figures with Companion Species' – is to make clear how incredibly complex are the connections and threads that set up a particular story; in this case a story about how potentially sustainable, collective interlinking experiences and interdependencies of species and critters could be managed – respecting the truth as it relates to all participants. What is crucial in this chapter is that Haraway's description of projects linking pigeons and humans not excluding the possibilities of others being involved, challenges any attempt to privilege a particular perception of the truth of these relationships. It addresses the sense in which the complexity of the stories about possible connections – in churches within changing human societies as in concentrations of pigeons in changing human societies – demands constant critical rethinking, decentring, realigning. Yet it also rings with a kind of hopefulness based on the thought that through negotiation and 'a kind of care for one another' we do not need to deny or demonize different (true) stories.

Haraway (p. 27) describes a small project in 'hatching control' set up in Batman Park in Melbourne, Australia. The park is a small reclaimed strip alongside the Yarra river that was part of the Wurundjeri people's territory before the white settlers arrived and took the land for the Crown, destroying the wetlands. It is now host to part of the city's attempts to manage feral pigeons – descendants of those brought by the first European settlers – and consists in a pigeon loft of 200 nesting boxes in which these urban so-called 'rats of the sky' can roost. Those who enjoy feeding the pigeons have ample encouragement to do so in this specific site but not elsewhere. The eggs are very largely removed and replaced by artificial ones. The birds produce a modest but constant supply of pigeon manure that people are free to take away. As Haraway (p. 29) suggests:

> the municipal pigeon tower certainly cannot undo unequal treaties, conquest, and wetland destruction; but it is nonetheless a possible thread in a pattern for ongoing, non-innocent, interrogative, multi-species getting on together.

This example points a willingness to exercise the kind of muscle critical for caring about flourishing to which Haraway (p. 29) refers in her view of a kind of truth that does not seek to dominate or exclude but to discover more about how we can, in truth, live together in this time of environmental fragility.

The Bible is a collection of texts written long before our current exigencies in terms of social and environmental changes. But as I indicated at the start, it does not reflect a world of unassailable, privileged notions of the truth since it too is marked with the tell-tale signs of truth's non-innocence – its implication in the messiness and compromise of daily living and dying. In thinking about how the Scottish Episcopal Church travels forward, therefore, I believe we should not shy away from these difficult texts in which truth is lauded as a principle but cannot be entirely protected from the corrupting impact of the unscrupulous both within the texts and within their reading communities. And we may also need some entirely new stories to try out for the new times.

Questions for discussion

1. What stories/passages in the Bible most reflect for you a complexity of assumptions and attitudes towards the truth? And which biblical passages/stories offer you the most assurance of truth? In what ways is it possible to reconcile these two insights on your own (or your 'biblical reading community's') biblical reading?
2. In one of her non-fiction essays on the work of writing fantasy literature ('The Critics, The Monsters and the Fantasists'), Ursula Le Guin talks about 'the limitations and falsity of ordinary perception' (Le Guin, 2018, p. 314). What ordinary perceptions would you most like to challenge in the name of truth and why?

Further reading/viewing

D. Haraway, *Staying with the Trouble: Making Kin in the Chthulucene* (Durham NC: Duke University Press, 2016). The chapter about pigeons, to which I refer at the end of my own chapter above, is Chapter 1, 'Playing String Figures with Companion Species', pp. 9–29. Science fiction aficionados might also enjoy Chapter 8, 'The Camille Stories: Children of Compost', pp. 134–68, which is in some ways a work of science fiction.

D. Haraway, 'SF: String Figures, Multispecies Muddles, Staying with the Trouble' https://www.youtube.com/watch?v=Z1uTVnhIHS8, 2014 (last accessed 27 November 2018). Haraway is a lively speaker. It might suit some readers better to try to engage with aspects of the same work electronically.

L. Gilmore, *Tainted Witness: Why We Doubt What Women Say about Their Lives* (New York: Columbia University Press, 2017). This is a relatively short work focussing on some particularly egregious cases in which women's testimony to bullying or sexual assault was denied or down-played. Although it was published in 2017, it can be read profitably as a commentary on the recent case concerning Judge Brett Kavanaugh and Dr Christine Blasey Ford as discussed in the chapter above.

U. K. Le Guin, *Dreams Must Explain Themselves: The Selected Non-Fiction of Ursula K. Le Guin* (London: Gollancz, 2018). Lovers of science fiction and SF related ideas might also enjoy browsing through this compendium of Le Guin's non-fiction. The essay to which I make reference in this chapter is called 'The Carrier Bag Theory of Fiction', pp. 158–62.

Y. Sherwood, and A. Fisk, (eds), *The Bible and Feminism: Remapping the Field* (Oxford: Oxford University Press, 2017). This is a good and recent introduction to feminist biblical hermeneutics.

Notes

1 It is difficult to make references to broad geo-cultural areas without encoding within these descriptions structures of power and privilege. The terms 'west' and 'western' have long been critiqued from the perspective of those who see the binary east/west as informed by a colonial history. By using 'minority world' here I intend simply to make a little more visible my own geo-cultural roots within a context of disproportionate power and privilege, identified with most of northern Europe, northern America and other Anglophone communities.

2 See J. E. Anderson, *Jacob and the Divine Trickster: A Theology of Deception and YHWH's Fidelity to the Ancestral Promise in the Jacob Cycle (Siphrut)* (Waco TX: Baylor University Press, 2011).

3 For a more extended view of the role of modern science in relation to truth see Chapter 10 (Priest) and Chapter 11 (Fuller).

4 See B. Latour, *Pandora's Hope: An Essay on the Reality of Science Studies* (Cambridge MA: Harvard University Press, 1999).

5 For some figures on the current rate of extinctions see http://wwf.panda.org/our_work/biodiversity/biodiversity/. See also the work of ecological philosopher and multispecies ethnographer, Thom Van Dooren, and the Extinction Studies group: http://extinctionstudies.org.

6 See I. Strenski, *Thinking about Religion* (Oxford: Blackwell Publishing, 2006); D. Jasper, *A Short Introduction to Hermeneutics* (Louisville, London: Westminster John Knox Press, 2004); J. Zimmermann, *A Very Short Introduction to Hermeneutics* (Oxford: Oxford University Press, 2015).

7 D. Haraway, *Staying with the Trouble: Making Kin in the Chthulucene* (Durham NC: Duke University Press, 2016), p. 169 n.1. Haraway uses the term 'critters' to include 'microbes, plants, animals, humans and non-humans, and sometimes even ... machines'. It reflects her concern to avoid human exceptionalism.

8 See L. Gilmore, *Tainted Witness: Why We Doubt What Women Say about Their Lives* (New York: Columbia University Press, 2017).

9 https://www.timeshighereducation.com/books/review-tainted-witness-why-we-doubt-what-women-say-about-their-lives-leigh-gilmore-columbia-university-press (last accessed 4 November 2018).

10 http://time.com/5408567/christine-blasey-ford-science-of-memory/ (last accessed 4 November 2018).

11 See S. Ullman, C. J. Najdowski, and H. H. Filipas, 'Post-Traumatic Stress Disorder and Substance Use: Predictors of Revictimization in Adult Sexual Assaults,' *Journal of Child Sexual Abuse*, Vol 18 (2009), 367–85: Samiera Saliba, 'Rape by the System: The Existence and Effects of Sexual Abuse of Women in United States Prisons,' *Hastings Race and Poverty Law Journal*, Vol. 10 (Summer 2013), 293–326: H. Feeney, R. Campbell, and D. Cairn, 'Do You Wish to Prosecute the Person Who Assaulted You?: Untested Sexual Assault Kits and Victim Notification of Rape Survivors Assaulted as Adolescents,' *Victims and Offenders: An International Journal of Evidence-based Research Policy and Practice*, Vol. 13 (5) (2018), 651–74.

12 https://www.theguardian.com/us-news/2018/oct/02/trump-mocks-christine-blasey-ford-at-mississippi-rally (last accessed 4 November 2018).

13 See also above, Chapter 11 (Fuller).

14 U. K. Le Guin, 'The Critics, the Monsters and the Fantasists,' in *Dreams Must Explain Themselves: The Selected Non-Fiction of Ursula K. Le Guin* (London: Gollancz, 2018), pp. 318–19.

15 Ibid., p. 163.
16 D. Haraway, *Staying with the Trouble*, p. 56.
17 Ibid., pp. 3–4.
18 Ibid., p. 46.
19 Ibid., p. 46.
20 Le Guin, 'The Critics, the Monsters and the Fantasists,' p. 163.
21 Ibid., p. 163.
22 Haraway, op.cit., p. 39.
23 Ibid., pp. 44–47.
24 Isabelle Stengers, *Cosmopolitics 1*. Trans. Robert Bononno (Minneapolis: University of Minnesota Press, 1997), p. 25.
25 Ibid., p. 24.
26 Ibid., p. 20.
27 C. Keller, *Face of the Deep: A Theology of Becoming* (London: Routledge, 2003), p. 190.
28 Ibid., p. 190; Ilya Prigogine, and Isabelle Stengers, [1984] *Order Out of Chaos: Man's New Dialogue with Nature* (London: Verso, 2018), p. 51.
29 Prigogine and Stengers, op. cit., p. 51.
30 Haraway, op. cit., p. 118.

31 Ibid., p. 118.

32 Le Guin, op. cit., p. 165.

33 Ibid., p. 165.

34 Tertullian, *De Cultu Feminarum*, 1, 1, in Migne, *Patrologia Latina* (Paris, 1944), cited by O'Falain and Martines, *Not in God's Image* (London: Virago, 1979), p. 14.

35 See P. Trible, 'Eve and Adam: Genesis 2—3 Reread,' in C. P. Christ and J. Plaskow eds, *Womanspirit Rising: A feminist Reader in Religion* (San Francisco: Harper, 1973), pp. 74–83; Caitlín Matthews, *Sophia Goddess of Wisdom, Bride of God* (Wheaton Illinois: Quest Books, 2001).

36 S. Ringe, 'A Gentile Woman's Story' in A. Loades, *Feminist Theology: A Reader* (London: SPCK, 1990), pp. 49–56.

37 L. Juliana M. Claassens, *Mourner, Mother, Midwife: Reimagining God's Delivering Presence in the Old Testament* (Louisville KY: Westminster John Knox Press, 2012).

38 Keller, *Face of the Deep*.

39 N. L. Eisland, *The Disabled God: Toward a Liberatory Theology of Disability* (Nashville: Abingdon Press, 1994); M. Althaus-Reid, *The Queer God* (London: Routledge, 2003); L. Isherwood, *The Fat Jesus: Feminist Explorations in Boundaries and Transgressions* (London: DLT, 2007).

40 Haraway, op. cit., p. 57.

41 Ibid., p. 10.

42 Pippin, *Death and Desire: The Rhetoric of Gender in the Apocalypse of John* (Louisville, KY: WJK Press, 1992): Pippin, *Apocalyptic Bodies: The Biblical End of the World in Text and Image* (London: Routledge, 1999); Donna Haraway, *Modest_Witness@Second_Millenium.FemaleMan©_Meets_OncoMouse™ : Feminism and Technoscience* (New York: Routledge, 1997).

43 Mayra Rivera, *Poetics of the Flesh* (Durham NC: Duke University Press, 2015), p. 19.

Afterword

JOCHEN SCHMIDT

In a post-truth era, it is ostensibly worthwhile to resort to the virtue of truthfulness. Many passages in this book reference virtue implicitly and explicitly, e.g. when 'truth and the continuances of virtue' are discussed (David Jasper), or when *aletheia* in the sense of an 'integrity of character' (Nicholas Taylor, Robert A. Gillies) or 'justice, fairness, integrity, and honesty' (Alison Jasper) and the need for mutual respect among those who advocate competing truths (Michael Fuller) are being referred to. The book also references the 'commitment one makes in the pursuit of truth' (Scott Robertson). In my brief Afterword to the book, I would like to take up this thread of thought and explore the virtue of truthfulness, which many authors of the book reference in their contributions (e.g. Nicholas Taylor, Scott Robertson, Jenny Wright). While there would be a plethora of responses to be made to the great variety of questions pertaining to truth and post-truth in the book, I decided to focus on this strand of truthfulness, as it appears to be one very important strand of the many contributions. I will argue that the virtue of truthfulness can adapt a range of different tones, and I will distinguish between two kinds of truthfulness in particular – one good and one bad – meaning that one kind of truthfulness is problematic, while the other kind is worth striving for.

Immanuel Kant's discussion of lying is the example that I will give for a problematic account of 'truthfulness'. Kant often refers to the duty not to lie in order to give an example for a moral law that is to be followed under any circumstances (that is, categorically). To lie is to be in conflict with duties that one has towards oneself, towards the other person, and towards humanity. To lie means to cast away one's dignity as a human being. Indeed, even if foreseeable harm is being done as a consequence of telling the truth (e.g. when I reveal the hiding place of someone hiding from unjust persecution), the ensuing injustice is something that I am never to be blamed for, it is solely in the responsibility of those who commit this injustice. Now not only does the example of unjust persecution prove Kant wrong. The claim that lying is always wrong is also at odds with ethical life in many other ways. Political reason, especially when it comes to economic crises, and also professional responsibility on the part of medical physicians, often forces people to negotiate between their responsibility for the common good or the good of the other person, on the one hand, and the value of truthfulness and transparency on the other hand. Even when it comes to intimate relationships, one may argue that we have a right to some privacy, that we are not always obliged to give an exhaustive answer when the other says 'a penny for your thoughts'. We have the right to and the need for a certain distance.

What are the consequences? It would be premature to conclude that there is no obligation to be truthful at all. Perhaps Kant is overdrawing a cause that is nonetheless generally a proper cause. One might claim that Kant is right in demanding that truth always be our main concern in our everyday dealings, home and work life, etc., but that we need to build the possibility of exception into Kant's account. If this were the route we wanted to take, Thomas Aquinas's and Dietrich Bonhoeffer's discussions of the lie, which Robert A. Gillies takes up, could prove helpful as they offered sound criteria for determining when a lie is acceptable or even when it is to be favoured ethically. So we could try to use moderate recourses to truth and somehow negotiate how to allow for exceptions and still stay true to the general Kantian conviction that we may never risk losing the foundation of truth and truthfulness. This kind of negotiation is certainly essential when it comes to dealing with everyday ethical problems that pertain to truth and lying. However, in this paper I will do nothing of that sort. My claim is that to *carry out* such necessary negotiations in concrete societal fields is not what *theological* ethics is about: theology does not have anything to put on either of the two scale pans that are being balanced in these negotiations. For one thing, theology is not committed to the Kantian position at all. It does not follow from biblical and/or theological concepts that there can never be a justification for lying, even if lies are often condemned in theological traditions and even if the truth is a high value in biblical rhetoric. And yet, on the other hand, theological ethics are not responsible for *deconstructing* Kantian ethical demands, either. One may well be tempted to think that the task of Lutheran theology is to make a case for *the good* – i.e. for compassion and solidarity with those who will suffer from rigorous adherence to truth – when *the good* is apparently in conflict with the right as determined by legalistic moral procedures. And yet, again: it is not the task of theological ethics to put weights *either* on the good-over-right scale pan *or* on the right-over-good scale pan. The task of theology is rather to contribute to a culture where human beings are empowered to decide responsibly – both compassionately and calmly – when the good of truthfulness and the good of compassion are in conflict. To be able to decide responsibly in such a situation requires personal qualities that are traditionally called 'virtues'. Now the virtue of truthfulness lies at the core of these respective virtues, but my point here is that the virtue of truthfulness must be embedded in a context of other emotional and cognitive virtues that enable human beings to enact and live the virtue of truthfulness in a way that will be for the good of people. Emotion, which is closely tied to justice, also plays an important role in many of the chapters of this book (e.g. Steven Ballard, Jenny Wright).

A strong normative claim for the demand to be truthful, as I have argued, does not get us anywhere. It is not always right to say the truth, it is not always wise to tell the whole truth, it can even be heartless or indeed plain wrong not to lie under certain circumstances. There is no ultimate yardstick by which to measure what kind of commitment to the truth is right, indeed 'truth is not simply "out there" to be plucked effortlessly like fruit from the tree' (Trevor Hart). This does not mean that truth is not a high value. But it does mean that this value can only be productive when considering how it is embedded in narratives of lives – fictional or 'real' – that demonstrate what integrity, sincerity etc. look like in the mess of everyday life decisions which are hardly ever perfect or clear cut. In an imperfect world, i.e., in a world in which to speak the whole truth is not always morally defensible, we need something like a commitment to truth and truthfulness, we need to ask 'how truth is best served' in face of this uncertainty (Robert A. Gillies), and we need a community that constantly challenges the sincerity of the commitments to truth that its members uphold, and we need moral visions that employ values in narratives that are in touch with the messiness of real moral life, like the biblical narratives.

This community needs to cultivate human qualities that enable us to be truthful in the first place, that is, the courage to be truthful (where truthfulness comes with a cost) and the generosity to let bygones be bygones when people have failed in their genuine, or maybe not so genuine, attempts at balancing the duty to be true and the duty to care for the well-being of other human beings. This would be a culture in which we grant each other credit. This credit works in several ways: first, it can mean treating each other as if each of us were capable of being truthful, i.e., as if we were all able to find sufficient motives within ourselves that incite us to be truthful, and as if we were able to withstand hearing the truth even when it will be hard and painful to do so. It takes courage to do that. It takes trust and courage to credit human beings with the strength to endure the truth. This credit can also work in a second way: it can mean letting each other off the hook of a rigorous demand of truthfulness, to trust that our community will not fall into utter mendacity if we allow ourselves and each other the luxury of suspending the demands of truth under certain circumstances. And finally, this credit will also consist of 'un-binding', releasing ourselves and one another from the weight that we must bear when we have wronged ourselves or someone else by failing to find the proper balance of truthfulness and care for the well-being of the other. To balance the demand for truth on the one side and the demand for compassion and solidarity on the other side is *not* a balance between the *rational* (i.e., the moral demand for truth derived from reason alone) and the emotional (i.e., the feeling of compassion for and solidarity with those for whom the truth may be harmful or hurtful). Either of the scale pans is to be loaded with both emotion and calm, rational deliberation. Compassion towards another can be a terrible adviser if it is not held in check with rational deliberation about what the other person actually needs; recent monographs on empathy have made this point compellingly. At the same time, and this will be my final point, striving for truth and truthfulness is not unemotional, at least if we move beyond Kant's 'cold' absolute demand for truth that is derived from his moral theory. Longing for truth is itself a moral emotion. In Psalm 119:163, the psalmist says: 'I hate and abhor falsehood, but I love your law,' and it seems that Amos expresses a similar idea: 'Hate evil, love good; maintain justice in the courts' (Amos 5:15, NIV). There is at least some evidence that striving for justice and the objection to lies are themselves *emotions*, biblically speaking (even if this claim begs for further exploration in light of the fact that emotions in the Old Testament are depicted as something that takes over the human person from the outside rather than springing from her interiority).[1] This striving is not merely a rational implication from a purely rational categorical imperative, as Kant wants to make us think.

Finally, it is important to bear in mind the role that emotion plays in the post-truth debate. When the Association for the German Language elected the term 'post-truth' as Word of the Year 2016 (just as the Oxford dictionaries had done in the same year), they pointed out in their press-statement that by post-truth they meant a 'felt truth': post-truth means that we still appeal to truth, but emotional factors become dominant when we assess what is true or what we deem to be a lie. It is extremely harmful for democracy when we let our evaluations of alleged 'facts' be hijacked by the emotion that we tie to these facts. And yet, as I pointed out, proper dealings with truth cannot be unemotional. What we need is therefore a cultivation of personal integrity in the sense that our moral emotions and our ability to keep our emotions at a distance are *both* strong and communicating moral forces inside of the moral personality that each of us is. Theory can never solve the question as to how this balance is to be achieved. This is a skill that we learn by trying and failing and trying again, and we do this in a community if we encourage one another to try.

Again, I think theology does not offer any formulae that allow us to pass judgement when it comes to balancing the truth on the one hand and the interests and rights of those who may suffer from the truth on the other hand. Good decisions in dilemma-situations are never developed on a drawing board, they are always embedded in concrete situations, and must rely on a moral person that is rationally fit and emotionally driven to pursue both the truth and the good, particularly when the two seem to be irreconcilable. To hate lies and to love truth does *not* mean automatically to avoid lies at all costs, it means to be driven to be truthful and to be encouraged to tell the truth when truth may come at a high cost. And this allows me to distinguish between two kinds of truthfulness, one good and one bad: bad truthfulness is the ideological, rigorous and uncritical adherence to say what one thinks is true no matter what. Bad truthfulness amounts to falling prey to an ideology of total transparency – as if transparency was going to heal the world from all social ills if only we act out our truthfulness without reserve. Bad truthfulness is very simple and very self-righteous. Good truthfulness in contrast is complicated. It means constantly to cultivate intellectual and emotional competences that may enable us to act well in the messiness of everyday life, when it comes to situations where the truth can be harmful and hurtful. The biblical traditions contain what I would like to call a moral vision of truthful life, as they hail truth without absolutizing it normatively. This moral vision is an idea or an ideal in light of which we grow both as individuals and as communities, not to become perfect but perhaps to create genuine relationships with ourselves and with others. 'Truth,' says Julian Baggini, 'is not a philosophical abstraction. Rather it is central to how we live and make sense of ourselves, the world and each other, day by day.'[2]

Notes

[1] Cf. A. Wagner, 'Gefühle, in Sprache geronnen. Die historische Relativität von Gefühlen am Beispiel von „Hass".' In A. Wagner, *Emotionen, Gefühle und Sprache im Alten Testament. Vier Studien* (Kleine Untersuchungen zur Sprache des Alten Testaments und seiner Umwelt, 7) (Kamen: Hasrtmut Spenner, 2006).

[2] J. Baggini, *A Short History of Truth: Consolations for a post-truth world* (London: Quercus, 2017), p. 108.

Index of Biblical References

Hebrew Bible

Genesis
1:26	88
11:6–8	33
12	177
15:6	4
27	177
42:2	4

Exodus
12:14	90
12:42	90
20:16	178

Deuteronomy
7:9	4
26:8	90
28:59	4

2 Samuel
7:16	4
7:28	5
11	177

1 Kings
8:26	4
19:12	33
21	177
22	5
22:16	5

2 Chronicles
1:9	4
6:17	4

Nehemiah
9:8	4

Psalms
31:5	5
89:29	4
119	5
119:163	193
132:11	5
146:6	5

Proverbs
8:7	5
25:13	4

Isaiah
8:2	4
33:16	4
43:1	5
49:7	4
55:3	4

Jeremiah
9:23	5
15:18	4
23:28	5
26:15	5
26:16–19	5
42:5	4

Ezekiel
11;16	5
18:8	5

Daniel
8:12	6
8:26	5
10:1	5
11.2	5

Amos
5:15	193

Micah
3:12	5

Zechariah
8:16	5

Apocrypha

Tobit
3:8	5
4:6	5

Judith
10:13	6

Ecclesiasticus (Sirach)
44:20	4

INDEX OF BIBLICAL REFERENCES

New Testament

Matthew
7:15	177
16:16	92

Mark
8:29	92
8:36	30
12:4	7
15:38	89

Luke
7:11–17	92
9:20	92
24:42–43	169

John
1:3	85
1:14	84, 85
1:17	84
2:19	86
2:6–21	86
2:21–22	86
3:4	7
3:33	7
5:31	7
8:32–36	6
10:41	7
14:6	1, 172
17:17	84
18:33–38	28–9
18:37–38	84
18:38	ix, 20
20:26	169

Acts of the Apostles
6;14	86
12:9	7
17:22–31	8
20:28	10

Romans
1:2	90
2:20	6
3:3–7	6
10:9–10	92

1 Corinthians
2:14–16	142
13:12	146, 172

2 Corinthians
4:2	6
6:8	7
11:10	6
12:2–4	104

Galatians
2:5	6
2:14	6
3:15–4:7	6

Philippians
1:1	10
2:5	131, 141, 143
2:5–11	92
4:8	7

2 Thessalonians
2:10–12	6

1 Timothy
3:2	10
6:5	6

Titus
1:7	10
1:13	7
1:14	6

James
2:18	173
3:14	7
5:19	7

1 Peter
3:15	172
5:2	7

2 Peter
1:12	6
2:22	7

1 John
2:27	7
4:15	92

2 John
1	7

3 John
3	7
12	7

Revelation
1:4–8	91
4:8	91
4:11	91
5:9–10	91
5:12	91
5:13	91
22:6–21	91

Index of Names and Subjects

Abhishiktananda (Henri le Saux) 102–3, 111
Aletheia 3, 5–6, 7, 22, 190
Alles, Gregory D. 123–4
Almond, Philip 125
Amen 4
Ampère, André-Marie 155
D'Ancona, Matthew 67
Anglicanism 69
Anselm 34
Anthropocene 181
Aristotle 22, 25, 152
Art of the Novel, The (Kundera) 17–18
Augustine of Hippo 43, 89, 111, 137–8
Ayer, A. J. 3

Babel, Tower of 36, 47
Bach, Johann Sebastian 150
Bacon, Francis 20
Baggini, Julian 17, 194
Barbour, Ian 149, 168
Barmen Declaration 62
Barr, James 94
Barth, Karl 115
Bauckham, Richard 77
Bauder, W. 141–2
Beethoven, Ludwig van 116
Belhar Confession (South Africa) 62–3
Bethge, Eberhard 141
Bevan, Aneurin 173

Blackburn, Simon x, 22, 26
Bok, S. 132
Bonhoeffer, Dietrich 62, 131, 137, 139–41, 142–3, 191
Book of Common Prayer 135
Brave New World (Huxley) 20
Brief History of Time, A (Hawking) 11
Brittain, Vera 23
Bultmann, Rudolf 96
Busch, Eberhard 62

Caillois, Roger 19, 20
Cartwright, Nancy 168
CERN (European Organisation for Nuclear Research) 169
Chekhov, Anton 28
Clinton, Bill 132
Cloud of Unknowing, The 108
Coherence theory 21
Coleridge, Samuel Taylor 27
Confessing Church in Germany 62
Confessions (Augustine) 43
Correspondence theory 21
Critical realism 167–8
Critique of Pure Reason, The (Kant) 118
Crumpher, Peter 63
Culture and Value (Wittgenstein) 43, 44–5

Darwin, Charles 10

INDEX OF NAMES AND SUBJECTS

Davidson, R. F. 120
Dawkins, Richard 24, 151–2, 171, 174
Derrida, Jacques 19, 21
Descartes, René 33–4
Deus Absconditus 19
Dirac, Paul 158
Doxology (Wainwright) 93
Dreyfus, Herbert 20
Drury, Maurice 45

Eagleton, Terry 19
Edward VI, Second Prayer Book of 21
Einstein, Albert 168
Elijah 47
Eliot, T. S. 146, 149, 159
Ellul, Jacques 19–20
Enchiridion (Augustine) 137
Enlightenment 3, 8, 72, 139, 156, 162, 164, 173, 178
Ephrem the Syrian 105
Episkopos 10
Ethics (Bonhoeffer) 139–41
Euclid 146
Euler, Leonhard 150
Euripides 25
Evagrius Ponticus 105
Evans, C. F. 94

Fagerberg, D. W. 97
Faraday, Michael 155
Fermat's last theorem 149
Feyeraband, Paul 170
Fish, Stanley 19
Fisher, Elizabeth 183
Ford, Christine Blasey 180
Foucault, Michel 23
Four Quartets (Eliot) 146
Fragility of Goodness, The (Nussbaum) 25
Francis of Assisi 104, 173
Fries, Jakob 117, 119

Future of Religion, The (Rorty and Vattimo) 26

Gadamer, Hans-Georg 36
Gates, Bill 77
Genova, Judith 42, 46
Gill, Robin 56
Gödel, Kurt 150
Gorgias (Plato) 29
Graham, Elaine 55
Grammar of Assent, A (Newman) 73–6
Griffiths, Bede 104
Grotius, Hugo 138–9
Le Guin, Ursula 180, 181

Haidbauer, Joseph 46
Hammond, Cally 95
Haraway, Donna 180–2, 183, 184, 185–6
Hardy, G. H. 149
Hawking, Stephen 10
Hecuba (Euripides) 25
Heidegger, Martin 22, 26
Hemming, Laurence Paul 86
Hitler, Adolf 121
Hooker, Richard 70–2
Hume, David 33, 153, 165

Idea of the Holy, The (Otto) 114–27
India's Religion of Grace (Otto) 122
Isaac of Nineveh 105

James, William 21, 106–7, 108, 110
Jerome 1
John of the Cross 104
Johnston, William 107–8
Julian of Norwich 104

INDEX OF NAMES AND SUBJECTS

Kant, Immanuel 33, 117, 118–19, 137, 139, 190–1
Kavanaugh, Brett 180
Keller, Catherine 182
Kepler, Johannes 173
Kerr, Fergus 46
Kierkegaard, Søren 39
King, Ursula 104, 111
King Lear (Shakespeare) 79
Klagge, James 37
Klare, Michael 181
Kuhn, T. S. 3, 148, 155, 166, 171
Kundera, Milan 17

Lacoste, Jean-Yves 87
Large Hadron Collider 169
Larson-Miller, Lizette 90
Latour, Bruno 23–4
League of Nations, The 121
Lewis, C. S. 75
Life and Ministry of Jesus, The (Otto) 125
Logos 7
Long, D. Stephen 53
Lord of the Rings, The (film) 96
Luther, Martin 118
Lyotard, Jean-François 19

Machiavelli, Piccolo 132
MacIntyre, Alisdair 52, 68
Malcolm, Norman 37
Marx, Karl 68
McGilchrist, Iain 105
McGinn, Marie 40
McIntyre, Lee 17, 18
Mercadante, Linda 103, 111
Merton, Thomas 111
Modest Proposal, A (Swift) 17
Monet, Claude 150
Monk, Ray 35, 38, 45, 46
Mooney, Edward 39
Moore, G. E. 34

Moore, J. M. 117
Moravians 104
Morse, Christopher 130, 135
Murdoch, Iris 24, 27
Mysticism East and West (Otto) 122

Naturalism and Religion (Otto) 115
Nature and Destiny of Man, The (Niebuhr) 57
Newman, John Henry 73–6, 78, 80
Newton, Isaac 153–4, 163
Nichols, Aidan 76
Niebuhr, Reinhold 53, 57–61
Nietzsche, Friedrich 22, 131–2
Nineteen Eighty-Four (Orwell) 17, 20, 121
Nussbaum, Martha 25
Nuttall, A. D. 28–9

Obama, Barak 18
O'Brien, Keith Patrick 133
O'Donovan, Oliver 79–80
Odyssey, The (Homer) 132
'Of Truth' (Bacon) 20
Orwell, George 17, 21
Otto, Rudolf x, 114–27
Oxford English Dictionary 29, 54

Paradigm shift 155
Pascal, Blaise 18, 138
Passover 90
Paul VI, Pope 88
Peacock, Arthur 149
Pensées (Pascal) 18–19
Phaedrus, The (Plato) 18, 29
Philo of Alexandria 6
Philosophical Investigations (Wittgenstein) 36, 39, 40, 41, 43, 45

INDEX OF NAMES AND SUBJECTS

Philosophy of Religion based on Kant and Fries (Otto) 117
Planck, Max 146, 152
Plato 18, 22, 29
Polanyi, Michael 148, 149, 156, 165
Polkinghorne, John 149
Pontius Pilate ix, 19, 20, 22, 24, 28–9, 84
Pontius Pilate (Caillois) 19, 20
Popper, Karl 3, 153, 165, 167
Postmodernism 152
Post-Truth (McIntyre) 17
Priest, Eric 163, 165
Prigogine, Ilya 164
Principia (Newton) 164
Professor Schmoot Has Lost His Keys Again (Morse) 130

Quinton, Anthony 24

Reformation 8, 21
Reich Gottes und Menschensohn (Otto) 125
Religious Essays (Otto) 122–3
Religious League of Mankind (*Religiöser Menschheitsbund*) 120, 122–4
Ritschl, Albrecht 119–20
Römerbrief, Der (Barth) 115
Rorty, Richard 26
Ross, Maggie 105–6, 109, 110
Roszak, Theodor 19
Royal Society, The 157, 167
Rudolf Otto: An Introduction to His Philosophical Theology (Almond) 125
Russell, Bertrand 34, 36, 37, 38, 45, 150

Sacrosanctum Concilium 88
Le Saux, Henri (Abhishiktananda) 102–3, 111

Schleiermacher, Friedrich 118, 120
Schmemann, Alexander 90, 97
Schrödinger, Erwin 158
Scientism 151
Scottish Episcopal Church 94–5, 184, 186
Scottish Liturgy (1982) 84–97
Secular Age, A (Taylor) 56
Short History of Truth, A (Baggini) 17
Smit, Dirk 63
Smith, Christian 169–70
Sovereignty of Good, The (Murdoch) 24
Speaking of God (Long) 53
Spinks, Bryan 97
Spiritual Autobiography (Weil) 103
Stein, Edith 108
Steiner, George 80
Stengers, Isabelle 182, 183
Still Point, The (Johnston) 108
Summa Theologica (Aquinas) 138
Swift, Jonathan 17

Tam, Henry ix
Targumim 1
Taylor, Charles 56, 75
Ten Commandments 178
Teresa of Avila 111
Testament of Youth (Brittain) 23
Theories of Religious Experience (Moore) 117–18
Theory of Religion (Wundt) 117
Theravada Buddhism 116
Thirty-Nine Articles of Religion 9, 71
Thomas Aquinas 85, 138, 152, 191
'Threefold cord' (scripture, tradition, reason) 69–70, 76–8

INDEX OF NAMES AND SUBJECTS

Tolstoy, Lev Nicholaevich 44
Torrance, Tom 149
Tractatus Logico-Philosophicus
 (Wittgenstein) 35, 36, 37, 38,
 39, 40, 41, 43, 44, 47
Tracy, David 106–7
Trent, Council of 70
Troeltsch, Ernst 120
Trump, Donald 18, 19, 20, 29,
 173, 178, 180
Turing, Alan 150
Tyson, Neil deGrasse 162, 174

Varieties of Religious Experience
 (James) 106–7
Vattimo, Gianni 26–7

Waaijman, Kees 108–9
Wainwright, Geoffrey 93–4

Warner, Martin 132
Weak Theology 26
Weil, Simone 103
Welby, Justin 132–3
Wesley, John 104
Whithead, Alfred North 182
Wigner, Eugene 149
Wiles, Andrew 150
Williams, Rowan 140
Wittgenstein, Ludwig 3, 33–47
Wolterstorff, Nicholas 62
Women's rights 179–80
Wright, N. T. 96
Wundt, W 117
Wurundjeri people 185–6

Zabala, Santiago 26
Zen Buddhism 107–8, 110

www.ingramcontent.com/pod-product-compliance
Lightning Source LLC
Chambersburg PA
CBHW021947290426
44108CB00012B/983